FEAR WAS MY ONLY WEAPON

By J. Dennis Papp

 PROLOGUE

Why me, Lord? Why Vietnam?

Everything had been wonderful at Fort Sill, Oklahoma. Annette, my wife, was with me. We were living off-base in Lawton. I had a great assignment as a personnel clerk—exempt from KP, guard duty, and any dumb details. Every time I was eligible for a promotion, I got it. Even when the special allotment came down for Spec 5, I was fortunate enough to get the promotion several months ahead of the minimum requirement for time in service and grade. I couldn't believe things could be so right in the army.

Then the dreaded phone call: the December levy for Vietnam.

In its infinite wisdom, the Army decided I had it too good for too long. It was time to screw up my life—like the countless thousands before me. And after me.

I didn't know how to tell Annette I was headed for Vietnam. So I rehearsed my speech by writing a letter to Chet Drangula, a Fort Sill buddy now stationed in Germany. As I wrote the dreaded word *Vietnam,* Annette chose that precise moment to peer over my shoulder and begin reading the letter. When she got to *the* word, her empty look gave me goose pimples. She shook her head and eked out a "No." I nodded. Without another word, she ran to the rear of the house, slammed the bedroom door, and sobbed in-between screaming "No!" over and over.

Knowledge soon became acceptance. In time, acceptance turned into goodbye. The final goodbye was a vow to return.

DEDICATION

This book is dedicated to my family, to the men with whom I served in Vietnam, and to everyone who experienced the tragedy of the Vietnam War.

CHAPTER 1

IN-COUNTRY

I was a personnel clerk—void of any infantry training—on my first guard duty in Vietnam. Armed with a rifle I not only couldn't fire without obtaining permission from the lieutenant in charge, I wasn't allowed to *lock and load* a bullet into the chamber. So, if I pulled the trigger, nothing happened. Not a damned thing.

For the ninth time since my nightly vigil began, I glanced at my Timex. The luminous hands said 3:09. If I could make it through the next four-hour sentence without getting killed, my nocturnal horror would be over.

3:10.

Without warning, a breeze swept through the bunker and caterpillars crawled up my back. I tightened my grip on my impotent M16, cursing the in-charge lieutenant snug and safe in the Command Post half a mile from our bunkers.

3:11.

Other than being aware of each rotation of my watch's sweep-second hand, one fact invaded my mind: No one could ever convince me that this flimsy sandbag barrier would protect me if we were attacked by the Viet Cong. No one.

Squinting at the moon-shrouded perimeter, I imagined Charlie, our elusive enemy, stealing his way toward me. My thoughts drifted to the likelihood of making it home in one piece. I calculated my chances at fifty-fifty. Maybe forty-sixty. Faced with the realization I was "armed" with a gun I first needed permission to use, I recalculated my chances at twenty-eighty.

Click. Click.

The faint metallic sound violated the graveyard-quiet perimeter.

Standing dead still, I braved a close look through the gun-port in the bunker's front wall. An eerie darkness consumed the area, although everything appeared tranquil. I stared harder into the shadows. Nothing. Peaceful or not, my hands dripped perspiration, and my heart pounded like a jackhammer on concrete.

If our bunker didn't reek like a cesspool, the two guys who slept during my watch would have been close enough to bolster my courage. In order to escape the pungent aroma, they moved their cots outside, near the bunker's rear entrance. Ten feet away. And ten feet might as well be ten *thousand* if you're alone in a bunker for the very first time . . . with fear as your only weapon.

3:14.

My lips twitched as I reminded myself everything would be okay. We weren't expecting any enemy activity tonight. There was a thirty-six-hour ceasefire in honor of Tet, the Vietnamese lunar New Year. Saying another prayer that Charlie would obey the ceasefire and celebrate peacefully his most-important holiday, I stared into the shadows. Nothing suspicious. Maybe, just maybe, God *will* let me survive the remaining hours of guard duty.

KABOOM!

3:15.

Maybe not.

The explosion shook my bunker. Even though its origin was well distant from our perimeter, it sounded close. Too fucking close. Evidently Charlie was celebrating Tet by trying to kill me and dozens of others.

High overhead, our choppers responded by firing red tracers into the tree line. Iridescent ropes danced before me. Flares turned darkness into daylight. Our artillery came to life. Chunks of jungle disappeared before my incredulous eyes. We were kicking back even harder.

"Hey, Papp! What's going on?" a sleepy voice whispered.

Looking over my shoulder, I glimpsed Dan Hoffman out of the corner of my left eye. It amazed me how lost his scrawny body appeared in the dilapidated cot.

"I don't know," I confided. "Looks like Charlie broke the truce."

He sat up and grabbed his M16. "What time is it?"

Without looking at my watch, I answered: "Time for you to relieve me." I tried to extend my left arm ten feet and drag him into the bunker. "So get your skinny ass over here. Quick," I demanded, angry that my arm wasn't able to stretch as long as my dick. (Even my fantasies followed me to Vietnam.)

"Okay, lard-ass. Okay."

Lard-ass? Granted, if I sucked in my generous gut, it would stick out my back. But that didn't make me *fat*, did it? At least I wasn't as fat as Hoffman was skinny. He could walk between the raindrops without getting wet—even during a monsoon.

The shelling stopped after Hoffman and I exchanged places in the bunker. Maybe things would quiet down the rest of the morning.

3:19.

KABOOM!

Maybe not.

I waited a few minutes for Charlie to mount a death-charge. Nothing. So I flopped on the edge of Hoffman's vacated cot. It replied with a groan. Nick Eaton—asleep in the next cot released a loud snort. Then a second. The son of a bitch could sleep through a war—excuse me, a *police action.* I studied the zombie and felt comforted by Eaton's presence. Even a sleeping body rendered reassurance in this godforsaken place.

Two mangy rats darted past the bunker and between my dangling feet. I tried to crush the slower one with the butt of my worthless M16. The only squish came from the gun hitting the muddy ground. Damn!

What the hell am I doing here?

A month ago I landed in-country with orders for the 309th Long-Line Communications Battalion in Pleiku. I ended up with the 9th *Infantry* Division. In Long Thanh. Two hundred miles *south* of Pleiku. Granted, I was still a clerk, but that job classification didn't put a warm spot in my heart. Charlie wasn't about to ask about my job before he squeezed the trigger. And I knew damned well *he* wouldn't ask *his* lieutenant's permission before he air-conditioned my forehead.

I swung my legs around and eased my distraught body onto the cot. The cot groaned a *who the hell are you?* Eaton completed the melody by adding a short snort, punctuating it with a longer one. Pillowing my hands, I stared at a lonesome star and began my nightly ritual: I squeezed shut my eyes, sterilized my mind of the day's events, and thought about the last time I held my wife: December 28th, thirty-four days ago. Annette and I had been married for eight months. We thought we would be together forever.

Wrong.

I held her, a magnet drawn to iron, struggling through my goodbye. The softball I swallowed made it difficult for me to breathe, let alone talk. Thank God she wasn't crying.

I'll come home alive and in one piece, I promised weakly. What else could I say? *Goodbye, I'm off to Vietnam to get killed?* Or: *Goodbye, I'll never see you again?* All I had to do was survive until the 16th of October, and I'd be on a plane headed for New Jersey. Back home where I belonged. Out of the Army. A civilian again. The chance to lead a normal life.

One minute I was in Annette's arms. The next I was three thousand miles away in California.

Processing out of the States in Oakland didn't take long enough. With only nine months remaining in the Army, every day I stayed in *The World* was one fewer day I suffered the inhumanity of being dropped in an unfriendly, hostile country, while enduring the stupidity of a military that handed me a weapon but denied me bullets.

SKA-rreeeech!

The grinding sound of a truck slamming its brakes woke me. I sat up in my cot and focused my mind and eyes on the disgusting sur-roundings.

3:24.

I was back to reality. It was Tet. I was on guard duty. Bunker 39A was under the watchful eye of Dan Hoffman. Nick Eaton hibernated in the cot next to mine.

Two men jumped out of the truck. One of them carried a Starlite scope. From what I remembered of weapons class at The Academy, a Starlite scope increased the intensity of light 10,000 times, turning total darkness into daylight. It provided a four-power magnification of the image—the better to see Charlie. All this for a mere $3,000.

"Over here," came the whispered shout of Tony Moritoni in the en-tranceway to the next bunker. There was no mistaking that New York accent—or his distinctive stance.

When they trotted over to him, Moritoni began babbling. I couldn't make out the conversation, but it didn't take a brain surgeon to know he was concerned about something outside the perimeter. His frantic waving and pointing painted a vivid picture. It coated my arms with goose bumps.

"Hey, Papp, what's going on over there?" Hoffman asked from inside the bunker.

"I don't know. But Moritoni sure is getting pissed."

The threesome disappeared into the bunker. After an agonizing five minutes, the two men exited the bunker, jumped in their truck and sped off. Moritoni waved his arms at their vanishing backs.

"Papp, wake up Eaton," Hoffman ordered. "Time for his watch."

"Hey, shithead," I nudged his shoulder, "time for your watch." No response. I kicked the underside of his cot. "Get up, troop."

"Huh?"

"I said get up. Time to relieve Hoffman." I boosted the side of his cot. He tumbled to the muddy ground.

"Okay, okay. I'm up," he mumbled, wiping his sleepy eyes with two muddy fists.

"You slept through a lot of activity." I bit my tongue to prevent me from laughing at his comical countenance. "Been some ass-kicking about a mile from here, and Moritoni had the O.D. out to his bunker with a Starlite scope." (O.D. was the Officer of the Day, who took charge after normal "working" hours.)

"Come on, Eaton," Hoffman complained, "get your ass in here. I'm not gonna take your watch, too."

"Okay, okay," Eaton moaned. "Too bad your patience isn't as long as your dick. We'd all be better off." He grabbed his M16 and reluctantly traded places with Hoffman.

"What the hell happened, Papp?" Hoffman asked, pointing an accusing finger at the overturned cot stuck in the mud. "How am I gonna sleep on that?"

"Use my cot. I want to see why Moritoni was upset. Let Eaton know I'm going next door, so he doesn't think he's got Charlie in his sights."

Walking over to the next bunker, I made enough noise so they knew *I* was coming and not the VC.

"Hey, Moritoni. It's me—Papp."

I waited for his reply.

"Okay. Come on over."

"What the hell's going on? Why'd you have the O.D. here?"

"Browning heard something outside the perimeter."

"And?"

"The O.D. saw a gook crawling away. He couldn't tell if Charlie had penetrated the wire." Moritoni's face turned a darker shade of crimson. "Then the gook stopped short of the tree line and set up a mortar tube."

"So why'nt you shoot him?"

"The asshole lieutenant wouldn't let us."

Perspiration turned to steam as it erupted on Moritoni's face. "What?"

"The shit-for-brains brown bar said it would be better just to *observe* Charlie. Unless the little fucker started shelling us," his hands mimicked dropping mortars into a tube, "we shouldn't open fire."

This was the reality of a paper soldier in Vietnam. This was how a dumb clerk helped to fight the war: with an M16 he couldn't fire.

First the Army said, *"Dennis, you're going to Vietnam."* Then it dropped me in this hostile environment and handed me a weapon. One with no ammo. An impotent weapon. *"You'd just shoots your feets off,"* the supply sergeant reasoned, *"cuz you a clerk."* I didn't bother reminding the idiot lifer that *he* was just a clerk, too.

Next the Army said, *"Dennis, you're going on guard duty. You're going to sit in a bunker and guard the perimeter. And this time, Dennis, the Army* will *give you ammo."* Great! Now I had an M16 with a magazine of ammo in it. But I wasn't permitted to chamber a round. If I pulled the trigger, nothing would happen. Zip. Zilch. Nada. This was like trying to get my wife pregnant while wearing an entire box of rubbers.

Now for the best part.

I've got my M16. I've got my ammo. I'm on guard, protecting my comrades. But . . . if I saw or heard something, I wasn't allowed to shoot unless I first got permission from the O.D. Even if Charlie was two feet away with his AK-47 pointed at my forehead, I had to pick up the field phone and ask for fucking permission to defend myself.

This was like being back in grammar school and raising my hand so the nun could give me *permission* to take a pee. Without *permission*, I couldn't go to the boys' room and empty my bladder into the urinal.

Okay. Okay. The worst that could have happened was I'd pee my pants. Big deal. Wet pants. A yellow puddle under my desk. I'd be embarrassed. The other kids would make fun of me. My mother would be angry because I soiled my pants. My father would be ashamed because his big boy wasn't big enough to pee in the specified place.

Now I'm in Vietnam, needing *permission* to shoot at the enemy before he shoots at me. And if I don't get *permission* in time, I'll get KILLED! But, before Charlie puts that bullet smack between my eyes—if it's any consolation to the O.D. and the nuns—I'll probably empty my fucking bladder in my pants.

On the return trip to my bunker, I repeated the noisy approach to let Eaton know who it was.

Hoffman was in his cot, staring at the empty sky. He turned his head towards me. "What'd he have to say?"

I related the idiotic incident with the lame-brained lieutenant. The amazement on Hoffman's face intensified as my story unfolded.

"I guarantee that fuckin' J.O.—er, O.D. will get his," Hoffman said, making an obscene gesture with a partially opened fist. "You can bet your last MPC on it." MPC were Military Payment Certificates—what we used for money in Vietnam instead of good old greenbacks.

"I hope so." God, I hoped so.

Our conversation drifted into silence. The sky began to light up—this time from the sun, not flares or artillery. The sun, aglow with its majestic power, began rising over the treetops. Its sudden appearance switched my thoughts from Vietnam back to Annette. This beautiful red-orange fireball brushed a rainbow of colors on everything it touched, turning the shroud of darkness into life. Its gentle warmth was awakening that which slept. Droplets of dew glistened in its caress. The welcome sounds of morning filled my head. The promise of being one sunrise closer to home brightened my heart.

Then reality cruelly slapped me in the face. All this power and beauty meant one thing: another fucking day in Vietnam. And this heavenly body, around which the earth rotated, would turn into a veil of heat within the next hour or two. But, at least guard duty would soon be over. Then it was back to the safety of the dilapidated dwelling known as The Pit. After the events of the last few hours, that pathetic tent would feel as comforting and secure as Fort Knox.

In a little while, Eaton stuck his head out of the bunker and said, "That's it. Guard's over. Time for the sweep."

Since this was my first guard duty in Nam, I didn't know what a "sweep" was. Reacting like a trained lab animal, I followed Hoffman and Eaton as they climbed over the berm—a mound of hard-packed dirt forming a shoulder-high wall from bunker to bunker. I couldn't help wondering how well this berm would stand up during the monsoon. *Would we have to import hundreds of little Dutch boys to finger-plug the holes?*

Eaton and Hoffman stopped in front of our bunker. I heeled and awaited further orders. Miracle of miracles. We were instructed to *lock and load* a round into the chamber. At least now we had more than an impotent weapon.

"Make your sweep," a voice barked.

On either side of me, Eaton and Hoffman trudged towards the barbed wire guarding our perimeter.

"What's going on?" I whispered, joining the parade.

"We have to see if Charlie's been around," Eaton said, cautiously looking left and right. "Check the concertina to see if it's been cut. Make sure the claymore mines are still pointed out towards the perimeter. And not towards our bunkers."

Claymores were nasty, as I had learned at The Academy. Classified as antipersonnel mines, they were packed with one pound of C-4 explosive behind hundreds of large BBs. Pushing the hand-held clacker detonated the explosive, and the BBs rocketed about one-thousand feet per second. If anything stepped into that 120-degree arc, it became instant Swiss cheese.

It was difficult walking over the coiled wire. Difficulty soon became comfort when I saw the concertina hadn't been cut. And our claymores were untouched.

"About face," the voice shouted.

We turned and headed back to the bunkers. My exposed back felt as big as a Mack truck. My fatigue shirt became a chameleon, changing from a dull-green nothing, into a brilliant red bull's-eye. Cement boots restrained me as I tried walking faster through the concertina.

I could hear a sniper's heart beat. Smell his starchy breath. Imagine him bend over. Put down his bowl of rice. Pick up his trusty AK-47. Slowly—confidently—take aim between my shoulder blades.

KABOOM!

I dove to the ground. Barbed wire penetrated my trembling body. Silence.

An eternity passed.

I finally worked up the nerve to lift my head and peek carefully over my shoulder. An enormous mushroom cloud filled the distant sky.

"All clear!" the voice yelled.

All clear? Half the jungle just blew up, and the voice says *All clear!?*

"All clear, troop," the voice again yelled. "Get up."

I pried myself off the barbed wire. Bits and pieces of my uniform stuck to its burrs.

"Clear your weapons," the voice commanded.

I looked to my left. Then my right. Everybody was taking the magazine out of his M16 and ejecting the bullet out of the chamber.

I couldn't believe it. We had our backs exposed to any Viet Cong (VC) in the tree line. We were standing knee-high in barbed wire. A Hiroshima-sized bomb just exploded. And "the voice" wanted us to castrate our M16s?

"You, troop," the voice shouted in my direction, "clear your weapon."

I took out the magazine and put it in the chameleon's mouth. I ejected the shell and caught it in midair. Then I double-timed it through the wire, over the berm, yelling the whole way: "FTA! All the way! Airborne! Up the Hill! Over the Hill!"

"Atta way to go, Papp," Eaton said, following me across the berm. "You were the first one over."

"No . . . shit, Sherlock." After catching my breath, I added: "When you get this much mass in motion, it moves."

"Sounds like you got a degree in physics, not advertising," he said.

"Nope. Though I learned enough to know when to get my butt in high gear."

"Did they also teach you the definition of torque, Papp?"

"Yeah, that's something like a measurement of force or pressure."

"Close, Papp. More specifically, it's when you wake up in the morning with a monster hard-on, and you've gotta take that first wicked piss of the day. You lift up the toilet seat," he patted me on the left shoulder, "cuz you're a gentleman. Then you push your dick down towards the bowl, and the force immediately drives your heels up off the ground, so you're standing on your toes. Now, *that's* torque," he laughed.

"Ouch!" Hoffman said, grabbing his crotch.

"Stop playing with yourself, Hoffman," Moritoni said, joining our threesome. "Jesus, Papp," his mouth fell open when he saw the front of my fatigues. "What happened to you? You look worse than one of the gooks."

"My fatigues needed some ventilation. So I rolled around in the wire."

"Looks like you left half of them *in* the wire," he laughed.

We headed for S-4 (supply) to turn in our ammo and the radio. Yes, we had to give back the ammo. Otherwise, *bang goes our feets!* Now I knew how Deputy Barney Fife felt when Sheriff Andy Taylor allowed Barney only *one* bullet for his revolver, which he had to keep in his shirt pocket. But, then, Barney at least had *one* damned bullet.

WHAHOOGAH! WHAHOOGAH! WHAHOOGAH!

Like a German shepherd to a bitch in heat, we raced to the closest bunker.

"If it's a mortar attack," Moritoni said, once we were safely inside, "it better not be because of that gook the O.D. wouldn't let me whack."

"Uh-huh," I said, shuffling my feet. I moved to the other side of Moritoni so I wouldn't be against the bunker's wall. Or up against any furry creatures crawling along it.

"What's the matter, Papp?" Eaton asked.

"Nothing." I inched away some more, stamping my feet in an attempt to ward off anything that might be on the ground.

"Why can't you stand still?"

"Never mind."

"What's the matter?" Eaton insisted. "Why do you keep pounding your feet into the ground?"

"What is this? A damned inquisition?"

"Easy, Papp," Eaton comforted. "We're okay in here."

"Sure, sure." I didn't have the nerve to tell them I kept moving around so a giant spider couldn't crawl up my leg. "Leg fell asleep," I lied. "That's all."

When we turned in our radio and ammo at S-4, the supply sergeant informed us that Charlie lobbed in a few mortar rounds—from the tree line at bunker 39. Moritoni's bunker. Fortunately, no one got hurt. That didn't stop Moritoni from volunteering to lead a lynch mob after the O.D.

Rrrrriiip!

"What was that?" Hoffman asked through a scrunched up face.

"Just a message from my anal orifice." I waved away the aroma. "Guess I'll hit the latrine before going to the tent."

In Vietnam, the normal bodily function of moving our bowels was an experience unlike any other. For one thing, we made every effort to go in the daytime. Never at night. During the day, the flies were bad enough. At night, the mosquitoes were murder. There was nothing worse than trying to swat a mosquito while it was biting an exposed right cheek. The first time I tried it, I ended up with more than just a handful of mosquito.

I opened the latrine door. It creaked a *come on in.* I was immediately overcome by the smell of fermenting feces—mixed with urine—that constantly hung in the air.

There weren't individual toilets or stalls in the latrine—simply one long wooden box or platform with five holes cut into the top. Beneath each hole was half of a fifty-five-gallon drum waiting for a GI's precious load.

I selected a vacant hole, dropped my drawers, and plopped my butt on wood. That was the three-step method. And this time I was lucky, *truly* lucky. Not only didn't I sit on a splinter, I even found some precious toilet paper.

Ahh, toilet paper.

All too frequently in Vietnam, the latrines would be void of this precious commodity. Except for the officers' latrines. They *always* had ass wipe.

By the time I got back to The Pit, the others had gone to the showers, and Moritoni's radio was blaring away.

> *Now people let me put you wise,*
> *Sue goes out with other guys.*
> *Here's the moral and the story*
> *From the guy who knows.*

Damn! They were playing the melody Rick Rodriguez, a medic I met in Oakland who was also on his way to Nam, and I coined as "our song." Wondering how my old buddy was doing in Dong Tam, I started singing half-aloud. I automatically changed the words from "Sue goes *out with* other guys," to "Sue goes *down for* other guys." Just like we revised the lyrics in high school.

Two envelopes were sitting on my cot. I got mail. I . . . got . . . mail! After one, miserable, lonely month in Vietnam, *I finally got mail.*

One letter—it felt more like a book—was from Annette; the other was from Rodriguez. Talk about a premonition. First, I hear "our song"; then, a letter's waiting from him.

I was tempted to rip open Annette's letter and immediately consume it. Instead, I decided to postpone the moment and get cleaned up. A warm shower and some clean fatigues would only help me to enjoy the letter even more.

When I returned from my shower, my tent mates were waiting for me to join them for breakfast. What the hell? I waited one month to read a letter from Annette. Another half-hour couldn't hurt.

When was I going to learn?

The bacon was educational. After sawing off a piece and trying it, I finally knew what shit really tasted like. Another selection was something green. Whether that meant it was rotten or Army issued, I didn't know. I pried up one end of it with my knife. Something underneath moved. Since I already had tried the so-called meat, I felt under no obligation to sample the moving green puke. When I stabbed the hash browns with my fork, the utensil bounced off it.

It was amazing how full I could get just by lifting and shifting various objects.

There was one thing left on my tray: a slice of something disguised as chocolate cake. Who'd serve cake for breakfast? Maybe it was the mess sergeant's way of saying he was sorry for the other crap. I guided my knife through the supposed cake. It gave way easily. I picked up my fork. Like a minesweeper, I cautiously broke off a piece. Holding my breath, I cracked open my mouth and eased the cake inside.

It was . . . delicious!

I washed down the cake and my chloroquine-primaquine antimalarial tablet (I gave up trying to say that three times fast) with a somewhat cold glass of milk. Could I survive nine months on chocolate cake, malaria tablets, and milk?

You better believe it.

With cake crumbs on my nose, and the hint of a smile on my face, I exited the mess hall with my buddies to scrape my tray. My smile did a one-eighty when I beheld the disgusting sight outside.

Three gooks were elbow deep in the garbage cans greedily fighting for the scraps. From the stench, either someone had forgotten to empty the cans for a few days, or the Year of the Vietnamese Bath still hadn't been celebrated.

When they saw me, the trio stopped foraging, cupped their hands, and pleaded for my rejects. There was no way to refuse their starving eyes. I scraped; they ate. Their hands moved faster than a teenager's in the back seat of a car at a drive-in theater. They treasured the last mouthful as though it were the *piece de resistance*.

This was what we were defending? This was why almost 20,000 GIs had been slaughtered since 1961? And over 60,000 wounded? Yes, the Army really knew what it was doing when it sent hundreds of thousands of us halfway around the world to Vietnam. To be maimed, murdered, or emotionally raped.

"Those cooks can screw up a wet dream," I complained, as we entered The Pit.

"I had a wet dream last night," Moritoni chimed in, sitting on his bunk. "Would have had another one, but I fell asleep."

We were acting like a bunch of kids again. I had to remind myself that we *were* kids—most guys were 18 or 19. I was an old man of 23. We were old enough to get shipped to Vietnam—and maybe die here—but we were still kids.

Moritoni turned up the volume on his radio. The memories of old songs filled my head—creating just the right mood for reading Annette's letter.

I considered tormenting myself a little more by reading Rodriguez's letter first. *Forget it!* I tore open the envelope from Annette and held twenty-two precious sheets of paper in my hands. *Twenty-two.* Written on both sides. If I could control my impulse to devour this letter, and instead enjoy it one page at a time, it might last until October.

December 28, 1967

> *Hon,*
>
> *I love you very much. I haven't stopped crying since you left. I know there are so many others in the same position we are and most will be separated longer. But that doesn't stop me from missing you and worrying about you. It even seems like the dog knows you're gone.*

I stopped reading the letter and gazed at the ceiling. My thoughts instantly turned to Honey, our dog. I pictured the first time I held the diminutive mutt up to my face and looked into her tiny eyes. Her reaction was to start licking my cheeks and nose with her scratchy little tongue. I laughed so hard, I cried. Then she licked away my tears.

> *I hope you end up in a safe place. I don't know what I would do if I lost you. We've been apart so much since we first met, but nothing like what we're going through now. Please stay safe.*
>
> *I hope all these months go by fast. I know that September will, because I'll be busy getting the new apartment ready for us. I can imagine how happy you will be in October. It will be the first time in 6 years you can lead a normal life. Not that the 4 you spent at Marquette weren't "normal." Just that you were always away from home—especially on your birthday.*
>
> *I wish October would come so that we could have a little time together and then start a family. I keep remembering one time in your Mom's kitchen when you came up and hugged me from behind and told me you wished I were pregnant. I miss hugging and kissing you.*

I put aside the blurry letter and got out my hanky. I wiped my eyes and the wet spots on the letter. Finding a dry part on the hanky, I blew my nose till my brains emptied into my hands. Then I buried myself in her letter.

Annette mentioned they had been getting a lot of snow. God, what I wouldn't give to see snow right now. To take thousands of flakes and crush them into snowball after snowball. To feel my hands turn ice cold. To see my palms become red from the frozen orbs. Then take those snowballs and toss them at a tree. At a fence. At a passing car. At anything I damned well pleased.

I was down to the last few pages of her epistle. Just before her closing paragraph, she asked *the* question no one could ever answer. Not even God.

> *Needless to say, I'm shook up now. After expecting you to go to a quiet, calm place, they're bouncing you around from place to place—and near where there have been attacks. I've read about the fighting that the 9th Infantry Division is involved with. Now I'm really afraid for you. I'm so sick of the damned Army.*
>
> *Why do they say they're going to do one thing, and then they do something entirely different?*

CHAPTER 2

AN ANNIVERSARY PRESENT

Putting aside Annette's letter, I reached for the one from Rick Ro-driguez, the medic I had met in Oakland. Our first encounter found us sharing a couple of beers at the NCO Club. He had departed for Nam the day before me. Tearing open the envelope brought back the mem-ory of seeing him my first day in-country, and his helping me find my temporary barracks at The Academy, where newbies to the 9th Infantry Division underwent a week of orientation. What remained stuck in my mind was his suggestion to take *two* blankets from the clerk at the barracks. I couldn't understand why I'd need one, let alone two, in this humid inferno called Vietnam. I found out that night, when I awoke around midnight, freezing my ass off. The temperature had dipped from around 100 to the 70s. Only in Vietnam was 70 *cold*.

> *Hey, Papp,*
> *I've been in Dong Tam for a few weeks now, and it*
> *looks like where you are in Bearcat. If you ever take*
> *the 70-mile or so trip down here, you'll see both*
> *places are a mirror-image of each other. But the*
> *big difference is that the 9th Infantry uses this place*

like a base camp for fighting in the Mekong Delta.
At times I go out with them on patrol and patch up
the wounded. Believe me when I say being shot at is
fricken scary as hell.

Rick went on about some of the horror stories he and the other medics had experienced. Then he ended his letter with a question of his own. Did he and Annette collaborate on how to end a letter?

On the trip down here, I saw something that made
me stop and think. There were two small boys play-
ing by the roadside, a short distance from a water
buffalo. One of the boys stopped playing, casually
pulled down his pants, and started taking a crap.
The buffalo and other child seemingly ignored the
call to nature and went about their business. As
soon as the last turd hit the barren ground, the child
pulled up his pants and went back to playing. No
sense in wiping his ass, I figured. It would only dirty
his already-filthy hands.
But on experiencing this event, I asked myself,
How do we begin helping people who have to live
like that?

I was getting sleepy from being up most of the night due to guard duty. But before I took a nap, I wanted to write a special-request letter to two friends back home.

Dear Joyce and Sam,
Everything is okay with me—as well as can be
expected. What can I expect when I'm stuck in this
hellhole called Vietnam?
Most of the time I'm perfectly safe. But the uncer-
tainty that things can explode at any minute scares
the hell out of me. Even though I'm safe, I don't
feel safe. Can you understand that? Neither can I.
Somehow I've got to convince myself that I'll make
it until October, when I'm scheduled to get out of
the Army and go home.

The plane to Vietnam left Oakland on New Year's Eve. We made refueling stops in Anchorage and Okinawa. A few of us were still awake when we crossed the International Date Line. It was 1 January 1968. We exchanged "Happy New Years" with as much enthusiasm as a caretaker tossing a shovelful of dirt onto a fresh grave.

I'm sorry if my ramblings are depressing, but it helps to get my thoughts on paper and off my chest—and out of my mind.

Even though I had orders for a communications battalion in Pleiku, I ended up with the 9ᵗʰ Infantry Division in a place called Bearcat. It's 25 miles outside of Saigon, near a village called Long Thanh. I wasn't surprised of my change in orders, because I always use "Rule #1" when it comes to the Army: Don't Apply Logic To The Situation!

During a week of orientation classes at The Academy, I learned the "basics" of dealing with the enemy and his jungle tactics. Nothing was said, however, about enduring the mental masturbation and the monotonous routine of each day. About trying to make sense out of the fact I've been dropped in this hostile environment and must deal with the inhumanity of it. About how to defend myself with an M16 but no bullets.

Sorry—rambling again.

After graduating from The Academy, I packed my gear and moved to my new unit. I live in a dilapidated tent now—it even has a name. It's called "The Pit." And it is the pits. But the guys in the tent are great. And their nicknames are inventive. For example, Nick Eaton, who's from Wisconsin and has a degree in accounting, is called Numbers. Then there's Tony Moritoni, a guy from New York City, who has the classic good looks of a Hollywood movie star. He's The Face. Another one is Dan Hoffman, who goes by the moniker of Boomerang— I can't mention why we call him that, because I haven't found out. And mine is Pinky, because I cut my little finger on a sharp edge of my footlocker, and bled all over my stuff.

Thanks for agreeing to help surprise Annette when we celebrate our 1st Anniversary on April 8th. It means a lot to me to know she at least won't feel forgotten on our special day.

I'm enclosing a money order for $15 to cover the cost of the dozen long-stemmed red roses ($7.50), and the box of good chocolate candy ($4). The remaining $3.50 is for the collect phone call from Oakland that you accepted. Can't see why you should have to pay for the call.

I wish I could be hiding somewhere in Annette's office, when the delivery man hands her the roses and candy and says, "Happy Anniversary, Mrs. Papp." I just hope she doesn't get too overwhelmed or upset by getting an anniversary present from her husband in Vietnam. It's bad enough we have to be separated—I don't want to make things worse.

Please remember to send me a card from the florist so I can sign it and have it accompany the roses.

Please tell Annette and my folks that you got a letter from me, and that I said I'm safe and every-thing. Please—PLEASE! —don't mention that I'm scared of some freak accident killing me—if Charlie doesn't do it first. Please keep my "uncertainty of death" to yourselves. Thanks.

Write when you get the chance. And be sure to let me know if the $15 is enough for everything.

In around 260 days, I hope to God that I'll still be alive—so that I can go home and be free of the Army.

Take care. Please pray for me.

The Wandering Hungarian,
Dennis

CHAPTER 3

THEY CALL ME PINKY

I awoke from my nap somewhat refreshed. *How good could anyone feel in Vietnam, anyway?* Selecting a stylish outfit—my jungle
fatigues and boots—I dressed and exited The Pit, clutching the letter to
Joyce and Sam. Once outside the limited protection of the tent, the sun
cloaked me immediately. Right. Left. Front. Back. Whichever way I
faced, the bright sphere beat down mercilessly and enveloped me with
its powerful heat. In spite of the relentless heat, my missive emitted a
cool comfort, overshadowing the mighty power of the fireball floating
in the sky.

On the way to the post office, I studied the surroundings. In two
words, Bearcat looked like a ghetto armpit.

Except for the "house" numbers, the buildings were identical:
wood, unpainted, two-storied, ample screening for ventilation, sandbags circling the lower three or four feet. The only thing missing was a
spray-painted name or obscenity on some of the walls.

Most of the roads were nothing more than hard-packed dirt, on the
shoulders, more dirt. Even weeds found it difficult to survive.

A truck drove past, kicking up mouthfuls of dust in its wake. During the monsoon season, this would be the only place in the world
where I could be up to my knees in mud and have dust blow in my
face.

A few feet ahead of me, several Vietnamese crossed the road. They looked like thermometers—minus the tomato juice. Their clothing was worse than the rags we scrubbed the floors with at home. The men wore only straw hats, sandals, and pajama-type pants. The women— thank God!—were covered below and *above* the waist.

I gently guided the letter through the OUTGOING mail slot at the post office. My spine tingled at the thought that a part of me went with the letter, making me feel a little closer to *The World.*

I didn't have to be at my assigned workplace—Personnel Actions/ Team #4—until later in the afternoon. So I painted a better-than-average smile on my kisser, did an about-face and headed for the PX. My mission: a can of black shoe polish. Since we were only clerks, and didn't go out on patrols, we were required to keep our boots spit-shined. Even if we *was jus' gonna shoots our feets off,* our boots had to shine like a new car in a showroom.

The PX was mobbed.

"They got some in," a PFC smiled, proudly holding up a six-month supply of deodorant.

"No, kidding," a beaming Spec 4 responded, uncovering his prized cache.

Hoping for a similar bountiful delivery of my treasured item, I elbowed my way to the FOOTWEAR aisle. As I searched frantically through cases of *brown* shoe polish—who the hell had *brown* shoes in Vietnam?—my blood pressure skyrocketed. Unable to find a single can of black, I began conceiving a plot to castrate all lifers. But I quickly realized my plot was futile: Lifers didn't have balls—otherwise they would be on the outside, making a living. Abandoning the hope of finding the one thing I sought, I wandered through the aisles. Eventually, I parted with a fistful of MPC for a box of Vietnam stationery, a bar of Ivory soap (the slogan automatically bounced through my mind: *99 and 44/100 percent pure),* Crest toothpaste, a handful of candy bars and three pairs of socks. A clerk dropped everything in a bag and I headed home.

Home?

Approaching The Pit, it dawned on me that this was the group of tents I vowed to stay away from when I first arrived at Bearcat. From a distance, the tents looked uninviting. Closer up, they were menacing.

Although most of the canvas on each tent was weathered, that unmistakable "O.D. green" still screamed ugly. Brighter patches of green revealed areas where hasty repairs had been made, giving the tents a checkerboard effect.

As with every other building, these luxury estates were surrounded by a four-foot-high wall of protective sandbags. Many of the bags were pocked with holes—leaking their protection on the ground like useless rubbers. Unidentifiable species of multicolored insects paraded in and out of the violated areas.

Bordering their front entrances, a wooden sidewalk permitted a dry path to the mess hall and other nearby buildings. This miniaturized boardwalk—a poor substitute for the real ones at the New Jersey shore—was the major sidewalk system throughout Bearcat.

Each tent had a wooden floor, raised about two feet off the ground. A sure blessing during the monsoon season. (Also a great place for creepy-crawlers and snakes to hide.)

These sorry dwellings had no doors or windows: flaps front and rear were the only means of ventilation. Bare light bulbs added to the minor illumination the flaps provided.

Our six-man tent slept eight. Each tenant had barely enough room for a cot and a footlocker. If two guys had a simultaneous erection, one would have to go outside—there wouldn't be enough room for extra maleness.

The one redeeming feature of these seven tents was that they were lined up arrow-straight. So they had a neat, military appearance. Something that would impress only lifers.

With my first step into The Pit, a musty aroma slapped me in the face, forcing me to swallow a long-forgotten breakfast.

Squeezing through the aisle way, I carefully sidestepped the footlockers, noticing the hand-printed signs stuck on all of them. Two of the signs were particularly amusing: *I'm Such A Short-Timer, I Left Yesterday—This Is A Recording*; and *If You Like Sex And Travel, Go Take A Fuckin' Hike.*

When I made it to the rear of The Pit, I dropped my purchases onto my cot, happy to be relieved of the awkward package. Figuring it was time to decorate my own footlocker with a sign, I pushed aside the dead specimens from the insect world that had collected on my locker, lifted the lid—careful not to cut my finger on a sharp edge—and grabbed some sign-making materials. I stared out the tent's rear flap, seeking inspiration. The view, however, was *un*inspirational: a urinal, the mess hall, and a scrawny yellowish-green plant desperately trying to survive. After a few minutes of pondering a catch phrase, I felt the urge to pee. I gently squeezed my crotch with my left hand and headed out into the backyard, letting my nose guide me.

An outdoor urinal in Vietnam amounted to a three-foot by three-foot hole in the ground filled with stones and gravel. A three-sided corrugated-tin wall—running from one's knees to one's waist—made a valiant attempt at providing privacy. A corrugated roof offered minimal protection from the sun or rain.

I stood on the awkward wooden platform in front of the hole, holding my breath and dick at the same time. Relieving myself was no simple matter. It would have been easier to pee in my pants. With all my sweat, the urine stain wouldn't have shown. Plus the odor would have blended with my surroundings.

Taking an average of two leaks a day—not counting the occasional one during a shower—I figured I'd have to go through this humbling ritual another six hundred times. Provided I lived that long.

Once relieved, I reentered The Pit and noticed Mike Grabowski had stopped by after having lunch—presumably to get some antacid pills—before heading back to work.

Upon first meeting him, I never would have guessed Grabowski was from Los Angeles. Although his hair appeared more sunburned than red, his fair skin looked like it had never seen the light of day. Even the ever-present sun in Vietnam couldn't give him a tan.

He had a unique nickname, the origin that was best told by Tony Moritoni.

As the story went, Grabowski was sound asleep one night, when an artillery barrage woke him. Startled, he didn't hear the first *BANG!* All he heard was the *WHIZ,* as the shell flew overhead. Moritoni's right hand then painted a trail to the horizon, turning his explanation in to a Hollywood production. Then another *BANG!* for the next shell going off. So Grabowski thought he heard *incoming* rounds, instead of outgoing ones. He began yelling: *INCOMING! INCOMING!* Then he ran for the bunker like a football player after a cheerleader. Everyone was still laughing when Grabowski sheepishly returned ten minutes later, forever more to be known as Incoming.

"Hey, Incoming, whatcha doing?" I asked.

"Looking for pills to settle my stomach after that damned meal." *Hah!*

"I'll walk back to the office with you," I offered. Incoming was in Team #3, which was within spitting distance of my workplace.

There were five teams in all, each working on different units of the 9th Infantry. My duties included preparation of special and emergency leaves, ID cards, OERs, TWIXes, and, reenlistments. I had been a personnel clerk at Fort Sill, but a lot of these new duties were foreign to me. Fortunately my teammate, Dennis Bohnny, trained me in what was unfamiliar. He was from Hamilton, Ohio, a little north of Cincinnati, and went by the nickname of Clyde—as in Bonnie and Clyde.

Our Madison Avenue office compound consisted of a row of seven buildings. Except for the center one, identified as the one-story office of the adjutant general, all were identical to the two-story hooches found in Long Binh and at The Academy. Across the street were a signal tower, three good-sized bunkers, some sort of garbage dump, and two latrines—one marked OFFICERS; the other, ENLISTED.

The $64,000 question: Did officers' shit smell different than lowly enlisted men's? Answer: Theirs didn't smell at all.

Off in the distance, past a signal tower, the telltale spire of the Post Chapel stood in solemn majesty. When given the opportunity, I went to Mass on Sundays, or at least stopped by for a chat with the Man upstairs.

Team 4 was in the second building from the left end. When I stepped inside, it struck me again that all these buildings were clones of one master hooch. The Army must have purchased the building plans from the developer of Levittown, Pennsylvania. The origin of that community, located near my hometown, was one big development with almost every house a twin of the other.

Bohnny got up from behind his desk, extending a 5' 10"-frame chiseled out of a redwood tree. Above a square jaw, his gentle-looking, bespectacled countenance was topped with thick brown hair.

"Mr. Blue wants to see you, Pinky." (Warrant officers were referred to as Mister.) While pushing up his glasses with his left index finger, he laughed and began singing.

I'm Mr. Blue when you say you love me,
Then prove it by going out on the sly,
Proving your love isn't true, call me Mr. Blue.
I'm Mr. Blue when—

"Enough, Clyde, enough. Do you know what the Chief wanted?" I asked.

"Didn't say."

I did an about-face, exited through the screen door, and headed over to a nearby building, entering through yet another screen door.

Mr. Blue wasn't in sight, so I propped my M16 against Staff Sergeant Dickson's desk and asked the Chief's right-hand man his whereabouts. Dickson's six-foot, stocky frame was planted board-straight in his chair. He was in his early thirties and had the same military appearance as the Chief.

"Where's the Chief? He wanted to see me."

He pointed to the chair across from his desk and said, "Relax, Papp. Mr. Blue is at H.Q." His soft-spoken voice and trusting brown eyes made me feel more comfortable than usual with someone of his rank. "I don't know what he wanted. Why not wait—oh, here he comes now."

When I turned and caught his eyes, Blue smiled and pointed to the chair next to his desk. "Sit down, Papp." Blue's tone of voice made it sound like an offer rather than an order.

I eased myself onto the wooden chair as requested. Unlike many officers, Blue was friendly, not a phony friendly, either. I estimated his age at forty. He was of medium build and height. His light brown hair was cut lifer-short, complementing the razor-sharp creases of his tailored fatigues.

"You've been assigned here for a few weeks now, and I wanted to know how things were going with Specialist Bohnny and Team 4." Blue shifted his weight in his chair, pain visiting his expression.

It was unusual for an officer to show an open concern for his men. My former commanding officer at Fort Sill, CPT Hill, gave frequent evidence of that quality. Blue was the only officer in Nam to be equally human. He sure as hell wasn't a prick like our HMFIC, the adjutant general. (HMFIC stood for Head Mother Fucker In Charge.)

"Bohnny's great, Sir. I've learned a lot from him."

"Yes, he's a good man," the Chief agreed. "He does his job very well." Blue rocked from side to side, trying to get comfortable in his chair. "Well, Papp. That will be all. Dismissed."

That's all he wanted? I thought. *To see how I was making out? Doesn't make sense.* Upon further review, I reasoned: *It does make sense—for the Army.*

Having been dismissed, I stood up, grabbed my impotent M16, did a smart about-face, and returned to my assigned workstation.

That afternoon Bohnny taught me about OERs and TWIXes, which we processed for four units of the 9th Infantry: the $2^{nd}/3^d$, $4^{th}/16^{th}$, $3^d/24^{th}$ and $1^{st}/32^{nd}$.

"There's nothing to 'em," Bohnny assured me with a smile. An OER is an Officer Efficiency Report. An officer's performance is rated by his superior at least once a year."

"How are they rated?"

"As with everything else we do, there's a form to fill out." He began digging through a foot-high pile of blank forms. "After you get the officer's 66 File—"

"66 File?" I asked, trying not to act too dumb.

"Enlisted men have a 201 File, and officers have a 66 File."

"Okay."

"Then you take this stupid form," he put it in my face and continued in a rapid-fire pace: "fill out the top half. In duplicate. Send the original copy to the officer's commander. For his rating. Keep the carbon in the 66. To cover your ass. And," he grinned, "that's a mighty big one to cover, I might add."

"Thanks, four eyes," I countered.

"Four eyes? You wear glasses, too, dickhead."

"Yeah, but at least my lenses don't have 'Made by the Coca-Cola Bottling Company' printed on the bottom of them."

"Never mind," he frowned, while using his index finger to adjust his heavy frames. "Do you understand OERs now?"

"Yeah. Sort of. I guess. Sure."

"Huh?"

"What's a TWIX?" I asked, changing the subject.

"A TWIX is like a Western Union telegram. First you type it up on this," he said, reaching for the proper form.

Just when he was about to grab it, the mountain of blank forms toppled over, and a gigantic spider climbed to the top. Its hourglass body was larger than a silver dollar and was completely covered with bushy, bluish-green-red hair that resembled fur. Eight vampire-like eyes held me in a trance while thick legs—more powerful than a track star's—reared for an attack. The thought of being caught in this predator's web made me vow never to consider any spider's web harmless—no matter how tiny it might be.

The instant the monster sprung at me, Bohnny swung his cap and knocked it down in midair. You could hear the spider cry out as Bohnny's jungle boot crushed the would-be assailant into brownish-green oatmeal.

"Thanks for saving my life, Clyde." I searched my arms and legs for a possible companion.

"You're welcome. Must have been one of your friends from the bunker." Bohnny hesitated when his hand reached for the forms again. Determining it safe, he grabbed one and explained what goes where on the TWIX form.

"Oh, shit," he exclaimed. "I just remembered. I gotta get Mr. Blue to sign these forms," he picked up a Manila folder, "and drop them off at the AG's. Why don't you come with me?"

"Okay."

We were a few steps out the door when Bohnny ordered, "Better snap a good salute."

After I returned my right arm to a relaxed position, I asked, "Who was that?" I wondered why that officer deserved such a military acknowledgement.

"CPT Enos Oscar—the fearful commanding officer of the 9th Admin."

"Oh."

"He's a real screw up. Oscar and the 1st Sergeant—John Smith—"

"John Smith? You gotta be kidding," I laughed.

"That's his name. Honest." Bohnny crossed his heart with his right thumb.

I laughed harder.

"Anyway, Oscar and Smith are the fifty-third and fifty-fourth cards in the deck."

"Fifty-third and -fourth what?" Another phrase new to me.

"You know. The two jokers."

"Riiight."

"Oscar is bad enough, but Smith rides us for no reason."

"Sounds like the kind of boss who lives up to the dirty diaper theory."

"What's that?" Bohnny asked.

"Bosses are like dirty diapers: full of shit and always on your ass."

"Bull's-eye," Bohnny agreed. "But as I was saying, Smith is a stupid asshole. You know how some guys have a high school GED?"

"Yeah . . . " I waited for the punch line.

"Well, Smith's got an *elementary* school GED."

"No kidding. Really?"

"The truth. I swear." He again crossed his heart. "He's so stupid he still thinks watermelons can grow inside your stomach if you swallow the seeds."

After taking care of signing-delivering the forms, we were back at the office when Sergeant Dickson opened the screen door and shouted, "Everybody outside for the ceremony."

"What ceremony?" I asked, reluctantly grabbing my jungle hat. I had no interest in having the afternoon sun crucify me while some lifers played Army.

"Some guy in the 9th Infantry is getting a medal from General Westmoreland and Nguyen Cao Ky."

"Who's New-yen—whatever?" Vietnamese names weren't my strong suit.

"Just call him Ky—like K-e-y," Bohnny suggested. "He was the prime minister of South Vietnam. Now he's something like their vice president."

"What's the medal for?"

"One of our guys saved a hamlet near Dong Tam. He evacuated the Vietnamese before the VC could come in and kill 'em all."

"Why would the VC kill everybody in a tiny village?" I didn't have a clue.

"Part of their terrorist activities. It stops a lot of the South Vietnamese from becoming our allies."

Becoming a well-trained puppy, I heeled and followed Bohnny outside and down the main road. Unconsciously, I lapsed into my human mode and made the Sign of the Cross when we passed the Post Chapel.

We stopped about a hundred yards from a huge stage. At least a thousand GIs were crowded around, waiting for the ceremony to begin.

"This is where Bob Hope performed on Christmas," Bohnny whispered. "It was a great show. Too bad you didn't get the chance to see it."

"Sorry I missed it." I didn't have the heart to remind him I was in *The World* for Christmas.

A board-straight, spit-and-polished buck sergeant, surrounded by a dozen officers and enlisted men, marched onto the stage. General Westmoreland materialized in front of the group, causing the sergeant to stand even more erect.

A chill ran through me when the proud recipient thrust out his chest and General Westmoreland pinned on the medal. At least this award wasn't presented posthumously.

We were ordered to stand at attention while the jeeps departed after the ceremony. A constellation of stars paraded by. I didn't recognize any of the generals, until I saw the four stars on Westmoreland's cap. My body turned to concrete.

Westmoreland's jeep mysteriously slowed to a crawl. Four stars and two eyes searched the crowd. When his penetrating glance riveted on me, goose bumps ran up my arms. Not knowing what to expect, I stiffened my board-like stance and returned his stare. As fast as puberty's first orgasm, Westmoreland's eyes released me and his jeep sped up.

I never thought I would see Westy, let alone get this close to him. Then again, I never thought I would get this close to Vietnam either.

FTA . . . all the way.

After work I joined Moritoni, Eaton and Hoffman for dinner. The evening repast consisted of hamburgers, fries, peas, and chocolate donuts. Plus the beverage of your choice: milk, or milk.

"This isn't too bad. Except," I picked at my tongue with my right thumb and index finger, "for the hair I just found." I extracted the culprit and proudly displayed it.

"You'll have to expect that. The cook forms the burgers by squeezing the ground meat in his armpit," Moritoni explained.

Spitting out a mouthful of hamburger and fries, I said, "Thanks a lot," and grabbed my donut.

"Don't mention it," he smiled, exposing a mouth full of fries. "But I guess now isn't the time to tell you what the cook uses to make the hole in the donuts."

I spit out half of a donut.

"Speaking of food," Hoffman chimed in, "what do you get when you cross an onion with a donkey?"

"I don't know, what?" I mumbled, trying to spit out more donut.

"Well, 999 times out of 1,000 you get a donkey that smells bad. But once," he held up a lone finger, "just one time in a thousand, you get a piece of ass that brings tears to your eyes."

Before I could stop laughing, Moritoni asked, "What did the South Vietnamese do with the 10,000 boxes of Cheerios the Pentagon sent over?"

"I don't know. What?"

"The gooks thought the Cheerios were donut seeds and planted them."

Deciding to keep the food topic going, I asked him, "What do you get when you cross a rooster with a jar of peanut butter?" Moritoni and Hoffman shook their heads. "A cock that sticks to the roof of your mouth."

"Enough, enough," Eaton complained. "Only three jokes per meal."

During the trip back to The Pit, dust and a mixture of tiny insects stuck to my sweaty body. Feeling increasingly grubby, I said, "I'm heading to the showers."

"I was going to take one myself," Eaton answered, "so I'll join you."

"I could use one, too," Hoffman said and smiled.

Eaton and Moritoni looked at each other and laughed. Spasmodically.

"Looks like the joke is on me," I said, shrugging my shoulders.

The showers were a good fifty yards past our tent. A box about five feet square and six feet high held the water. The words NONPO-TABLE WATER were stenciled in two-foot-high red letters on each of its sides. The container sat on top of a small storage trailer, elevating it about eight feet. The added height enabled the shower water to be gravity fed.

I put my ditty bag on a small shelf and unwrapped the towel from my waist—anxious for the cleansing relief of the expectant shower. When Hoffman removed his towel, I finally understood the reason for his nickname. He had a dick that would have made a porn star jealous. More outstanding than the titanic length, its shape had a gentle upward bend to it. Thus the obvious reason for the name Boomerang.

"That's some tool you have, Boomerang."

"Thanks, Pinky. But it almost caused me to break up with my girlfriend."

"Why?"

"Well, she said she wanted nine inches."

"You've got no problem there."

"Yeah, I know. But I was damned if I was gonna cut it in *half* for anyone," he boasted.

"Why," I asked, with a hint of sarcasm, "didn't you have a machete handy?"

"Forget the machete, I'd need a chain saw."

"Enough, already," Eaton pleaded.

"What's the matter, Numbers?" Hoffman laughed. "Pissed cuz you couldn't satisfy your girl when she said: 'Give me 12 inches and make it hurt'?"

"Nah," Eaton responded quickly. "I just gave it to her twice and smacked her on the ass."

Stealing another peek at Hoffman's monument to manhood, I noticed it bore the name *Wendy* in crimson letters. Whether this was a past or present lover, he must have thought a hell of a lot of her to go through the agony of being tattooed in such a delicate place.

Pointing to the symbol of affection, I asked: "What made you tattoo your girl's name on your dick?"

"That's not my girl's name," he smiled, gently touching the emblazoned area.

"Then whose is it?"

"Let me show you." He stroked his tool.

"God help us," I exclaimed, jumping back as his dick blossomed, exposing the full meaning of the tattoo. *Wendy* suddenly became *When on R&R, have a nice day.*

Trying to push Hoffman's accomplishment out of my mind, I unzipped my ditty bag and dug around for my soap. "Damn," I complained. "I forgot my stupid soap."

"Wanna use some of mine?" Hoffman offered.

"No, thanks. I'll just use my Prell."

"Hey, Numbers," he called, "we're gonna hafta watch this new guy. He takes a shower with shampoo."

With my tube of Prell in hand, I pushed Hoffman out of the way and defended my strange bathing technique with a "Screw you, it's an old Hungarian custom," and walked nonchalantly over to a dripping shower head, my flip-flops making sucking sounds as I stomped through the puddles on the concrete floor.

Turning the shower handle and releasing tepid water, the gentle spray caressed my body. Using a generous amount of Prell, I lathered my head, arms and armpits, then the rest of my body. Looking like a dog gone completely rabid, I quickly cured the affected areas under the cascading water and was miraculously cured.

Another new face was just leaving The Pit when we got back.

"Hold on, Small," Eaton said, "I want you to meet a new guy."

Small? *Was this another nickname referring to a body organ? How small was he?*

"Dennis Papp—now known as Pinky—this is Len Small, our official short-timer. Len DEROSes 14 February," Eaton added for my benefit. (DEROS was the date eligible for return from overseas.)

"Hi, Pinky." He doffed his jungle hat and eagerly shook my hand.

This guy was all smiles. Anybody would be, though, with only a couple weeks to go before leaving this hellhole. How I envied his status . . . so close to leaving Nam and returning to the sanity of *The World.*

"How many days you got?" Small chuckled. "Three hundred and fifty what?"

"Three-fifty, my ass. I've got around two-sixty," I stated proudly. "I DEROS the middle of October."

"You son of a bitch!" Eaton grumbled. "You just got here, and you DEROS before me? I don't get out until 16 November."

"That's what happens when the asshole Army sends you to Nam with less than a year to go," I explained, flashing a smile almost as broad as Small's. My expression quickly reversed itself, because I realized being in Vietnam was nothing to smile about. Unless you were a short-timer.

"Nice meeting you, Pinky," Small said, replacing his jungle hat. "I'm off to have a few beers. FTA."

Yeah, *Fuck the Army.*

"I've met five of the guys so far, Numbers." I pulled on a pair of boxer shorts and hung up my wet towel. "What about the two that are missing?"

"The other two are Joe Dorsey and Bill Williams—on R&R in Bangkok."

My thoughts drifted to that distant place and to the fun the missing duo was having.

"They'll be back tomorrow. You won't see much of them when they get back, though." Eaton stepped into his fatigue pants and buttoned his fly.

"Why's that?"

"They've been assigned special duty with finance." He traded his flip-flops for jungle boots, then guided his arms through the sleeves of his fatigue shirt. "They'll be working the night shift to get the year-end records straightened out—plus they both DEROS the middle of April."

"Seems like everybody is getting short—except us."

"Our turn will come soon enough, Pinky."

As the final step in his getting dressed, he checked his crown of hair in a mirror and announced: "I'm going to the mess hall to see the movie. Wanna come?"

"What's playing?"

"*How to Succeed in Business—*

"Already saw it," I cut him short, "so I'll pass."

"You sure? I'll even buy the popcorn," he kidded.

Did we have popcorn in Vietnam?

"Think I'll just stay here and write a letter to my wife," I responded. "Maybe next time."

"Okay, Pinky. Good night." Toping off his head with a crumpled jungle hat, he waved and exited The Pit.

<hr>

I had barely written a few lines—telling Annette that maybe the camaraderie of the guys in The Pit would help me make it through the next nine miserable months—when "Mr. Lonely" started playing on Moritoni's radio. The song evaporated the thoughts of camaraderie and brought me back to the reality of my crummy existence.

Putting pen and paper aside, I rested my head on my laced-up fingers and listened to Bobby Vinton . . . while tears made their unbroken journey down my cheeks.

> *Letters, never a letter,*
> *I get no letters in the mail.*
> *I've been forgotten, clear forgotten,*
> *Oh, how I wonder, how is it I failed?*

Had I, too, been forgotten? Had I somehow failed? Was it my fault that I ended up in Vietnam?

My tears turned to acid and burned more deeply. Feeling sorry for yourself came at a price. Especially in this damned place. So I did the only other thing I could: I drifted off to sleep to the song's closing stanza.

> *Now I'm a soldier, a lonely soldier,*
> *Away from home, through no wish of my own.*
> *That's why I'm lonely, I'm Mister Lonely.*
> *I wish that I could go back home.*

CHAPTER 4

"Well, Pinky, S.S.D.D.," Bohnny proclaimed, as he flopped into his chair the following morning.

"S.S.D.D.?"

"You know—Same Shit, Different Day."

"Not the same to me," I complained. "I still don't know anything."

"Then let's see if I can impart some of my infinite wisdom on a newbie," he said, patting me on the back. "We'll start with an OER, which I just glossed over yesterday."

His hands searched carefully through the drift of papers in our IN basket—making sure a relative of yesterday's hairy creature wasn't lurking in the pile.

"Have you met Spec 5 White yet?" he asked, adjusting his glasses with an expert's touch.

"No."

"He's one of the officer records clerks for Team 4. Let's get him to pull the 66 Files for these three OERs," he held up a typed list, "and I'll introduce you."

We walked to the front of the office, to the left of the screen door. Bohnny had an awkwardly graceful spring to his step. Like a duck after dancing lessons.

File cabinets lined the front wall and part of the side wall.

Standing guard over them was a mountain of a man. His black skin glistened with perspiration, tiny drops falling from a once-broken nose. He looked up as we approached; two liquid-brown eyes glowed like a full moon in a midnight sky. Standing up, his muscular frame filled the hooch.

"Hi, Clyde," his voice smiled.

"Hi, Fudgsicle. Want you to meet my new partner. Cliff White, this is Dennis Papp—Pinky."

"Pinky?" he asked, his big paw swallowing my right hand.

"Near lost my right pinky the other day."

He gently relaxed his grip and apologized with a soft-spoken, "Sorry."

"No problem. Doesn't hurt much any more." False pain etched my face. "How'd you get your moniker?" I imagined his ability to devour dozens of ice cream bars in one sitting—although that seemed unlikely, because his stomach was as flat as a slice of bread.

"The Face gave it to me, cuz I'm cool, chocolate, and deeelicious," he grinned. "What can I do for you guys?"

"Gonna show Pinky how to do OERs. Need these three 66s."

White surveyed the names. Pointing to the second one, he said, "Lieutenant Maven—he just died."

"Doesn't matter," Bohnny replied unemotionally. "Still gotta do an OER on him."

Without hesitation, White made an about-face, went to the file cabinets, and pulled the required records. Within seconds he handed us the three files.

"As I mentioned yesterday," Bohnny said, settling in his chair, "we have to do an OER whenever an officer changes duties, or his superior is replaced."

"Even if the guy dies?" I prompted, wondering why rate a dead officer? If his superior gave him a bad rating, what would happen? They'd demote him?

"Still have to do one to officially close out his records." Adjusting his glasses, he added: "If neither happens in a twelve-month period, we do an OER anyway."

After killing yesterday's furry visitor, Bohnny carefully restacked the blank forms into six smaller piles. We agreed nothing could take refuge behind any of these paper anthills. It was more hope than agreement.

He selected the proper form—in duplicate, of course—and proceeded to walk me through it. In reality, we crawled through it. I had three questions for every block of information we filled in. More than two hours later, we finished the first OER.

"Bohnny," Sergeant Dickson called through a partially opened screen door. "The Chief wants to see you. Now!" Dickson disappeared before the door closed.

"This shouldn't take long—I hope. Why don't you look through the next 66 and try doing an OER by yourself?"

Bohnny got up, dissecting the umbilical cord of knowledge.

I reached into the appropriate anthill, selected two blank forms, slipped a piece of worn-out carbon paper between them, and snapped my right wrist to insert the set into the typewriter.

The next 66 File opened by itself. The name MAVEN, JONATHAN DOUGLAS stared at me. I had selected the dead officer's file. Slamming it shut as though it were contaminated, I flipped it aside. I squeezed my eyes shut—to erase all memory of MAVEN and death—and blindly picked up the last of the three files.

MAVEN, JONATHAN DOUGLAS again filled my vision.

This was crazy. I refocused my eyes. MAVEN, JONATHAN DOUGLAS. Somehow I chose the same folder I had just flung aside. Forgetting the OER, I thumbed through the paper history of this dead warrior.

He was born on my birthday, 26 February 1944, in a town less than ten miles from where I came out of the womb. Goose bumps erupted on my arms. My fingers trembled as I flipped to the next page. The forms were stuck together. I licked a dry index finger with a sandpaper tongue and tried to separate them. No luck. I was stuck on this page. Something was forcing me to read on.

The hell with this! I tossed the file aside—again—got up, and gazed out the window. What little I saw was as morbid as the file I didn't want to read. I tried to concentrate on something besides Maven's file and my depressing surroundings. Even with my eyes closed, my mind held both images like a photograph. Giving in to the inevitable, I slid back into my chair.

I stared at Maven's closed file. I still didn't have the balls to touch it; to know the feeling of death. Minutes passed. I sucked up my fear and reached for it. My trembling hand stopped in midair—five hesitant fingertips unwilling to move closer. Miraculously, the folder jumped into my hand. I squeezed it, to keep the contents hidden, but it resisted and opened to where I had left off.

Maven was married. He had two children. Girls. Infants. I imagined his wife cradling their daughters when she was notified of his death. Tears overflowed, blurring my vision.

How does a mother explain to her children that their father had died?

Since the two girls were infants, she was probably spared the explanation. But the emptiness of a child never knowing her father—or mother—was the saddest tragedy of all. Empty memories.

DEROS: 16 FEB 68. The poor son of a bitch had a couple weeks to go. He would have been home for his birthday—my birthday.

My tears fell on his folder. Wrinkled puddles popped up on the forms. I lubricated a finger on one of the puddles and turned to the next page.

DECORATIONS, MEDALS AND CAMPAIGN RIBBONS AWARDED OR AUTHORIZED: National Defense Service Medal, Vietnam Campaign Medal, Vietnam Service Medal, Silver Star, Purple Heart, Good Conduct Medal, Army Commendation Medal. He was well decorated. For whatever good it did him now.

I paged through the rest of the forms, searching for a mention of how he died. None. It simply said: KIA/1 JAN 68. What a sickening way to begin—end—the year.

I jumped out of my skin as a hand gently touched my right shoulder from behind. Was this the angel of God calling me?

"Hey, Pinky," echoed a melodic voice, "ready for some chow?"

I turned around and saw the non-angelic face of Eaton. His smile became a frown when he saw my weird expression.

"What's the matter?" he asked tentatively. "You look like death warmed over."

"I was just looking through this dead officer's file," I offered it up in both hands, "to do an OER. Got kinda wrapped up in it. You just put tire tracks in my shorts."

"Huh?"

"You scared the crap out of me. Guess I'll have to change my underwear now."

"Sorry."

"That's okay. It was that time of the week anyway."

Halfway to the mess hall, I finished telling Eaton about Lieutenant Maven dying a month before his DEROS.

"There have been worse stories than that," he mumbled.

"What can be worse than spending eleven fucking months here," my voice became a shout, "and dying the month before you're scheduled to go home?" I couldn't comprehend anything worse than that. Nothing in the world could compare with dying with one month left on a twelve-month sentence in Vietnam.

"One of my buddies put in his damned year and was on his way out of here." Eaton searched the sky with swollen eyes. "Before his freedom bird took off from Bien Hoa, he got bumped from the plane and sent back to Long Binh." He took a deep breath and struggled to continue. "That night . . . Long Binh . . . took . . . some . . . heavy mortaring, and . . . my . . . buddy was killed." The last word was whispered with a mixture of sorrow and rage.

I made no response. Not even a "sorry." Sorry just wouldn't cut it now.

Eaton was right: There were worse things than dying after spending eleven months in Nam. Being bumped from the plane after completing your tour—and then dying. That was an even bigger tragedy. When I get on the plane in October—I would, wouldn't I? —nothing or no one will get me off until we land in *The World*. Nothing. Nobody. No fucking way.

We walked in silence, each step a hollow echo. Eaton's suggestion finally broke the silence: "Let's stop by The Pit for a minute."

Two guys in flowered shirts and Class-A khaki pants sat on their bunks, laughing as they unpacked their satchels.

"Dorsey, Williams, welcome back," Eaton's greeting rang out as we entered The Pit. They stood up and shook hands with Eaton as he repeated their names.

Williams was about my height—5' 9"; Dorsey was at least a head shorter. So short, that if he sat on a footstool, his feet wouldn't touch the floor.

"Who's this?" Williams asked, exposing amber teeth, while pointing a nicotine-stained finger at me.

Eaton made the introductions and asked: "How was Bangkok?"

"Bang-your-cock was great," Dorsey answered through a toothbrush mustache.

I couldn't imagine diminutive Dorsey banging his cock. He was more suited to walking into doorknobs and banging his forehead.

"We hired two girls for the week," Dorsey continued. "Only cost us 70 bucks each. Mine was great—"

"She had flat feet," Williams chided, grabbing a pack of Camels off his bunk and lighting up.

"Yeah, but she had round heels," Dorsey smiled. "Anyway, you should have seen the knockout Williams had."

"What was she like?" I urged, hungry for the description.

"The kind of woman you dreamed about since your first erection," Williams began, slowly and deliberately. He stuck the Camel in his mouth and inhaled deeply, filling every air sac in his bronchial tubes with poisonous smoke. "She had long, perfectly shaped legs that went all the way up to a tight, little ass." Dangling the Camel from his lips, he gradually raised two cupped hands to my face and whispered, "Her upturned tits were just the right size to fit into my eager palms."

The image took shape in my mind. And in my pants. Eaton's reaction was as obvious as mine.

"Her perfectly straight, golden-blonde hair caressed her soft shoulders," Williams continued in a louder voice—to drown out our panting. "Each time she looked at me, her deep-blue eyes shimmered. Best of all," he smiled, grasping his loins with his left hand, "she had a moist, sensuous mouth that could suck the chrome off a trailer hitch."

It was time for Eaton and me to go outside—the tent could no longer contain our maleness.

"What was the first thing you said to her?" I asked.

He took another drag on his butt, slowly exhaling smoke in my face. He finally answered in a hoarse, raspy voice: "I stared her right in the eyes, inhaled her cherry blossom aroma, and told her that as long as I had a face, she'd always have a place to sit."

"Let's get some lunch," Eaton pleaded, wiping his brow.

When I returned to the friendly confines of Team 4, Bohnny was pounding away on his typewriter.

"Bad news," he said, "I've got guard tonight. You'll be on your own after 1500 hours. How'd you do with the OERs?"

I told him about the eerie experiences with Lieutenant Maven's file and reluctantly explained that I didn't get a damned thing accomplished.

After reassuring me I'd eventually get the hang of filling out OERs and completing the other paperwork in our effort to fuel the paper war, he handed me a booklet entitled ARMY REGULATIONS and cautioned me to study the ARs this afternoon in preparation for tomorrow's inspection with the adjutant general.

"I'm not going to let some asshole lifer scare me," I promised.

"Just be careful, Pinky. There isn't a rational bone in his body—and he especially likes to pick on new faces."

"Other than that, I bet his only talent is picking his nose and ass at the same time."

I spent the next few hours being tortured: Bohnny rattled off an AR, and I attempted to cite the corresponding number. Then he'd give me a number, and I'd stumble through the description.

"Gotta go to guard duty now." He pushed up on the bridge of his glasses. "If all else fails, just look Murphy right in the eye—without laughing—and shout a response at him. Even if it's wrong, he'll be impressed with your volume."

Bohnny's suggestion about shouting appeared to be the only way I'd get through Murphy's inspection. Even if I studied through the night, I'd never get all the damned ARs memorized.

"Here's one more AR to study." He handed me a slip of well-wrinkled paper. "Good luck."

After Bohnny left, I unfolded the paper and read the words of wisdom.

> *The 23d AR*
> *The Army is my crutch, I shall not think. It al-*
> *loweth me to lie down on responsibility. It leadeth*
> *me blindly. It destroyeth my initiative. It leaveth me*
> *in a path of the parasite for my country's sake. Yea,*
> *though I walk through the valley of laziness, I shall*
> *fear no achievement.*

It was 0630. I had been parked behind my desk for over an hour . . . trying to memorize yet another AR. Ready to throw in the towel, I felt I had one shot at surviving the inspection: If my knowledge didn't impress the colonel, maybe my appearance would.

I was wearing a pair of fatigues that had sharper creases than Mr. Blue's. My belt buckle shimmered like a forty-carat diamond. Thanks to some borrowed shoe polish, my boots had a mirror finish. I had shaven especially close—taking off all evidence of a beard and two layers of skin. My desk was perfect. Even the concrete floor around my area was spit-shined. My typewriter glistened like the morning's dew—back in The World, that is.

"Morning, Pinky," Eaton said. He surveyed me from crew-cut to boots. "Looks like you've got your shit together."

"Atsa Rog!"

"Good luck."

Trying to take my mind off the never-ending list of ARs the colonel could stump me with, I went back to retyping the OER Bohnny and I had done yesterday. Each time a finger hit the wrong key, my thoughts returned to the inevitable: ARs; Colonel Murphy; Saturday-morning inspection; wrong answers; court martial; dishonorable discharge; firing squad.

"Tenhut!"

Mr. Blue's booming voice brought me back to reality.

Zero hour.

Except for a little sweat, I still looked razor-sharp. My area still sparkled. I still didn't know my damned ARs.

The circus fat man, whom I presumed to be Lieutenant Colonel Murphy, stopped at Cliff White's desk. I couldn't hear the dialogue, but White looked like he was getting through it okay.

I tried to whitewash my mind of Murphy's appearance, thinking it might eliminate his existence. Instead, my mental paintbrush created a monstrous mural. Packed into a six-foot height were a horseshoe of brown hair; a well-rounded, jutting stomach; a flat, pants-fall-down ass; and a pair of awkwardly long, flamingo-thin legs that even baggy trousers couldn't camouflage.

A couple minutes passed. It wouldn't be too much longer before I changed places with White. Beads of perspiration broke out on my forehead; my armpits became water-laden sponges.

Suddenly, Murphy turned and approached me. He wore his clown pants cinched under his generous gut, making the cuffs sweep the floor as he walked.

Two, vacant, battleship-gray eyes riveted on me. His expression said: new meat—all mine.

He stopped a foot from my desk. His chrome dome caught the light, nearly blinding me.

"What's your name, soldier?" he barked through a small mouth hidden under a beak of a nose. He was close enough to read my name tag, but evidently decided to begin the inquisition by being a bigger prick than his reputation.

I was unable to open my mouth—fearful that my heart would fall out. Finally, I shouted: "Specialist Papp, Sir!"

"How long have you been in Vietnam?"

"A month, Sir!"

"Which forms do you use for a reenlistment?" Typical question for a lifer.

"Sir! You use a 221, a 415, and a 121." My reply echoed throughout the hooch, putting a mile-wide smile on Mr. Blue's anxious face.

The colonel fired a couple ARs at me. I miraculously responded with the correct answers, faster than an altar boy answering a priest. Each reply turned up the volume one more notch.

How the hell was I remembering this stuff?

Seeing that he couldn't stump me, Murphy pushed me aside and stared at the objects on my desk. Leaning over my typewriter, he ran a pointy index finger over the keys—not the keyboard, the metal letters that actually struck the ribbon.

"Aha!" He inspected the bony digit. "Just as I thought. Filthy."

He thrust his blackened finger in my direction, and then shoved it in Mr. Blue's face. Blue cowered.

"Doesn't this excuse for a soldier know enough to have his machine clean for my inspection?" the maniac threatened.

"The specialist knows that, Sir," Blue answered weakly, awkwardly shifting his stance.

What the hell was I supposed to do? Clean my machine at 0630 and not use it until this asshole showed up?

"Who's the ranking man on this team, Mr. Blue?" Murphy asked, smoke pouring out of his flabby ears. He was looking for somebody else to chew out.

"Specialist Papp is, Sir." Blue looked at the floor and shuffled his feet. Drops of perspiration rose like boils on his spit-shined boots.

Even though I was new in-country, and there were three other Spec 5s on our team, I was the ranking man on the team because I had been Spec 5 longer than any of the others. Except for a few ARs, they knew more about Personnel Actions than I did. This was typical of the Army: most rank, least knowledge.

"Next Saturday, this specialist had better be ready for *my* inspection," he ordered.

The colonel stared at me, daring me to respond. I knew enough to keep my mouth shut. I wasn't the type who only opened his mouth to change feet.

"Yes, Sir," Blue shouted.

Colonel Murphy spent another five agonizing minutes chewing out Mr. Blue and me. He spit the pieces all over my tarnished typewriter. Then he turned his gut and followed it to the next victim. His side view gave the impression that he had once sat down too hard, pushing his buns up and out his belly button.

When the colonel began his inquisition on a pitiful PFC in Team 5, Eaton whispered: "You came through your first inspection okay, Pinky. But next time you'll know better. Clean your typewriter, and don't use it until after the inspection."

"What am I supposed to do? Sit on my thumbs and wait for him?"

"You got a better idea, Pinky?"

"Yeah, next time I'll give him a six-foot rubber, so he could go to a costume party as himself: a prick."

<hr/>

When Bohnny returned to Team 4 in the afternoon, he mentioned hearing all about my adventure with the colonel. Rather than dwelling on the subject, he smiled and said, "Saw a dynamite-looking Red Cross girl on the way back from guard duty this morning. She had flaming-red hair and a body like a goddess. Wanna know what else she had?"

"The hell with Red Cross broads," I replied. "Some of them are just money-grubbing whores."

I had heard dozens of well-documented stories that many of these ladies of aid were charging GIs $40 a throw for their *virginity*. The most infuriating incident happened a few weeks ago.

The ladies' fenced-in hooch was so popular on New Year's Eve, it had a waiting line of more than 100 officers and enlisted men. They eagerly anticipated their turn for the taste of a $40-piece of American apple pie. More expensive, if you wanted it a la mode. Or with whipped cream. And a hell of a lot more if you desired a cherry.

"Yeah, I guess you're right," Bohnny nodded. I read something in *Stars & Stripes* about the luggage of a Red Cross girl falling off a truck in Bien Hoa." He mouthed the words as though he had memorized the article. "Ten thou in American money came tumbling out of one suitcase causing a panic worse than the Crash of 1929."

"That's what I mean."

It was a shame that so many of us generalized and condemned the whole lot when only a few of them were rotten. But it served them right for charging their own guys forty bucks.

"You know what you need, Pinky?" Bohnny asked.

"What? Go back to New Jersey?"

"Well, I can't do that for you," he sighed, "but how 'bout I brighten your spirits and buy you a beer?"

"I guess I could settle for that," I replied, forcing a half-smile.

A few feet from the NCO Club, I noticed that, other than the jungle, the only things lush and green were the drunks stumbling out of the club.

We entered the darkened oasis and pushed our way to two empty stools at the bar. A dumpy Spec 5 waddled over to us. Too many free beers had taken their toll on him.

"Draw two cold ones, he's buying," I smiled, pointing a thumb at Bohnny,

Turn. Waddle.

"I should hang around with the bartender," I said. "He makes me look skinny."

Less than a minute later, the Spec 5 returned. Sausage-like fingers released two, long-awaited, sweaty mugs of beer.

Turn. Waddle.

I took a long swallow. The beer felt ice-cold as it slid down my throat and chilled my empty stomach. I closed my eyes. The next mouthful tasted like home. Even the sweaty glass felt comforting. One more gulp and the mug was empty.

"Ahh! That hit the—." I froze. "Do you hear that?"

"Hear what?"

"Listen," I prompted, music filling the air.

> *I'ma should have known it from the very start,*
> *This girl will leave me with a broken heart.*
> *Listen people what I'm telling you,*
> *Keep away from runaround Sue.*

"That's 'Runaround Sue,' " Bohnny said.

"I know," I replied, mesmerized. "It's my favorite song." Responding like a trained laboratory mouse, I stopped talking and just listened.

> *So if you don't want to cry like I do,*
> *Keep away from runaround Sue.*

"I would have liked to keep away from this place," I sighed.

"Bartender," Bohnny shouted, "two more beers."

Turn. Waddle.

"Sitting here reminds me of the time this guy walked into the NCO Club carrying an alligator," Bohnny said, evidently trying to cheer me up with a joke. "He went up to the bartender and bet him a drink he could pry open the alligator's jaws, stick his dick into the alligator's mouth, keep it in there for five minutes, and extract his manhood before the alligator slams his jaws shut and rips off his dick."

I winced, guarding my crotch with my right hand.

"'You're on,' the bartender replied, a crowd gathering around."

Without asking, Waddles delivered two more beers. I took a swig of the amber liquid and licked the foam off my lips.

"So the guy pried open the alligator's jaws," Bohnny mimicked the action with his hands, "stuck in his dick," he thrust out his pelvis, "counted off five minutes on his watch, and pulled his manhood out," he clapped his hands with a loud *pop,* making me jump, "just before the alligator slammed his massive jaws."

Bohnny grabbed his beer and emptied half the mug in two swallows.

"The crowd started applauding and patting the guy on the back," he continued, "and the bartender reluctantly gave him the drink."

Bohnny raised his voice a few octaves: "'That was remarkable,' said a guy, walking daintily over to the owner of the alligator, with admiration and desire dripping from his mouth. 'I just know *I* couldn't do anything like that.'"

Bohnny then dropped his voice a few octaves: "'Trust me,' said the brave man, 'there's nothing to it. Want to give it a try?' "

Again, a few octaves higher: "'Oh, no, I couldn't. I just know I couldn't keep *my* mouth open that long.' "

I laughed—making sure to keep my mouth closed—so hard, I nearly fell off the barstool.

"That joke deserves another round," I said, pushing our near-empty glasses towards the bartender.

Ten sausages grabbed the mugs. Turn. Waddle.

"How's the chow here at the club?" My stomach was sending alarm signals to my brain.

"The cheeseburgers aren't half-bad. I'm game if you are."

"Waddles—er, bartender," I shouted. Turn. Waddle. "*Four* of your finest cheeseburgers." I shot Bohnny a glance that said, *me hungry, want food.* "Make my two rare. Clyde?"

"Make 'em all rare," echoed Bohnny.

When the food arrived, we sipped our beers while inhaling the burgers. Then we topped off the meal with two more beers—for dessert.

"That wasn't too bad," Bohnny burped. I agreed, even louder.

Pushing back my barstool, I said over a held-back burp: "I'm ready to call it a day." The buzzing in my head signaled quitting time.

"Okay, John—oops. Sorry, Den," he corrected, "I momentarily forgot you don't use your first name."

Even though the Army forced me to fill out its stupid forms with *first* name, *middle* initial—thus the John D.—I still went by my civilian version of *first initial, middle name*—or J. Dennis. The Army had the power to pluck me out of civilian life and send me to this hellhole called Vietnam; but it didn't stand the chance of making me use my first name instead of my middle one. If the mighty nuns in grammar school couldn't force me to do it—even with repeated threats of being whacked with a ruler, or by calling on the Almighty—the lowly Army never stood a chance.

When I stood up, my left foot slipped off the bottom rung of the stool, and I bumped into Bohnny.

"Let me guide you back to your tent," he offered. "And if you promise to be good," he added in a fatherly tone, "I'll even tuck you in."

I giggled. "Only if you promise to tell me a story, daddy."

We eventually said our goodbyes in front of my tent—foregoing the bedtime story and any tucking-in ceremony.

Sunday morning shined brightly. I took advantage of not having to be at work until the afternoon by sleeping to 0930 and enjoying a leisurely shower—with soap, not Prell. Decked out in my civvies, I took a stroll to the Post Chapel.

A sign out front said Catholic services were at 0800 hours—almost three hours ago. I decided to try the door anyway—hoping I could at least make a visit. It opened without resistance.

Inside were ten rows of pews and a generous center aisle. I walked up to the second row, making sure to genuflect before entering the pew.

Sitting in the serenity of the chapel, I could hear the gentle beating of my heart. For the first time in about a month, I was at ease.

Other than God, I was the only one in this sanctuary. He stood before me, nailed to His cross. His eyes embraced me, filling me with a rainbow of visions: my wife . . . my parents . . . home. A burning within me cleansed a path from my swollen eyes to my dimpled chin.

A gentle, trusting voice said everything was going to be all right. I would live to see October. My freedom bird would lift me over the clouds to the waiting arms of a tearful wife. I would see the smiling face of my mother. Feel the firm grasp of my father's embrace.

A blurry vision appeared before me. It was the two soldiers who had guarded our convoy from Long Binh to Bearcat. Because of their menacing looks and protective powers, I termed them my "guardian angels," hoping they would keep watch over me during my tour. Now, though, their once ominous looks became as gentle as snowflakes. They smiled and gave a nod of reassurance. One extended his right hand, offering me my plane ticket home. I accepted it. Its warmth and promise soothed me. The harder I squeezed the ticket, the more reassured I felt. Even though I knew my hand was empty, my heart told me the vision would replay itself in October.

At this very moment, I realized nothing would stop me from leaving Vietnam and returning home. Alive.

Chapter 5

Weeks later, the atrocity of the Tet uprising invaded our collective minds. Or at least as much as the Army brass would tell us. Some reports came from what we were told; others from clippings out of hometown newspapers. It was hard to know which reports to believe, regardless of their source.

First, it was necessary to understand the significance of Tet. This was the most sacred Vietnamese holiday, bigger than a combination of our Thanksgiving, Christmas, New Year, and the Fourth of July.

In its glorious honor, the U.S. high command issued a ceasefire and stand down. Tens of thousands of Vietnamese rejoined their families to exchange gifts and celebrate the Year of the Monkey. However, someone forgot to pass the word to 70,000 VC soldiers who violated the truce. They hit the U.S. Embassy in Saigon. Blew up the ammo dump in Long Binh. Rendered inoperative the airport at Bien Hoa. Attacked General Westmoreland's headquarters. Destroyed the South Vietnamese general staff offices. And occupied Hue, South Vietnam's third largest city, for three weeks, infiltrating other strongholds: Nha Trang, Da Nang, Cam Ranh Bay, and Pleiku, where my orders originally had me stationed. In all, they penetrated thirty provincial capitals.

Three days after Tet began, President Johnson labeled the VC offensive a complete failure.

Why?

Vietcong leaders had counted on popular support in the cities, and—according to LBJ—they found little or none. In addition, more than 10,500 VC were killed by midnight on 1 February.

The real numbers told a different story, especially in Saigon and Hue.

By the time the VC withdrew from Saigon, large chunks of the city lay in ruins. More than 130,000 were homeless. The most political damage was to the U.S. Embassy. By attacking this stronghold, the VC proved to the South Vietnamese people that the United States was vulnerable, despite its immense power.

The attack began along Thong Nhut Boulevard at 0300 hours on 31 January. Using a fifteen-pound explosive charge, the Vietcong C-10 Sapper Battalion blew a three-foot-wide hole in the eight-foot-high wall surrounding the Embassy compound. Their commandos penetrated the defenses and killed five GIs. Four Saigon policemen, on guard outside, fled as soon as shooting began.

The most intensive fighting of the Tet uprising was in Hue, a northern province 50 miles below the DMZ.

This onslaught began an hour before the one on our Embassy and lasted until we regained control of Hue on 24 February. During those three weeks, the VC crushed the ARVN (Army of the Republic of South Vietnam) garrison and killed—or brutally executed—3,500 civilians. Three-quarters of its homes were destroyed, leaving 100,000 of its 145,000 residents to become refugees in their own city.

And Johnson said Tet wasn't successful!

According to the newspaper clippings, the significance of Tet was that half a million U.S. troops couldn't provide the South Vietnamese government with sufficient strength to fight the enemy. Even though the VC took the combat out of jungle cover into formidable urban areas.

All during Tet, the atmosphere at Bearcat was pregnant with anticipation of Charlie's visit. Especially after someone discovered a tunnel by the 9th Supply and Transportation Battalion leading out under the berm. Charlie had been using the tunnel to steal our supplies. Did he have plans to use it as a mass infiltration point for Tet? We never gave him the chance. A few grenades took care of Checkpoint Charlie.

For added security, the even-numbered bunkers were on twenty-four-hour guard. Even to take a leak, we wore our flak jackets and steel pots, a.k.a. helmets. In spite of these precautions, we were not provided ammo for our impotent M16s.

Bang . . . ouch! . . . there go our feets.

After the evening meal, if we weren't on guard duty, we went back to the office to process mountains of paperwork for guys wounded or killed in action. That was the most devastating part of my tour.

Horror stories circulated throughout PA. Like the tragedy of not finding dozens of 201 Files because the records were still in IN-PRO-CESSING. The guys had been killed less than a week after landing in Nam.

Another whispered story concerned two lieutenants in the same unit killed minutes apart. One was in-country thirteen days; the other, twenty-five. The twenty-five-day "veteran" died because one of our 105mm artillery rounds fell short and exploded in his back pocket.

Lost in these numbers and reports was one fact: While I was on guard duty, on the evening of 30 January to the morning of 31 January, 1,500 VC hovered around Bearcat. Had I known that lone statistic while standing guard with an "empty" M16, I'd have shit green bricks all night. And for many weeks to come.

Charlie left Bearcat alone, except for a few mortar rounds. We got through it okay. On the other hand, the Tet uprising took its toll on one member of The Pit: Jim Dorsey.

His brother, Tom, had twenty-three days left. After eleven months of fighting in Vietnam, he was on the last leg of his tour when his luck ran out on his last scheduled patrol.

Technically, the patrol was over. The squad was on its way back to the safe boundaries of base camp. Half a mile from sanctuary, Tom stepped on a land mine and blew himself to pieces. Many, many pieces. What body parts his squad could find were collected in a poncho and carried back to base camp. The pieces were reassembled in a coffin.

Jim left on 6 February to escort the body home. That morning, The Pit bade Jim a silent goodbye. Even though we never saw him again—he received a compassionate reassignment—he and Tom remained in our thoughts for a long time.

Not only did the VC kill Tom, they ruined the only thrill Jim looked forward to: going home.

CHAPTER 6

" . . . to you. Happy birthday, dear Pinky, happy birthday to you."

It was the early hours of 26 February, my twenty-fourth birthday. I opened my eyes to the smiling faces of Eaton, Hoffman, Moritoni, and Grabowski.

"Close your eyes, and put out your hands," Grabowski ordered, holding his hands behind his back, while Hoffman and Moritoni lifted my mosquito net.

How sweet. They chipped in for a present.

I did as instructed. Nothing touched my outstretched hands. Ten seconds went by. Fifteen. Nothing. As I was stealing a peek, a waterfall engulfed me.

"Da-damn, that's cold!" I clacked.

"Since we couldn't give you breakfast in bed," Eaton said, as Hoffman and Moritoni put down a humongous canvas bucket, "we decided to give you a bath."

"It's almost the end of the month anyway," Grabowski chimed in. "So we figured it was about time for one."

"Th-thanks," I shivered.

Changing the subject, Moritoni asked, "Did you get the bottle, Pinky?"

"Yeah, finally," came my unenthusiastic reply.

Because I was only a Spec 5, I couldn't buy a bottle of booze. I could suck up all the mixed drinks I wanted at the NCO Club, but I did not have *permission* (there's that damned word again) to purchase a bottle of booze. That was another stupid rule of the 9ᵗʰ Infantry. Had I been an officer, or at least an E-6 (staff sergeant), no problem. Even if I were a lowly 19-year-old brown bar (2ⁿᵈ LT), I could buy all the bottles my fat paycheck could afford. But as an E-5, I was not given permission to buy a bottle of anything but soda or beer. After being turned down by other lifers, Mr. Blue gratefully agreed to purchase the nectar of the gods for me. I gave him my $1.25 (in MPC, of course), and he got me an imperial quart of 100-proof vodka. As a birthday bonus, he threw in an extra bottle—proving that, on rare occasions, some officers actually could be human.

"Did you guys get the mix?" I asked.

"Yeah," Moritoni said. "I conned a couple cans of orange juice and tomato juice from the mess sergeant."

"How?"

"Told him it was for Mr. Blue," he laughed.

"Great! Remember," I added, "we celebrate tomorrow night." Since I had guard duty on my birthday, we postponed the celebration until the next night. Some guys would agree to anything if free booze was involved.

"Well, we gotta go to work," Grabowski pointed out. "See ya later, Pinky."

"Yeah," Moritoni added sarcastically, "we don't have the whole day off."

I already had the afternoon off because of guard, so Mr. Blue gave me the morning off for my birthday. Why was Blue being so nice to me? Did he have bad news in store?

Half-drenched, I sat on my cot, with no choice other than to get up and finish the dousing given me. Since it was only 0600 hours, the water was colder than a witch's tit in a brass bra in a snow drift on New Year's Eve. So I showered fast and toweled off.

Deciding not to screw up my birthday, I skipped breakfast—except for my malaria pill (nine down; thirty-two to go)—and headed to the PX for a haircut.

The post barber shop was in a king-sized hooch—similar to all the other two-story wooden structures—attached to the rear of the PX. It had twenty chairs and seldom a wait. When I approached, I was surprised to find a long waiting line. A quick glance through the double-wide screen doors revealed the reason: six of the chairs didn't have barbers.

"What happened to the missing barbers?" I asked an impatient Spec 4.

"Killed during Tet."

My heart sank. Unpleasant memories of Tet resurfaced, eating at my soul like acid. Would the insanity of this place never end?

"Poor bastards," I sighed.

"Don't feel sorry for 'em," he shot back. "They were NVA officers."

His words left a red handprint on my cheek. Sorrow changed to disgust at the reality of this conflict: Our barbers were officers in the North Vietnamese Army. They cut our hair during the day. Our throats at night.

A gruesome war story flashed through my head. Six months before I got to Nam, not twenty feet from where I now waited, a major was getting his monthly haircut. He watched impatiently in a nearby mirror as papa-san clipped away. When the old gook finished the major's trim, he finished him for good. Instead of using the straight razor for the "cutout" around his hairline, papa-san slit the major's throat. Blood gushed everywhere, splattering the mirror like a teenager popping a juicy zit. Thanks to a sergeant's handy .45 pistol, the barber was killed on the spot. The gook's brain tissue and blood mixed with his victim's blood, generating a crimson-white mess on the officer's limp body.

From that time on, higher-ranking officers—majors and above— didn't get their haircuts at the post barber shop. They trusted one of their own men with a razor.

After about fifteen minutes of indecision, I made up my mind to forget the haircut—and save not only my scalp, but my throat.

"Next, GI," a barber shouted at me. The look of executioner was carved on his wizened face. "Next," he demanded. "You come."

I was trapped. If I turned and left, it would look chicken shit. So I pushed one wobbly leg in front of the other—carefully stepping over a faded crimson stain—and walked the longest, slowest twenty feet of my life.

Was it only my imagination, or were there wrist and ankle straps on his chair? As well as a head restraint?

Inspecting every inch of the chair beforehand, I cautiously plunked down my butt. Spinning my head a full 360 degrees, I kept a watchful eye on my diminutive barber as he circled his prey.

"GI want works?" he interrogated.

"Ya-yes," I stuttered.

Although I never had "the works" before, I knew that it consisted of a haircut, a facial, and a body massage. The haircut cost 30 cents; another 95 cents for the mugging.

Bzzz. The clippers danced up my neck. The gook smiled, revealing mustard-colored teeth. Bzzz. Now he bore the clippers into my left temple. Bzzz. Then the right. Bzzz.

"Easy with the top," I instructed, as he swooped down like a kamikaze aiming for my destruction.

"Okay, GI," came with another mustard grin.

Bzzz. He took off the top layer of skin.

The ancient Oriental mercifully put the clippers on a counter and picked up a pair of long, pointy scissors. As he whirled around, I caught a glimpse of a dark red stain on the tip of one blade.

I froze.

He took a snip here, a snip there.

I relaxed.

Returning to his counter, he exchanged the scissors for a straight razor.

I morphed into an icicle.

He turned ever so slowly and crept over to me, poising the blade above his panther-black eyes. I stared into them and beheld the anger of five generations. Then I looked back at his weapon. The overhead light danced on the lethal edge of the razor, momentarily blinding me. When I regained my sight, he was at my feet, coiled and waiting. I cringed and slammed shut my eyes, bracing myself for the inevitable.

My assailant grabbed my throat, ensuring instant tire tracks in my shorts. Then a quick scrape, scrape, scrape, and . . . my haircut was over.

I survived.

Thank God Spec 5s weren't worth killing in the open arena of a barber shop.

The gook overturned a bottle of pungent blue liquid into his calloused left palm and worked the substance into my face and hair. Now I smelled like a French whore. So much for the facial.

He came at me with two empty hands. He slowly put his fingertips together and spread apart ten bony digits. Making sure the heels of his hands were still in contact with each other, he chopped at my shoulders. My neck. My back. Tensed muscles suddenly relaxed under his Paul Bunyan pounding. I felt renewed. And a gentle swelling in my loins. This was almost as good as sex. Whatever that was.

"All done, GI," he said, holding out an empty palm.

I gave him $2.00. Without waiting for my change, I covered my prize boner with my jungle hat, hastened down the crowded aisle, and pole-vaulted through the double doors to freedom.

"You, troop," screamed the First Sergeant as he entered The Pit. "Why are you on your ass, doing nothing?"

I was relaxing on my bunk, reading *Fahrenheit 451*. About three hours remained before I had to leave for guard duty.

"I have guard today," I explained, jumping to attention, "and Mr. Blue gave me the extra time off for my birthday, Top." Top was a nickname for a first sergeant, but SFC Smith was the bottom. He was as popular as a fart in church.

"No excuse, Specialist," he barked, spraying me with his alcoholic breath. His big, black cigar did nothing to disguise the booze. "And my name is First Sergeant Smith, not Top," he growled.

"Yes, First Sergeant—Smith."

Top was a triple-threat in red: straggly carrot hair, bloodshot eyes, a Rudolph-the-Reindeer nose. Like Colonel Murphy, Smith was big and fat. He weighed at least 240 pounds; credit his gut with about 80 of it. He resembled an over-ripe melon with arms and legs.

This dumb asshole soaked up liquor like a sponge. Even though he was with the 9th Admin for only a few months, Top had been caught drunk on duty three times. Prior to transferring to the 9th, he'd been thrown out of more units than Army-town whores had crabs.

He stuffed the unlit cigar in his mouth and chewed furiously. Then he dropped his clipboard and bullhorn—his constant companions—on Eaton's bunk. The clipboard was his security blanket; the hollowed-out bullhorn was a great place to hide his flask of booze. He rifled through his pockets, found the needed match, lit his stinking black rope, and dropped the burning match on the floor. Puffing intently, he surveyed the interior of the tent.

"This place looks like hell," he complained, flapping his right arm, cigar ashes falling in its wake. "Inside, out, and underneath."

Tough shit, Top.

"I want it cleaned. I want it to shine," he demanded. "I'll be back in two hours."

He dropped the cigar on the floor, crushed it with his right boot, and flashed a shit-eating grin. With two doughy hands, he picked up his clipboard and bullhorn and bounced out of The Pit.

Thanks, you son of a bitch. There goes my afternoon off.

As much as I hated to, I swept and mopped every inch of the floor. I Brassoed the nails, washed the baseboards, and dusted the Venetian blinds. Then I scrubbed the walls, shook out the welcome mat, and spit-shined the sandbags and door bell. Next I repainted the front and back doors, made sure the front porch light worked, crawled under The Pit, and picked up all the garbage and dead animals. That done, I hung up exquisitely framed pictures of Top—excuse me, First Sergeant Smith—Captain Oscar, and Colonel Murphy.

Dream on.

All I did was pick up a couple empty beer bottles, shove the remains of Top's raunchy cigar in one of them, straighten my bunk, and leave early for guard. FTA, First Sergeant Smith.

Guard was a pisser. We were on gray alert most of the night: two guys had to be on duty, while the third one slept.

Sometime after 0300 I woke up shivering. I couldn't tell the exact time because my watch had stopped. The crystal was frosted over, tiny dew drops trapped inside. I didn't know whether it was broken or not, but I had a psychic feeling the watch would tell the right time only twice a day from now on.

I sat up in the cot and put my arms into my field jacket and snapped the buttons from top (first sergeant?) to bottom. Still shivering, I grabbed a smelly blanket and tossed it on over my shoulders. The cold gnawed at me. The temperature had to be somewhere in the 70s, yet I was freezing my ass off.

Reluctantly, I busted out of the cot and started walking in small circles. Not feeling any warmer, I began flapping my arms. Maybe I could fly back to New Jersey? Gradually, the numbness subsided.

Out of the corner of my left eye, I saw a flare explode and the grass in front of the next bunker caught fire. The growing inferno resembled a lighthouse beacon as it swept up to the bunker and ignited the front wall of sandbags. Less than a minute later, the fire mysteriously went out. Brief as the episode was, it lasted long enough to make me take off my shorts and ring them out.

When I got back to The Pit, there was a box on my bunk. My eyes eagerly measured it: a foot, by two feet, by about another two feet. Neatly printed on a red-framed Dennison® label were four words: " FROM ALL OF US." My first package from home.

I eased myself onto the edge of my bed and visually caressed the parcel that had traveled more than 12,000 miles. For about five minutes, I stared at it, rereading every word on the wrapping.

When I was at Marquette, I appreciated getting a CARE package. But it wasn't a big deal. In Nam, anything from home was cause for celebration. Especially a package. Letters were like the warm, happy feeling you got from a wet dream. But a package . . . that was like real sex: something you could hold, touch, taste, and smell. More than just words on a page, it contained real stuff from The World.

My heart raced as I tenderly ran my fingertips over the box.

I picked it up. It felt like ten pounds of solid gold. I lovingly cradled it in my arms—like a first-time mother holding her baby. I gently unwrapped it with the expectations of a couple on their wedding night.

On the top was a note from Annette. Tears stung my eyes. I tried reading the words, but it was like looking through the exasperating line on a pair of bifocals. From what I could make out, the package contained gifts from Annette, her parents, mine, her Aunt Betty, and Sam and Joyce Tarcza.

My first selection was the present from my in-laws. It was a little bit bigger than a bar of soap. And about as heavy.

I tore off the bright wrapping paper. It was a Timex. Great! I took off my waterlogged watch and replaced it with my shiny new one. I pulled out the stem, set it—guessing at the exact time—and wound it. Tick, tick, tick. Back in business.

I took out something wrapped in aluminum foil. It had a little tag on it. "We love and miss you, Son. Love, Mom and Dad."

Carefully unfolding the flaps, I discovered two dozen *kiflis*: Hungarian fruit-filled cookies. Selecting an apricot one, I bit it in half. It tasted sinfully delicious. I finished it and then put two lekvar (prune jelly) ones in my mouth. I chewed them slowly—letting my saliva make them good and mushy. I held back the impulse to finish them all and quickly refolded the foil.

The next gift, neatly wrapped in red paper with white " Happy Birthdays," was from Joyce and Sam.

I gave in to my first reaction and shook it. It sounded like cookies. Or something broken. My first guess was closer. Unwrapping the paper revealed a box of my favorite crackers: Chicken in a Biskit. I tore off the box top and stuffed a handful into my mouth. God! they were good.

After wiping my hands on my fatigues, I took out an envelope marked "Open Me Last" and obediently set it aside.

The bottom of my CARE package held a box from Annette. Little ducks covered the wrapping paper. More quackers?

Instead of taking a shaking-guess this time, I held it to my nose and inhaled deeply. A mixture of aromas filled my senses. My fingers anxiously exposed a collection of cherished items: six packets of Kool-Aid, some iced tea mix (both were great because the water here tasted like bat piss), an individual-sized box of Fanny Farmer candy, a small homemade fruitcake, a paperback by John Dickson Carr, and . . . a can of black shoe polish. Yahoo! I could look like a lifer again.

Now for the "Open Me Last" item. It was from Aunt Betty.

I held the envelope up to the blazing sun. A vague object—about three inches by six inches—was enclosed. I opened my footlocker, got my P-38, and carefully slit open the envelope. Inside was a letter. When I unfolded it, a new $5 bill fell into my lap.

> *Denny,*
>   *Didn't know what to get or make for your birthday. I know that giving money can be "tacky," but I thought you'd enjoy having a little piece of home to carry around in your wallet.*
>   *We love and miss you. We pray for your safety every day.*
>   *Enjoy your birthday—as best you can.*
>   *Love,*
>   *Aunt Betty*

I picked up the $5 bill. Its crispness was familiar, and comforting.

It had been about two months since I held real money. I never was so happy to see the expressionless face of Lincoln with the lock of hair dangling over his forehead.

I turned over the bill. Above the picture of the Lincoln Memorial were the familiar words "IN GOD WE TRUST." Even though the silhouette of a seated president was barely recognizable through the columns, the colossal statue of Lincoln was emblazoned in my memory, thanks to my two trips to Washington, D.C. As school kids, we memorized the emotional words on the wall behind our sixteenth president. Squeezing the $5 bill, I repeated them aloud: "In this temple as in the hearts of the people for whom he saved the Union the memory of Abraham Lincoln is enshrined forever."

This little piece of paper was the best gift of all. Not being allowed to have real money made it all the more special. I quickly hid it in my wallet—before someone saw it and made me exchange it for MPC.

I repacked the gifts into the box and lovingly placed the CARE package in my footlocker.

"Hi," a voice behind me gasped.

I looked over my shoulder and saw a PFC standing inside the entrance to The Pit. His chest pounded as he balanced everything he owned—including the proverbial kitchen sink. An enormous smile exposed snow-white teeth.

"I . . . was . . . told . . . this was my tent."

I returned his constant smile.

"Which bunk . . . should I take?"

"Second one on your right," I pointed. "It belonged to Dorsey."

"Belonged?" he hesitated.

"He went home." He was obviously shaken by the " missing" occupant, so I told him Dorsey DEROSed.

"Oh. Thanks," he said. The squeaky cot almost collapsed when he dropped his worldly possessions on it. "Private First Class Chris McGuire at your service," he bellowed, with a touch of Southern accent.

Again he smiled, lighting up The Pit like a Christmas tree at midnight.

Without even knowing him, I instantly liked him. He made me feel comfortable. As though he could somehow find a nice way to tell me I had a piece of spinach stuck between my teeth.

"Dennis Papp." I returned his smile and extended my hand. He pumped it warmly.

McGuire was an inch or two my senior, a couple-three years my junior. His slender frame carried a little extra around the middle. Hidden behind his radiant smile were crystal-clear blue eyes, a full head of medium-length blond hair, and peach fuzz for a mustache.

"Where ya from?"

"Atlanta," he grinned.

Damn, this guy was all smiles. He seemed happier than a pig in shit. "Don't you ever stop smiling?"

"I try not to. Life's too short to take seriously. Don't get me wrong," he quickly added, "I'm not happy to be here. It's just that there's nothing I can do about it, so I try to take it in stride."

"I just got back from guard. I need a shower." McGuire nodded agreement. "Why don't you get settled it, and I'll buy you a cup of coffee after I scrub off the stink and put on clean fatigues."

"Thanks, I'd appreciate it," he smiled.

"You, Private," an unknown sergeant ordered, sticking his head inside our tent. "Follow me. You just volunteered for my detail. On the double!"

"Yes, Sergeant." McGuire looked back at me and shrugged. "You still owe me that cup of coffee," he reminded me.

Like it was drilled into him during basic training, he made an about-face and hustled after the sergeant, his smile disappearing into the glowing sun.

Chapter 7

ALL THE REST HAVE 31

"Who's that?" Moritoni asked, pouring himself another healthy drink.

My birthday party was in full swing. Grabowski had already exceeded his limit—two—and was babbling to himself in his bunk. A frustrated Eaton, holding an empty glass, was quizzing a smiling Hoffman, our resident trivia expert, on insignificant facts about the planets.

I turned in the direction of Moritoni's nod and saw McGuire, head hung low, drag himself into The Pit.

"That's Chris McGuire. He joined us today, while you guys were at work. They put him on a detail five minutes after he arrived." Motioning with my free hand, I shouted, "Hey, McGuire, come on over and get a drink."

McGuire summoned all his strength and plodded over to us. "Couldn't handle a drink right now," he smiled. "I'd pass out after the first sip. Even when I'm not tired, I get drunk reading the label."

"At least let me introduce you," I offered.

Through a fading smile, he replied: "Okay."

"This ugly turd is Tony Moritoni—from New York."

"Hi." McGuire extended his right hand with noticeable effort and turned up the volume on his dim-witted smile.

Moritoni switched the drink to his left hand—spilling a quarter of it—and accepted McGuire's limp greeting. "Hi . . . Smiles. Welcome to Vietnam." He returned the drink to his right hand and licked the spilled nectar that remained on the left one.

McGuire perked up at the mention of his new nickname. "Thanks," he beamed. "Do I still get the drink?"

Surprised at the sudden about-face in his mood, I pointed to the makeshift bar on my footlocker and said, "Help yourself."

He mixed a weak screwdriver, pointed a thumb over his shoulder, and asked, "Who's the babbling brook?"

"That's Mike Grabowski," Moritoni said. "Had two too many."

At the mention of his name, Grabowski lifted his head, grinned, turned on his side, attempted to sit up on his right elbow, and fell out of bed.

"Nice meeting you, too," McGuire nodded.

With drinks in hand, Moritoni and I took McGuire to meet Hoffman and Eaton.

"Okay, smart-ass," Eaton complained, "how far is *Mars* from the Sun?" He attempted a sip from his empty glass.

Hoffman winked at us and answered, "Approximately 141,600,000 miles."

"What about Pluto?" Eaton shot back.

"3,666,000,000," Hoffman grinned. "And, Specialist Eaton, if you meant the distance from Pluto to *Mars*," he kiddingly added, "that's about 3,524,400,000 miles."

Eaton took another empty swallow, stared into his glass, and blurted: "What's the diameter of the Sun, *Specialist* Hoffman?"

Almost before Eaton finished his question, Hoffman responded: "865,000 miles."

"What's the tem—"

"At the Sun's surface, it's about 10,800 degrees—Fahrenheit! 25,200,000 degrees at the center."

"How do you know all this shit?" Eaton shouted, taking another mouthful of air from his empty glass.

"Just do." Hoffman gave us another wink.

McGuire leaned over to me and whispered into my right ear: "How does Eaton know Hoffman's telling him the truth?"

Pointing to Eaton's red face, I whispered back: "At this point, I don't think it matters." Raising my voice, I added, "If you two can stop your verbal war for a minute, I'd like to introduce a newbie. This is

Chris McGuire—or as the Face coined him, Smiles."

"Hi, Smiles. I'm known as Boomerang," Hoffman stated proudly. "This dickhead," he put a friendly hand on Eaton's shoulder and had it immediately shrugged off, "goes by the name of Numbers."

"Boomerang?" McGuire questioned.

I explained the meaning by spreading my hands apart the appropriate length, then making a gentle U-shape with the right one.

"Wow!" he exclaimed. "You could put out a three-alarm fire with that hose." Then he gave Eaton a sympathetic look and continued, "But take it easy on Numbers, because it's rough being a dick."

"Oh?" Hoffman prompted.

"Yeah," McGuire's smile brightened, "you always have to hang around with two nuts," he stared at Hoffman and then at Moritoni, "and," nodding towards Grabowski, "your best friend is a pussy."

"Hah!" Eaton laughed and slapped Hoffman on the back.

Obviously remembering his bunk was next to mine, Eaton patted me on the shoulder and grinned. "Worst of all, my closest neighbor is an asshole." He lifted his glass to take a drink, realized it was empty, and let his arm fall limply to his side.

I smiled at Eaton's rebuttal and realized when guys get together, they degenerate to the lowest common denominator and act like a bunch of kids. But then, we *were* a bunch of kids. At 24, I was the oldest one in the group. Most of the others were scarcely out of high school—some hadn't graduated yet. Compared with World War II vets, who averaged something like 24, we were babies . . . sporting pimples instead of facial hair.

"So where ya from, Smiles?" Hoffman asked.

"Georgia. Atlanta."

"I've been to Atlanta," Hoffman said. "What part do you call home?"

"Let's just say it was a tough neighborhood," he replied cautiously. When McGuire saw my expression turn to concern, he winked at me.

"How tough can Atlanta be?" Moritoni scoffed.

"We used to steal hubcaps from—"

"Big deal," Moritoni cut in. "You think we didn't steal hubcaps in New York?"

"From *moving* cars?" McGuire challenged.

There was a soft thud behind us. We turned and saw Grabowski trying to climb back onto his bunk. Defying the law of gravity, he sprung to his feet, sprinted the few steps outside The Pit, and with an "Oh, shit!" tossed in, puked all over the backyard. To show our appreciation for holding it until he got outside, we gave him a resounding round of applause.

"Thank you, thank you," Bohnny said, entering The Pit through the front door flap. "Didn't expect such a warm greeting. Happy birthday, Pinky." He held up two six-packs of beer and two pizzas.

"Thanks, Clyde. I'll take the beer, and you can put the tomato pies on the closest empty bunk."

"*Tomato pies?*" he frowned, pushing up the bridge of his glasses with his now-free right hand.

"That's what we call a pizza back home," I explained.

"You're *dinky dau*, Pinky," Bohnny said.

"I am not crazy," I shot back, swinging a six-pack at his head.

"Anybody who calls pizza tomato pie doesn't have his shit together." He put the boxes on Hoffman's bunk. "But you still get the first slice of *tomato pie*, because it's your birthday."

"Since nobody was kind enough to get me a birthday cake, I will deem it an honor to take the first slice of birthday *pie*."

"Ahhh . . . birthday cake," Eaton sighed. "Home is made of cake and icing . . . " He attempted another drink from his still-empty glass, muttered a few choice obscenities, swung around, and headed for our makeshift bar.

While Eaton was going through his diatribe to his empty glass, I gratefully grabbed the first slice of pizza and gobbled half of it in a single bite.

"Yuk! This pie needs some help," I complained.

"Wait a sec," Moritoni said and went to his footlocker. He dug around for a few seconds and eventually held up salt and pepper shakers. "Here, try these."

Bohnny grabbed them and said, "Let me." As though he were masturbating, he shook on generous amounts. "There, taste it now," he challenged, and immediately adjusted his glasses.

I took a bite, scrunched up my face, said, "Just right," and spit an empty mouthful onto the floor. "Garlic is what it needs."

Without hesitation, Moritoni returned to his footlocker, rummaged around, and proudly offered me a small bottle labeled GARLIC POWDER.

"Where the hell did you get that?" I asked.

"Don't ask. But what kind of Italian would I be without it?"

"You sound like my wife."

"Your wife's Italian?" he beamed.

"Half. The better half is German."

"Got any more vodka?" Eaton yelled, holding up an empty bottle and shaking it.

"There's another one in my footlocker," I replied.

"Good thing Mr. Blue got you the extra bottle," Bohnny said.

"Yeah, Clyde, you're right," Eaton agreed, attacking my footlocker. After ten seconds, he pulled his head out—gasping for air—and shouted: "Where the hell is it, Pinky?"

"It's right under—"

"Never mind," he dove back in, "I got it."

Fortified by nearly two bottles of vodka and a couple six-packs of beer, we began a verbal assault on officers and lifers. When the comments turned to Mr. Blue, and changed from sarcastic to mildly complimentary, it reminded me of a question I had since the first time I met Blue.

"Speaking of Mr. Blue," I said, "is there something wrong with his feet or legs? He—"

"Why do you ask?" Moritoni interrupted.

I gave Moritoni a dirty look and continued.

"I've noticed that he keeps shifting his weight when he stands or sits for a long time."

"I remember reading something in his 66 File," Hoffman said, "about him getting frostbite in Korea. The doctors wanted to amputate his feet, but Mr. Blue wouldn't let them."

The thought of a saw tearing away at my ankles made me shiver.

"He has to wear padded boots. And he's supposed to soak his feet every few days," Hoffman added.

"Sorry I asked."

Changing the subject, McGuire smiled and said, "I didn't know today was your birthday. How old are you?"

"Yesterday was actually my birthday. I'm 24."

McGuire looked up at the ceiling, waved a finger in the air as though he were calculating, and said, "You were a leap year baby."

"Yup."

He again stared at the ceiling, as though he had taped a crib sheet there, and searched his memory. Then he looked me in the eyes and recited: "Thirty days hath September, April, June and November—"

"I know, I know. All the rest have 31, blah, blah, blah," I responded in a monotone.

"And since *this* is a leap year," McGuire said, "you get to spend an extra day in Vietnam. Special birthday present from the Army."

"Son of a bitch! You're right."

I eyed four footlockers stacked in a corner to give us extra room for my party. Holding back the urge to take out my frustration on them with a few well-placed kicks, I slurped down my glass in one gulp.

"Just like the damned Army to squeeze something extra out of me," I complained, wiping my mouth with the back of my right hand. "Thanks for reminding me."

"Don't mention it." Seeing that the extra day obviously bothered me, he looked at my generous waist and quickly added, "Twenty-four, you say?"

"Uh-huh."

"God! you're ancient. You must be at the stage where your knees buckle, but your belt won't." McGuire flashed one of his patented smiles.

"Not really." I mirrored his smile. "But when I see a great-looking woman, my mind *does* make promises that my body can't keep."

"Is it true," McGuire asked, trying to gain the upper hand, "that when you paint the town red, you have to take a long nap before you put on the second coat?"

"That's right." I leaned toward him so that our faces almost touched, and added, "But the nap, no matter how *looong* it is, will still be over before the day *you* DEROS."

McGuire bent his head, shuffled his feet, and sighed, "Cruel, Pinky. Really cruel."

"Sorry," I laughed, giving the back of his neck a fatherly squeeze.

"What's going on?" Spec 4 Bill Williams asked, pushing his way into The Pit.

"Having a little party for me. Where ya been?"

"At work," he muttered, his voice more raspy than usual. "Just came back for a minute because I ran out of smokes."

He made a bee-line to his footlocker.

Bending over, Williams used a nicotine-stained right hand to toss open the lid. Exposed were six cartons of Camels and a pile of socks and underwear. He ripped off the end flap of one carton, grabbed two packs, and calculated out loud, "This should get me through the rest of the night."

"Got time for a drink?" I asked.

Williams closed his footlocker with a slam and replied with an abrupt "No."

Balancing the two packs of cigarettes in his left hand, he opened one with obvious precision and greedily extracted a coffin nail. He fumbled in a lower pocket in his fatigue shirt and found the needed torch. In a single, fluid motion, he flipped open the cap, spun the wheel of his scratched Zippo, raised his eyebrows, and carefully applied the four-inch flame. After inhaling half the cigarette in one drag, Williams stuffed his Zippo and the two packs of Camels into the same generous shirt pocket. Then, like the Lone Ranger, he left in a cloud of smoke, without uttering another word.

"What's his problem?" McGuire asked.

"He recently got a 'Dear John' letter from his girlfriend," Hoffman explained.

As though he were reciting Shakespeare, McGuire held up an opened hand and proclaimed: "Well, it's better to have loved and lost, than to have paid for it and not liked it."

"It's not that easy, Smiles," Hoffman said. "Williams DEROSes in about a month, and he was gonna get married when he got home."

McGuire's head drooped. "Sorry, I didn't know."

"What's going on in here?" demanded an unidentified voice from the back of the tent.

"Who the fuck wants to know?" Hoffman yelled.

"*I* do," the voice said with an extra layer of sarcasm.

Turning to face the voice, we saw Sergeant First Class Smith bouncing up to our little group at the front of The Pit. His left hand held the bull horn; his right gripped the clipboard. Smoke belched from a black cigar.

"Oh, sorry, Sir. Didn't know it was you," Hoffman apologized and came to attention. The rest of us straightened up like uncooked spaghetti.

"Don't call me *sir*," Smith bellowed, "I *work* for a living."

Since when, I thought.

"Sorry, Top," Hoffman corrected himself.

"Don't call me Top," the first sergeant yelled, blowing rancid smoke into Hoffman's face.

Tiny drops of perspiration erupted on Hoffman's forehead. "S-sorry, First Sergeant."

Smith shoved the clipboard under his left arm, grabbed the cigar with his freed hand, and flicked ashes onto Hoffman's boots.

"Well, what the hell's going on in here?" he demanded again.

"Uh . . . well . . . you see, First Sergeant," Hoffman hesitated, "it's Pinky's—uh, Specialist Papp's birthday, and we were—uh, having a little party for him."

Sweat ran down Hoffman's forehead, making him squint.

"Well—uh, yesterday was actually his birthday," he quickly corrected, "but—uh, he had guard duty yesterday, and postponed his party until tonight so he could—uh, be here for his own party. *You know*," Hoffman pleaded, totally exhausted. He started to raise his right hand to wipe the sweat from his eyes, evidently thought better of it, and quickly returned it to a stiffened position at his side.

Thud.

All heads turned to the back of the tent. Grabowski had tumbled out of his bunk, again. In his effort to get up, he overturned the cot on top of himself. Flailing away at his covers, he resembled a cat trying to get out of a pillow case.

It would have been easier to settle this damned war than hold back our laughter. Somehow, not a ripple emerged.

"Where were we? Oh, yes," Top's eyes lit up, "*yesterday.* I remember now."

Keeping the clipboard pressed in his left armpit, he pushed Moritoni aside with his bullhorn and bellied up to me.

"I came in here and told this sorry excuse for a soldier," he spat cigar smoke at my face, "to clean up this shit house. Apparently, *he* didn't do what I ordered."

I alternately stared at his whiskey-ripened nose and the beady eyes above it, calling to mind a few, choice defamatory expressions of my affection for him. Without warning, Top's eyes met mine. I had the sickening feeling he had just read my mind, because the rest of his complexion suddenly matched the color of his lumpy proboscis.

"Sorry . . . F-First Sergeant," I stammered, "I guess I didn't do a good enough job. I'll make sure it's done right the next time," I promised with faked sincerity.

"Well, Specialist Papp, that next time is now! So put that booze away," his eyes searched the back of the tent and covetously embraced the top of my footlocker, "and clean up this fuckin' mess! Or I'll have your ass in the morning. You got that, troop?" Tiny pieces of soggy cigar whizzed past my right ear.

"Yes, First Sergeant!" I screamed.

He tossed his smoldering cigar on the floor and crushed it with his right boot, repeating yesterday's exit. Before leaving, he sucked in his gut, leaned over, and grabbed the two remaining slices of pizza. Overturning one on top of the other, he consumed the "sandwich" in three bites. Using his dingy sleeve, he wiped tomato sauce from his chin, smiled, and squeezed through the doorway, dramatically ending my twenty-fourth birthday party.

Chapter 8

It was mid-March. I'd been in-country nearly three months. That left me six months to go before I returned to The World. So far I'd survived with getting shot at only twice, and getting the crap scared out of me two other times. Being "scared" doesn't sound like much—but remember, I was stationed in this godforsaken hellhole with nary a bullet for my powerless M16.

My first big scare was right after our plane landed in Vietnam. Being on shipment roster 13 should have been my first warning, but I was just a clueless clerk. One way of going was the scenic route via Hawaii. We took the over-the-top route, with refueling stops in Anchorage and Okinawa.

When we stopped in Anchorage, no one was allowed to step foot off the plane during refueling. It had nothing to do with safety. The Army wanted to make sure the *full* plane of replacements arrived in Vietnam.

After we crossed the International Date Line, I dozed off, hoping I could sleep through the next nine months. Then a voice boomed over the intercom: "Fasten your seatbelts. We'll be landing in a few minutes."

Oh, God, I prayed, please make this just a bad dream.

"The local time is 2:30 p.m.," the voice droned. "The temperature is a hot 87 degrees."

No sooner did I look out the window, the wheels touched down, and we were in-country. A barrel-chested sergeant in the first row stood up and shouted: "Listen up! Grab your personnel records and your asses and assemble in a single file by the buses waiting at the terminal. Now move it!"

We jumped at his command, trying instinctively to be the first one off the plane, while it still taxied to the terminal.

A stewardess with a bright-yellow scarf cried when saying good-bye to each passing soldier. Her "good luck" was barely audible over the whimpering. I nodded and half-smiled as she bade her farewell. Her glazed eyes and hollow voice evidenced she had gone through this awkward departure too many times. As I passed her, she clutched my right arm. When I looked back, vacant blue eyes stared through me. "Be careful," she begged. "Please," she added, grabbing my right hand as well.

Why did she single me out to plead her warning? What ghastly premonition did she have?

"I will," I shuddered. Her nametag said JOAN. "Joan," I added, prying my crushed appendage out of her fierce grip.

Using my left hand to guide me, I descended the stairs with as much confidence as a pirate walking the gangplank. The heat enveloped me immediately, turning my armpits into swollen sponges. When my feet touched the tarmac, I spun a full 360 degrees. There were a thousand places Charlie could be hiding. I couldn't see him, but I felt his breath.

A billboard, big enough to make any motorcycle cop happy, stood in front of the terminal. WELCOME TO BIEN HOA AIRBASE, it said.

Then came the scare.

KABOOM!

The logical reaction to this Hiroshima-sized explosion was to run and hide. I froze. Was that sweat or piss running down my legs?

I relaxed a little when I saw a huge ball of black smoke rise above the horizon well outside the airbase. This time, evidently, Charlie wasn't trying for me.

When my eyes focused on the welcome sign (some welcome!), I

saw them: the guys who had put in their time and were waiting for our plane, their freedom bird, to take them home. They stared at us with the same vacant eyes as the stewardess, most likely wondering if we would live through our tour and return home. Unlike the stewardess, they weren't crying. Although I just landed, I knew that anyone who had spent a year in Nam had already shed all the tears possible. Except, maybe, for tears of joy upon leaving.

A few of them taunted us by yelling, "Short!" and "300 and how many days?" In spite of their short-timer sarcasm, I heard the compassion in their voices.

"Move it, soldier!" a voice behind me ordered. "Get your ass on the bus. Any bus."

"Yes, sir!" I shot back automatically. When I swung my head around, I realized the voice belonged to the barrel-chested sergeant, not to an officer.

"Don't call me *sir*," he screamed. "I work for a living."

I flew into the nearest bus and double-timed it down the narrow aisle, searching for an empty seat. I dove over a frozen PFC, hitting my head on the luggage rack as I landed in the seat next to the window.

The door slammed. Our fearful trip was underway.

The jungle was a blur as we sat in a trance. No one said a word. The only activity was an occasional hand wiping off endless sweat, even though the bus was air-conditioned. In very few minutes, a planeload of cool, crisply uniformed soldiers were transformed into wet raisins.

Without warning, the bus came to a screeching halt. I pried my bruised forehead from the seat in front of me and glared at the driver. I called him every Hungarian cussword my mother had taught me.

"Oh, my God," someone a few rows in front of me groaned, his face glued to the window. "Oh . . . my . . . God."

Reacting to the cry of concern, I peeked out the window. The result of the Hiroshima-sized explosion blocked our way. One glance was all I could stomach.

A jeep and its driver were ripped apart. The driver's left eye dangled from its socket. A second body was trapped under a rear tire. I didn't have the guts to take another look. Had we landed ten minutes earlier, this carnage could have been us. I made the sign of the cross and thanked God. With delayed embarrassment over my good fate, I whispered a prayer for the soldiers who'd died. There was nothing anyone could do. Our driver bypassed the smoldering heap of flesh and metal and sped down the stretch of blacktop that passed for a highway in Vietnam.

Scare number two was more *emotional* than *physical*.

"When I call your name, fall out," the lieutenant ordered.

It was 0700, and we were in formation in Long Binh, awaiting unit assignments. The sun had already caused our uniforms to become soggy. Somehow, the lieutenant's remained crisp. *Lifers.*

Since leaving California, each time someone called Specialist Palmer's name, mine followed, since the alphabet ruled and we were both headed to the 309th Communications Battalion in Pleiku.

"We'll start with the 101st Airborne Division. ABBOTT, Julius L.; CARSON, Donald—"

"I hope he gets this over fast," a PFC in front of me whispered. "I gotta take a wicked piss."

"TROUT, Benjamin A." The lieutenant flipped a page and continued. "Next unit is the 20th Engineer Brigade. ARMENTI, Anthony P.; DOORE, James F.; HALL, John K.—"

"Come on, you dumb brown bar, I've gotta piss like a race horse."

"All right, listen up." The lieutenant licked an index finger and flipped to another page. "The next unit is the 309th Communications Battalion."

Whether it was the expectation of having my name called, or the broiling effect of the sun, I sweated even harder.

"AARONSON, Joseph M.; CHESTNUTT, Charles L.; LAHAIE, Donald D.; NIXON, James J.; PALMER, Ralph D."

I dragged my feet and headed to the front of the formation, expecting my name to be next.

"ROGERS, Donald F."

I froze.

"SCHMIDT, Michael L. That's it for the 309th."

That can't be it for the 309th, I almost shouted. What happened to PAPP? I've got orders for the 309th. Why didn't you call my name for the 309th, you dumb shit brown bar?

"Listen up. Next unit is the 9th Infantry Division."

What's going on? WHAT HAPPENED TO PAPP? You were supposed to call PAPP.

"GALLAGHER, John R.; JOHNSON, James—"

"Come on, L.T., I really gotta piss now."

"Shut the fuck up," I screamed at the PFC, now standing along side of me. His crotch became soaked.

"OCHELTREE, John S.," the lieutenant continued, undaunted by my outburst. "PAPP, John D.—"

What the hell was I doing in the infantry? Me . . . an overweight typewriter jockey with no combat training.

My numb legs carried me to the front of the formation, following others headed for the 9th Infantry. I tried to stop. To grab onto something. My fingerless hands did me no good. I was a zombie on a collision course with self-destruction.

A faceless sergeant bellowed, "Those of you headed for the 9th Infantry, fall in here."

We plodded over to him.

"Go back to your hooches, get your gear, and meet me by truck #33. Over there," his left arm shot up 90 degrees. "You got three zero minutes. Your next destination is Bearcat, headquarters for the 9th Infantry." As though he expected the question, he added: "It's about twenty-five miles northeast, near the village of Long Thanh. Now move it!"

So now that I had the shit scared out of me twice, I was ready to get shot at. Twice.

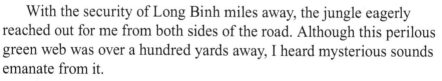

With the security of Long Binh miles away, the jungle eagerly reached out for me from both sides of the road. Although this perilous green web was over a hundred yards away, I heard mysterious sounds emanate from it.

I looked at my empty hands and wondered when the hell the Army was going to give me a rifle and about a thousand rounds of ammo. And a few grenades, plus whatever else they stored in the supply arsenal.

A quick survey of the truck revealed two men armed with M16s, plus the M60 machine gun mounted above the cab. Even though this wasn't enough firepower for the middle of a war zone, the armed men were sufficiently menacing to make up for any shortness in firepower.

The one sitting directly across from me had a right cheek that was a web of scars; the intersecting lines resembling a road map. Steel-gray eyes shot through me whenever he looked my way. His aura said he was the kind of man who would rip off your head and crap down your neck.

The other armed guardian had muscles packing every inch of his tailored fatigues. Rolled-up sleeves exposed biceps as hard as a morning's first erection. Massive hands caressed his M16. Surveying the passing landscape through horn-rimmed glasses, like a gambler, his face gave away nothing, yet took in everything.

If I never saw either of them again, their memory would be my constant companion. They became my guardian angels, making sure I would use the return half of my round-trip ticket to Vietnam.

KAPOW! KAPOW! KAPOW!

A series of shots rang from the jungle. One of my guardian angels opened fire with his M16, then grabbed his M-79 grenade launcher. That little beauty could accurately propel a grenade three hundred meters. At shorter range, it was deadly.

After sending the first red-orange fireball into the foliage, he reloaded and fired a second round into the jungle. My other guardian angel traded his rifle for the M60 mounted on top of the cab and sprayed the living hell out of the tree line.

The driver took the hint and gunned the engine, rushing us to safety. The jungle soon became a large clearing. A vast encampment was within reach. Barbed wire and massive bunkers fortified its main gate. A lookout tower, strategically positioned in the right-hand corner, boasted two machine guns of its own. A hand-carved wooden sign identified the fortress as Bearcat.

Three heavily armed guards signaled our truck to enter. Quickly. When the security of Bearcat embraced us, my two guardians relaxed.

Maybe I would make it home—alive—after all.

A week later, the enemy's bullets found me again.

On Monday, 8 January, we had our final major class at The Academy: the infamous night patrol. Classified as a routine exercise, it turned out to be more than we bargained for.

We packed the appropriate field gear, making sure to take enough C-rations to last three days, though we would be gone only overnight. We included such delicacies as ham and limas, beef and potatoes, beans and franks, and assorted desserts better left unmentioned.

Our convoy departed the sanctuary of Bearcat shortly after 1500 hours for a rubber tree plantation a few miles outside the main gate. Only in the Army did rubbers grow on trees.

I kept my head down, keeping an eye on my boots and the variety of bugs crawling around them. Otherwise, I wouldn't have to know how far away Bearcat really was. With each passing minute, the jungle's noises climbed further under my skin. Goose pimples popped up on my legs. Myriad bugs of undecipherable ancestry worked their way up my boots.

"GI, GI," children yelled, "chop-chop. We want chop-chop."

We were at the edge of the rubber tree plantation. Fifty children swarmed our convoy. They wanted our food and wouldn't let us get off the trucks until we shared some. Even though this greeting party acted more like a lynch mob, it was difficult not to feel sorry for them.

They were more undressed than dressed. Dirt covered every inch of their little bodies. Their odor rivaled the latrine's. To say they were skinny wouldn't be descriptive enough. These kids rattled when they farted.

Each of us tossed a few cans of C-rations well past them. Once off the trucks, we huddled together for safety. Why did I fear a bunch of kids? The little mob kept us separated into groups of twos and threes. A few of the urchins isolated me from the rest of my group.

"GI got smoke?" one begged. He was barely old enough to pee standing up. "Give me smoke, GI," he insisted.

"I have no smoke," I explained. "This GI no smoke."

"GI lie. GI have smoke. Give me smoke."

The little monster was getting on my nerves. Another one of his gang came over. Now it was four against one.

"GI have candy," I said, trying another avenue of approach. "You want candy?" I unbuttoned my bulging shirt pocket, took out a Butterfinger, leaned over, and offered it to him.

When he yanked it out of my hand, two of his partners in crime grabbed the other candy bars out of my pocket and ran.

"Little bastards," I shouted. I started after them, but made the prudent decision to remain within the safety of our ranks. There went my midnight snack. Or maybe even my dinner. Damn!

"GI give me chop-chop?" someone behind me whispered.

I carefully turned around and lowered my eyes to a little girl. She was five. Maybe six. She couldn't have had a decent meal in months. Maybe never. She was as frail as a twig you can snap between your fingers. What was left of her tattered clothes hung from her like a wet dish rag. Beet-red scratches covered her swollen ankles. Her bare feet were caked with mud.

She cautiously raised her filthy, upturned left hand. Part of her index finger was missing. Unconsciously, I guided my thumbs over my index fingers—reaffirming mine weren't mutilated.

"Chop-chop, GI?" she gently pleaded again.

Along with my heart, I gave her my two biggest cans of C-rations, hoping they were enough. I didn't have many more to spare.

"More, GI?" she whimpered, lowering her eyes.

"That's all I can give you." I would have given her everything were it possible.

"More, GI?" A tear worked its way out of each sad eye, turning her dirt-caked cheeks into little mud puddles.

"Sorry, no more. That's all," I repeated, displaying empty hands.

"Fuck you, GI," she shouted, then ran away.

"Listen up! I want a formation over here," demanded Sergeant Rutherford. "It'll be dark in two hours, and we've got a mile to go before we set up our perimeter outside of Long Thanh. In a column of twos, forward, ho."

We marched down a narrow path through the rubber trees. This was more of a forest than a plantation. The farther we went, the darker it got. Spooky dark. I imagined VC hiding behind every tree.

Out of the corner of my right eye, I saw a body dart from one tree to the next, slowly working its way closer. Then the body jumped right out in front of me.

"GI want boom-boom?"

This urchin was about twelve or thirteen. He hadn't missed a meal in a long time. By the way he carried himself, he must have been the leader of this band of thieves. He wasn't dressed like a pimp, but that was his role right now.

"Have Numah One boom-boom for GI."

"No want," I answered, suddenly wondering what was happening to my vocabulary.

"Have Numah One sister. Only 500 P."

He was selling his sister for 500 piasters, a little less than $7.00.

During orientation, we were warned to stay away from Vietnamese women. Many of these lovelies gave GIs strains of venereal diseases that hadn't yet been diagnosed. Until diagnosed and then cured, our guys couldn't go home. Some of them had been in Nam for more than three years. Dripping and waiting. No way did I want any part of that.

"No want," I repeated eloquently.

"Only 400 P," he bargained.

"No want. Didi mau," I shouted. He ran away as instructed.

KAPOW! KAPOW!

Two shots rang out from my left, grazing a nearby tree. I jumped on the ground. My stomach came up through my back. Here I was again with my impotent M16. When the hell were they going to give us ammo?

Always on the alert, Sergeant Rutherford opened fire. Another M16 rang out. Get the gook, I pleaded, making sure to keep my head down.

Minutes passed. Nothing.

"He's gone," someone shouted. "Let's move out. Now!"

The "now" wasn't necessary. None of us had to be convinced to get the hell out of there. Fast.

About eight weeks had passed since those encounters. What horrors did the next approximate thirty weeks hold? Only God knew. And He wasn't talking to me.

Chapter 9

"Goooooood morning, Viet-naaam!" the radio shouted. "This is Army Specialist 4 Jim Burnside. It's 0615 hours on Sunday, 31 March 1968."

"Oh, shut up!" Moritoni yelled, pulling on his left sock.

"Yup, 0615," Burnside repeated. "That's the latest it's been all day."

"How the fuck can that guy be so cheerful every morning?" Moritoni bitched, throwing his left boot at the radio, missing it by a pubic hair. The boot slammed against the tent wall with a hollow *smack*. "Damn." He flashed his middle finger at his misguided missile.

"And a good morning it is," Burnside continued, "because we're all one day shorter. Annnd, it's payday."

"That's right," Moritoni said, brightening up as he retrieved his boot. "The eagle shits today."

"Now look who's so *damned* cheerful," I mocked.

"Screw you, Pinky," Moritoni shot back, faking another missile launch.

I ducked the intended liftoff and thumbed my nose at him. Unwrapping a stick of Juicy Fruit gum, I made a wad out of the foil wrapper and threw it at The Face, hitting him square in the nose.

"Hah!" I laughed, chomping on the gum. "Bull's-eye."

31 March.

It was hard to believe that another month was only eighteen hours short of being entered in my DOWN column, leaving six more in the TO GO.

So far, March was National Rumor Month. The craziest ones included Lieutenant Colonel Murphy being kicked out of the Army, peace talks ending the war, and the entire 9th Admin relocating to Dong Tam.

All of us rooted for the peace talks. Murphy being booted out of the Army ran a close second. *Nobody* wanted to move to Dong Tam.

Keeping the mill going, I started a rumor (why not?) that all R&R's would be postponed until the prophesied Dong Tam move was settled. This got Eaton pissing in his hat, because he put in for in-country R&R to Vung Tau.

"Where ya been, Pinky?" Bohnny asked, when I approached our work station. "Chief's looking for you." He put down his paystub and adjusted his eyeglasses.

I shoved a fresh stick of Juicy Fruit in my mouth and said: "I'm only a couple minutes late. What's the big deal?"

"Didn't ask. He came through about ten minutes ago and wondered where you were."

"What did you tell him?" I shot back, chewing faster and faster.

"Said you just went to take a piss," he laughed.

"Thanks, Clyde. I'll try to look relieved when I see him."

"Welcome." He readjusted his bulky frames and buried himself in his paystub.

Although the sun wasn't out, it was a steamy morning. The sky had a strange, foreboding look. Like sour milk poured into a cup of coffee. A few raindrops—the size of quarters—began falling. It wouldn't be much longer before monsoon season arrived, and every day would look as menacing. The rain stopped as suddenly as it had started.

I approached the adjutant general's building and spun my head around. Seeing no one, I inhaled noisily and let loose with dark-green spittle—plus my well-chewed gum—smack on the AG's doorstep. *And a good morning to you, Lieutenant Colonel Murphy.*

A few steps farther on, I heard a screen door open behind me, and a "What the hell?" shouted as a boot hit the ground.

I quickened my pace to the PA headquarters building and rushed up the rickety stairs. When I reached the top, I stole a glance at the AG's building. I swallowed a laugh, letting only a smile express my reaction to seeing LTC Murphy inspecting the stringy mucus-gum mixture that violated the sole of his right boot.

Quietly closing the second-floor screen door behind me, I exchanged my smile for a just-took-a-great-piss look, marched over to CWO Blue, stood at attention, and said, "You wanted to see me, Mr. Blue?"

He looked up from a neatly stacked pile of paperwork and responded, "Yes, Papp." I flinched when he flung his right arm at me. "Here's your paystub."

I silently cursed Bohnny for not telling me the real reason Mr. Blue wanted to see me. I also made a mental note to castrate the four-eyed bastard with a rusty P-38 can opener.

Opening his bottom desk drawer, Blue took out a metal cash box, lifted the squeaky lid, counted out $35.05—in MPC, of course—and held it out to me. After I took my month's pay, he handed me a clipboard and a pen.

"Sign here," he ordered.

"Thank you, Sir," I said, signing the pay voucher. *Why was he so formal today?*

"Another thing, Papp," he continued. "I'm postponing your R&R to Vung Tau until the planned move to Dong Tam is settled."

"*My* R&R, Sir?" Move to Dong Tam? But that was only supposed to be a rumor. So was cancelling all R&R's. *That* was a rumor for sure, because I started it.

"Don't look so stupid, Specialist." He shifted his weight in the chair, carefully repositioning his feet. "I'm talking about next month's R&R you and Eaton put in for."

"Oh, *that* one, Chief," I replied, trying to regain my composure. "It entirely slipped my mind," I lied, handing back the clipboard.

As I turned to leave, he stopped me with a: "One more thing, Papp. Team 3 is backlogged because they're a man short. So I volunteered your services. See Specialist Cohen."

"But what about working with Bohnny?" I pleaded.

"That'll be all, Papp." He returned to his paperwork, totally ignoring my question.

Son of a bitch! After Bohnny and I had worked ten seventy-hour weeks to get the mountain of backlogged Team 4 paperwork squared away, this lifer switches me to another team. *What the hell was the sense of our busting our asses to get our shit together? Just to move me to another team and start all over?*

FTA! FTA! FTA!

I raced back to Team 4 to give Bohnny a piece of my mind. Approaching our work station, I noticed Eaton walking toward us balancing a mountain of 201 files.

"Guess what Mr. Blue wanted, dickhead," I fumed at Bohnny.

"T-take it easy, Pinky," he stammered. "I was only busting your chops."

"I don't mean about getting my pay."

"What then?" He defensively adjusted his binocular frames.

"I'm moving to Team 3."

"What? Why? When?"

"They're a man short and up to their asses in paperwork—"

"Hi, Pinky. Why so glum?" Eaton asked, trying to maneuver around my bulk without dropping the stack of files.

"Mr. Blue just told me I'm moving to Team 3."

"Oh?" He dropped the paperwork on my desk and applied his right sleeve to a sweaty forehead.

"A-n-d," I continued, "the Chief also said he's postponing our R&R to Vung Tau." I shot Eaton a dirty look that had *rusty P-38* and *castration* written all over it. (The same P-38 I had first planned to use on Bohnny.)

"Uh—well—uh," Eaton mumbled, "I was gonna tell you—uh about that. It was a surprise. Yeah, that's right," he recovered his composure, "a big surprise."

"Well," I scoffed, "the surprise is on you and—"

"You don't have to act like a prick, Pinky," Eaton interrupted. "I was just trying to get you out of this godforsaken place for a few days—"

"Sorry," I apologized.

"—to enjoy some decent food and hot showers," he finished.

"Sor-ree," I repeated. "Guess I'm just pissed about having to go to Team 3."

"You're forgiven. But," Eaton added quickly as he picked up the

201 Files, "the drinks are on you the first night when we go to Vung Tau." He flashed me a shit-eating grin and disappeared before I could refuse.

"So when do you desert me and go to Team 3?" Bohnny sullenly asked.

"Right now. I'm supposed to see a Specialist Cohen."

"Cohen? He's in my tent. He's a nice guy. Not as great as me, of course, but he's got his shit together."

"Well," I sighed, "guess I'll shove off. Nice working with you, Clyde."

Cutting the umbilical cord and exiting Team 4, a prophetic black-ened sky and pelting rain greeted me. I was soaked by the time I climbed the precarious steps to the second floor and Teams 2 & 3. Reaching for the screen door, I had the sickening feeling I had just landed in Nam and was starting all over again. Without a friend in the world.

My heart brightened when I saw the beaming countenance of McGuire sitting behind a smoking typewriter. His fingers were moving faster than a groom's on his wedding night.

"Hi, Smiles," I called out.

He looked up. His fingers slowed to a halt. Through pearly whites, he beamed a: "Hi, Pinky." Crackling expansion noises filled the room as his typewriter cooled off. "What brings you to the penthouse?"

"The second floor can hardly be considered a penthouse," I pro-tested, spraying raindrops as I took off my jungle hat. His lukewarm typewriter hissed a complaint.

"I don't see any building higher than two stories," he challenged.

"Okay, okay," I gave in. "I'm here to see a Specialist Cohen."

"The Coach?"

"Whatever."

"He'll be back in about ten minutes. That's his desk back there," McGuire pointed to a table two rows back.

Before I could say another word, McGuire's fingers were a blur. The rain-dampened typewriter turned white hot, emitting a cloud of steam.

When I plopped into Cohen's chair, I realized I had been holding my pay stub all this time. Even though it was dimpled from the rain, I could still read the meager figures.

```
E-5 Base Pay***************** $211.50
Separation Pay *************** $30.00
Overseas Pay****************** $16.00
Hostile Fire Pay ************** $65.00
Allotment ******************* $110.00
Total Pay ******************** $432.50
Social Security/Deductions ****** $47.45
Net Pay ********************* $385.05
Less Spousal Check *********** $350.00
Payable Amount ************** $35.05
```

I grabbed a blank sheet of typing paper and did some quick calculations.

The $350 I was sending Annette each month would amount to a little over $3000 for the nine (hopefully) months I'd be in Vietnam. I made about $1950 in 1967, while I was Stateside serving in "this man's Army." So my "fat" paycheck in Nam would just about double last year's pitiful earnings.

Delving into fantasyland, with expected raises and promotions, I could make about $108,000 if I stayed in the Army for 20 years. Not counting all the great food I'd eat, sharp clothes I'd wear, and exotic places (like Vietnam again?) I'd visit.

"Can I help you?" an unfamiliar, soft-spoken voice questioned.

I looked up, blinked to clear the lifer fantasy out of my mind, and saw brown wavy hair, glasses, and a nametag that said COHEN.

"Hi," I responded weakly, standing up and extending my hand. "I'm Dennis Papp. The Chief told me I'm on Team 3 now and to see you." His muscular grip released my throbbing hand.

"Hi." He looked down at my scribbling. "Planning your retirement?"

"Definitely not. Just passing the time in fantasyland while you were on R&R."

He smiled warmly. "Yeah, Philadelphia was great."

"You're from Philly?"

He nodded.

"I'm from Trenton."

"Really?"

I nodded.

"Were you home for New Year?"

"No," I responded sadly. "I was on a plane headed for this dump."

"Oh."

"Why?"

"Was wondering if you saw a good parade."

His smile broadened. There was a twinkle in his eyes. My gaze locked onto his twinkle. I read his thoughts.

I unbuttoned my fatigue shirt.

He unbuttoned his.

I grabbed my opened shirttail.

He grabbed his.

Holding onto my shirttail with both hands, I extended my arms away from my sides, raising them slightly.

He mirrored the technique.

I began humming "Oh! Dem Golden Slippers."

He joined in.

I danced in circles, joyously flapping my arms.

He mimicked my ritualistic movements.

As we strutted noisily, a crowd gathered, watching in amazement. Some of them clapped in synch with our movements; others picked up on the words to "Oh! Dem Golden Slippers."

Cohen and I laughed as our frenzy grew.

Spying a yardstick on a nearby desk, I let go of the shirttail with my left hand. Bending my knees and back ever so slightly, I grabbed the yardstick and thrust my left arm straight up as though I held an umbrella. I took one step forward, half a step backward. After repeating the footwork a few times, I spun around from left to right, cranking my left arm up and down the whole time.

Cohen smiled at my expertise.

Freeing both hands, he skillfully duplicated my movements using two imaginary umbrellas. But instead of spinning around, he turned slightly, then repeated the footwork backward, all the while keeping his head perfectly upright. *Then* he spun around and started all over.

After ten minutes and endless choruses, I tripped over Cohen's left foot. We both ate plywood. Rolling on the floor, our laughter turned into tears of joy. My throat burned from pleasure.

Cohen managed to reach his feet first. He bent over and yanked me up.

"What the hell was that?" Smiles asked.

"You . . . " I couldn't talk. My throat ached.

"You never heard of the Mummers Parade?" Cohen asked easily, obviously in better shape.

"No."

"Well," he explained, "there's this big parade in Philadelphia on New Year's Day—"

"The Mummers Parade?"

"That's what I like about you, McGuire," Cohen kidded, "you have a firm grasp of the obvious."

"Thanks," he beamed, missing the feigned sarcasm.

"Anyway," Cohen continued, "there's this big parade down one of the main drags in town. About 15,000 people, dressed in bright, multi-colored costumes, strut down Broad Street."

"Like you two were doing?"

"Yup."

"Do they do anything besides just dress funny and dance like idi-ots?" McGuire laughed.

"Not just—"

"Don't they have bands or music, or something?" McGuire interrupted.

Cohen and I looked at each other and smiled. Broadly.

"Music?" I exclaimed. "Bands?" I was amazed at his naiveté.

"They've got dozens of bands," Cohen shot in. "The String Band Division is one of the biggest parts of the Parade."

"*String* band?" McGuire asked. "You mean like violins, guitars, and—"

"No, shithead." Cohen's tone had a touch of annoyance. "More like steel-stringed banjos, mandolins, and a variety of other instruments, like flutes, saxophones, drums, and even a glockenspiel or two."

"Glockenspiel?"

"Yeah. It gives the music a distinctive tone—"

"But it gets cold in Philadelphia in January. Don't the banjo play-ers' hands freeze?" McGuire asked. "Or do they play with gloves on?" he laughed.

"Yeah, it gets cold. But we Yankees aren't pussies like you guys from Atlanta," Cohen poked me with a friendly elbow. "Anyway, the old-timers are proud to strum their banjos in the coldest of weather, without gloves."

"How'd they keep their fingers from falling off?" McGuire asked. It was something I always wondered, too.

"They rub a mixture of Vaseline and camphor-ice on their hands."

"What's camphor-ice?" I asked.

"Never mind," Cohen replied abruptly. "The important thing," he explained, "is that their music can be heard for miles around."

"And it's great!" I added.

"Atsa Rog," Cohen beamed. He looked at McGuire, expecting another interruption. Getting none, he continued smiling and said, "Although, one of my neighbors played in a string band—"

"Which one?" McGuire asked.

Cohen shot him a dirty look, ignored the question, and finished his sentence: "But he preferred marching with one of the Comic Clubs."

"W-w-wh—"

"Because," Cohen went on before McGuire could complete his umpteenth interruption, "he just had more fun. He and some of the others would have a few drinks before the parade. To get in the mood, as it were," Cohen grinned. "Anyway, they'd get half-loaded and just have a lotta fun with the crowd. Without a worry about hitting the right notes on their instruments."

Somewhere in the back of my mind, I heard a screen door slam.

"Oh," McGuire nodded an understanding.

The admiring crowd that had gathered around us thinned out.

"And they could use their theme to get away with making fun of people and stuff," I said. The hint of an acrid aroma attacked my senses. "Like in '67, when they made fun of the White House wedding of Luci Johnson and Pat Nugent."

One by one, the remainder of the crowd casually disappeared, leaving Cohen, McGuire, and me "alone."

"Right, Papp," Cohen said. "And remember what they did to Mia and Frank Sinatra?"

"Yeah," I laughed. My jovial response echoed in the near-empty room.

"What did they do?" McGuire asked.

"What's going on here?" an irritated voice behind me demanded.

Oh, no, not him again, I begged.

"Why are you out of uniform, Specialist?" the voice asked with increasing irritation.

Cohen quickly buttoned his fatigue shirt. I started doing the same, trying not to face the origin of the interruption.

"So you're part of this, too, *Papp*," First Sergeant Smith bellowed. Spittle mixed with cigar bits flew past me as he enunciated my name. "I might have known *you'd* be involved," he hissed.

McGuire nonchalantly took a few steps to the side and attempted a retreat to his desk.

"Where do you think you're going, Private?" Smith shouted.

"Er, back to work, Sir." McGuire's expression verified he knew he had chosen the wrong appellation for Smith.

"Don't call me *Sir*," Smith erupted. "I work for a living."

Yeah, right, you asshole, I thought.

"I'm g-going b-back to w-work, First Sergeant," McGuire cowered.

"Well, then, move it, troop." He threw his putrid cigar on the floor and ground it out with the heel of his left boot. "Before I put you on report."

McGuire melted away.

"Now for you, Papp," he sprayed. "What the fuck was going on?"

"We were—"

"Never mind. Don't answer back, smart ass."

"I was only—"

"Shut it," he demanded. "Before I have your big ass on report."

I swallowed my lips.

"I'm tired of running into you, Papp. And your wise-ass remarks."

Fuck you, Lifer.

"The next time, I won't be so nice," he leered. "Now get back into uniform," he leaned over, putting his bulbous nose a hair away from my nasal organ, "and do some work for a change."

I threw myself into Cohen's chair and fumed at the overflowing IN box. Waiting until Top turned to leave, I bid the worthless asshole goodbye by flashing him the bird with both hands.

Chapter 10

"Hey, Pinky, wanna give your wife a special belated anniversary present?" Moritoni plopped down in the chair next to me and grinned like the evil devil he was.

For the past week, I'd done nothing but think about Annette. Monday, 8 April, was our first anniversary. I'd emptied my tear ducts a few times since then, picturing the deliveryman giving her my present of the red roses and candy while she was at work.

"What have you got in mind?"

"Well, since she and I are both Italians, I thought something extra special was in order."

"Like a pizza or spaghetti?" I kidded.

"No, asshole. I can pull a few strings with a buddy at MARS—."

"I didn't know you had friends on other planets."

"Not that Mars, dickhead. The *telephone* MARS."

My eyes lit up. "Oh, you mean the Military Assistance Radio Service?"

"That's them."

I leaned toward him and lovingly put my hands on his shoulders. "You mean I can talk with my wife today?"

Talking on the phone was another of the commonplace events taken for granted . . . like electricity and indoor plumbing. But to us, banished to Vietnam, talking to *The World* was like a jailbreak. Especially when it was to our wives or parents.

"Yup."

A kiss was out of the question. So I thanked him by using my right hand to distort his cheeks and lips with an Italian aunt's squeeze.

"Hey, don't mess with the face," he kidded.

I stood up. "What do we have to do to place the call?" I sat down.

"I just have to phone my buddy and let him know what number you want to call."

I stood up. "That's all?" I sat down.

"Yup."

I stood up. "How long's it take?" I sat down.

"About half an hour."

I stood up. He pulled me down by my fatigue shirt.

"Stop it with the damned yo-yo imitation already."

"Sorry. I'm a little excited. Not to mention nervous." I began rocking back and forth.

"Sit still, Pinky, you're making *me* nervous."

I stopped rocking and apologized again.

"What's you wife's phone number?"

I ripped off a piece of a blank OER form, wrote the number on it, and handed it to him.

Moritoni got up and grabbed me by the collar. "Come with me."

He dragged me to a corner table at the rear of Team 3. He picked up what passed for a telephone in Vietnam and spun the dial a few times.

"Let me talk to Rocky," he ordered in a throaty voice.

Pause.

"*Ciao*, Rocky. *Si,* Moritoni. *Come sta?*"

Pause.

"*Magnifico*! *Molte grazie.*"

Pause.

"*Scusi.*" Pause. "*Si. Si. Non importa.*"

Grabbing his left arm, I asked, "What the hell you doing? Placing a call to my wife, or ordering a hit?"

"Cool it, Pinky. You gotta ease your way into these things."

"Sorry, Face, but all this *gaba, gaba, gaba*, is making me nervous."

Switching to English, Moritoni said, "Rocky, you still there? I need a favor. Want you to call a buddy's wife for me."

Pause.

"No, shithead. The guy's standing next to me. *He's* gonna talk to her, not me." Moritoni put his hand over the mouthpiece and whispered, "He thought I was fooling around with someone's wife and wanted to call her." Moritoni got out his paint-by-numbers set, put on an innocent face, and asked: "Now, would *I* do something like that, Pinky?"

"Does McDonald's have golden arches?" I answered. "Does a bear shit in the woods? Is the pope a Catho—"

"Enough, Pinky. I get the point. Maybe I should just hang up?"

"No. Don't." I sat down and began rocking.

Taking his hand off the mouthpiece, he continued, "I'm still here, Rocky." After searching his pockets for the slip of paper I gave him, he read off Annette's phone number.

Pause.

"Okay. Call us back at—" Moritoni tried reading the extension number on the phone, but it was too faded to be recognizable. "What's the extension here, Pinky?"

I blurted it out.

"Got that, Rocky? *Si, trenta minuti. Arrivederci.*" Moritoni hung up the phone.

"Well?" I shook him by the shoulders. "Well?" I demanded.

"You're all set." Moritoni forcibly removed my hands. "He'll call us back in thirty minutes."

"That's it?" I was amazed it would be only half an hour and I'd be talking with my wife.

"That's it, Pinky."

"That's great. Only twenty-nine more minutes," I beamed.

Moritoni grabbed me by the collar when I began rocking back and forth and dragged me back to my desk. "Sit. Wait," he commanded.

"Aren't you gonna wait with me?"

"Okay. Okay."

"Thanks."

Five minutes passed.

I looked back at the phone. It sat there. Quietly.

Ten minutes.

Fifteen.

I stared at the phone, defying it to ring. Nothing.

Twenty-three minutes.

McGuire got up from his desk, walked past me, and headed for the telephone.

"Get away from the damned phone," I shouted.

"Take it easy, Pinky. I was just getting a 201 File." He continued past the phone and pulled out the top drawer of a nearby file cabinet.

"Sorry, Smiles."

"Calm down, Pinky," Moritoni said. "It's only a phone call."

"Only a phone call? *Only a phone call?* I haven't talked to my wife in over three months." I looked at my watch. "Don't tell me it's *only* a phone call." I stared at my watch. "It's been *27* minutes, Face. What's taking so long?"

"Here." He handed me a piece of paper. "Why don't you write down a few things you want to say to her. Or some questions you want to ask her."

"Good idea."

With a shaky left hand, I jotted down what I wanted to ask in my last few letters, but kept on forgetting. Gluing my right eye on the paper, so Moritoni wouldn't be the wiser, I turned the left eye to my watch and peeked at the time.

"The half-hour is long gone, Face. Why hasn't Rocky called us back yet?"

"Just a min—"

"Hey, Pinky," Bohnny shouted from the front door, "you just had a call from MARS."

"What?"

"Some guy named Rocky called and—"

"Oh, shit," I said, "I must have given him Team 4's extension, instead of Team 3." I began rocking. "I just automatically thought of Team 4's number."

"Relax, Pinky," Moritoni soothed. "I'll just get Rocky on the phone, and we'll try again."

"But we don't know the extension here."

"Then we'll give him Team 4's number again, and you wait over there."

"Can we do that?"

"Sure. Why not?"

"I can't just wait there, doing absolutely nothing, and have asshole Colonel Murphy, or Top walk in. They'd have my butt for sure. Especially that prick Top. He spells vendetta with a capital P-A-P-P."

"Don't you remember, Pinky?" Bohnny asked. "Murphy was reprimanded and reassigned to the States for trying to get phony awards put on his record."

"Yeah," I smiled, "I remember now. A Silver Star and something else."

"Right."

"But what about Top? That rotten bastard is still with us."

"Guess you forgot that, too," Moritoni said.

"What?"

"He's on R&R until Tuesday."

"Oh, God, yes." My heart brightened. "Then let's do it. Okay, Face?"

"Atsa Rog, Pinky."

Then remembering the time, I again found something to complain about.

"But won't it be too late? I mean, if we have to wait another 30 minutes, it'll be close to midnight in New Jersey."

"Maybe I can get Rocky to speed it up."

"And I'm sure your wife won't mind how late it is," Bohnny said.

"Yeah, but she's living with her folks, and I don't want to terrify the whole house when the operator says it's a call from Vietnam—in the middle of the night." I stood up. "They'll immediately think it's a death notice. Cuz people only call in the middle of the night to give somebody *bad* news." I sat down and started rocking.

Moritoni grabbed me by the shoulders and shook me convincingly. "Listen, stupid, I'm sure your in-laws will be just as happy to hear from you as your wife will. No matter what time it is. And the operator isn't gonna give the impression that the call is a death notice. Okay?"

"Okay." I stood up.

Moritoni pushed me down.

"*Okay.*"

"Great. I'll call Rocky. Clyde, you take this bundle of nerves back to Team 4. Hold his hand while you're waiting, or tie him in the damned chair if you have to. Do anything just to keep him quiet."

"Thanks, Face. I'm sorry to be such a pain."

Bohnny had a firm grasp of my arm as he shoved me in a chair and slid the telephone squarely in front of me.

"Sit. Stay. Wait for it to ring," he ordered. "And remember to say *over* each time you finish talking, so your wife will know it's her turn to talk. Okay?"

"Yes. Over. Sorry."

Bohnny turned and walked back to his mountain of paperwork.

I put my hand on the receiver, so that I could answer it the second it rang, and waited with what little patience I had.

Rrring!

"Hello?" Then I remembered to add: "*Over.*"

"This is Nick Loretucci in San Francisco."

San Francisco?

"I'm a ham radio operator, and I've got an Annette Papp on the line. Are you her husband? *Over.*"

"Yes, I am." Pause. "*Over.*"

"Great! Always happy to connect you guys in Vietnam with someone back home."

My left hand was clammy. The phone almost slipped out of my tight grip. So I choked the receiver a little harder.

"When I say 'over,' I'm going to end my transmission, and then your wife will be on the line. I can hold the line open for only about five minutes. So be prepared for me to cut in and end the call. *Over.*"

Pause.

"Denny, are you there? *Over.*"

"Net, is that you?" Pause. "*Over.*"

"Yes, it is. *Over.*"

"Oh, God, I can't believe it. I'm actually talking to you. Are you okay? I'm sorry I called so late. I called earlier. But they put the call through to the wrong extension. I'm sorry. I hope I didn't wake the whole house. I'm sorry. Are your parents mad? I'm sorry. Please tell them I'm sorry." My aching throat finally stopped my babbling. Pause. "*Over.*"

"Don't worry," she said. "Everything is okay here. My parents aren't mad. Just the opposite. They're very happy that you could call. *Over.*"

"Good. I'm sorry I rambled on." Pause. "*Over.*"

"Stop saying you're sorry, and tell me you love me. *Over.*"

"I love you, Annette." I squeezed the phone a little harder and held it closer. "I love you. *Over.*"

"I love you, too, Denny. Happy Anniversary. *Over.*"

"I'm sorry. Happy Anniversary. Did you get the flowers and candy? *Over.*"

"Yes," she said, with only a trace of tears. "I was so surprised. The flowers are beautiful. I'm looking at them right now. Thank you. I love you. *Over.*"

I exhaled a sigh of relief, grateful that my planned surprise hadn't gone astray. For the thousandth time, I pictured the delivery man handing her the roses and candy . . .

"I love you, too. And I'm safe and okay here. Please believe me when I say I'm safe. Okay? *Over.*"

"It's hard for me to believe anyone could be safe in Vietnam, but I know that you're as safe as you can be. And that we pray for you every day. *Over.*"

"I understand how you feel. The important thing is that I'm not going out in the jungle every day and risking my life." Trying to sound a little more cheerful, I asked: "What were you doing when I called? *Over.*"

"The first time you called, it was about 10 o'clock, and I was ironing my father's barber jacket, so he could use it tomorrow. When the second call came," pause, "I was watching TV, hoping you'd be able to call again. *Over.*"

Her telltale pause made me feel that she was hiding something. Like she was really crying her eyes out after the first call, wondering if something had happened to me. I couldn't picture her sitting calmly on the couch, just watching TV . . . waiting for her husband to make another phone call from Vietnam.

"Good. I'm glad the first call didn't disturb you." I heard her cough (gag?) in the background. "This call is as much of a surprise to me as it is to you." I explained how Moritoni was able to make it possible. "Are you okay? *Over.*"

"Denny, I'm as good as I can be. All I want is for God to answer my prayers and bring you home to me—"

"Sorry for the interruption, folks. This is Nick Loretucci again. You've got about 30 seconds. Then I'll have to pull the plug. *Over.*"

"Denny, I love you. Please take care of yourself. See you in 180 And A Wake Up. *Over.*"

Unbelievable. I surprise the hell out of my wife with an unannounced phone call in the middle of the night, and she has enough wits about her to say *180 AAWU*. What a woman!

"I love you, too, Annette. I'll find out when I'll be able to call you again. I'll let you know in one of my letters. You'll have some advance notice that way. *Over.*"

"That would be great! *Over.*"

"Tell your folks hello for me. And please call my parents tomorrow, and let them know I called you and I'm okay. *Over.*"

"I would have done that without your asking. I love you. Goodbye. *Over.*"

"Me, too—I love you, too. Goodbye, Annette. *Over* . . . "

I pried the receiver out of my ear, looked at it, and smiled. Then I gave it a big kiss and hung up. Taking off my glasses, I wiped my eyes with both hands.

"Everything okay, Pinky?" Bohnny asked.

"Just great, Clyde. Just grrreat." My ear-to-ear smile emphasized my feelings.

Slam went the back door.

Oh, no, I thought. Not *him*. Then I remembered: Murphy was long gone and asshole Top was on R&R.

"Hey, dickheads," Williams called out. "See, ya."

"Where you going?" I asked.

"*The World.* Got a chopper waiting to take me to my freedom bird," he grinned, exposing nicotine-stained teeth.

"I was just talking to *The World.* My wife," I smiled back.

"Big deal, dickhead. Talk all you want. I'm *going* there. You've got another six fuckin' months in this dump. Hah!" he laughed. Then he flashed me the finger and let the door slam behind him.

Six more months . . .

Chapter 11

KA-LAP! FLASH! KA-LAP! KA-LAP!

A cacophony of thunder and lightning had been visiting us since 0600. Seven continuous hours of *spit, boom,* and *blast.* Monsoon season arrived on the auspicious occasion of my brother's birthday: 10 May. Not that any of us were looking forward to it, the monsoon, not my brother's birthday. The only saving grace was, since these two-story, wooden buildings had screening instead of windows, we were spared the *rattle, crash* of glass from the storm's violent winds. But then, the screens did nothing to stop the wind from playing havoc with all of the foolish paperwork that fueled our paper war. Or cause a sudden updraft to lift the roof to the heavens.

KA-LAP! FLASH! FLASH!

"That's my 19th one today, Pinky," Cohen sighed, pushing his chair away from his desk.

"You're two up on me, Coach."

The monsoon didn't keep away the parade to Team 3. We had been getting hit with ID cards all morning and into lunch. No sooner did one GI leave, then two more came in, leaving us low on blank cards. Based on the phone calls we received, so were the other teams.

"Here come two more. I'll take the taller one," I suggested to Cohen, "you get the other one."

"What makes you think they want ID cards?"

I stared at him in disbelief.

"We're both here for ID cards," *Taller* said.

FLASH! KA-LAP! KA-LAP!

I smiled at Cohen, thumbing my nose at him.

"Sure, sit down and I'll take care of you. Doubting Thomas," I pointed a finger at Cohen, "will take care of your buddy."

KA-LAP! KA-LAP!

Cohen's customer wiped his head and neck with a green towel that showed signs of being wrung out several times.

"What's your unit? And your name?" I asked *Taller*, his fatigue shirt was minus the nametag.

"I'm attached to the 9th Medical unit. My name's Scott Kingston."

"*Attached?*"

"Yes. I'm a doctor. A civilian."

KA-LAP! FLASH!

"Hot damn!" I pumped his right hand. "Hey, Coach, this guy's a civvie," I half-shouted over the latest outburst from the heavens.

"You don't have to yell, Pinky." Suddenly realizing the importance of what I had said, Cohen jumped up, grabbed Kingston's right hand, and shook it like he was trying to get the last drop of pee off his pecker.

KA-LAP! KA-LAP! FLASH!

"Does it always pour like this?" Kingston asked.

"Only during monsoon season," I replied. "Where you from, Dr. Kingston?"

"Please, call me Scott."

"Scott."

"I'm from Chicago."

"That's a great, great place," Cohen said. He absentmindedly added: "I was never there."

"That's why it's so great," I laughed.

"When did you get to Nam, Scott?"

He looked at my nametag. "About three days ago, Mr. Papp."

"Holy shit. The guy called me mister, like I was a real human being or something."

KA-LAP! FLASH! KA-LAP! KA-LAP!

"Well, you are, aren't you?"

"We're not too sure," Cohen chimed in.

"Three days ago?" I said. "Damn. Let me shake your hand again. Jeez, you even smell like *The World*." Realizing how I was acting, I asked: "You're not a *psychiatrist* by any chance, are you?"

"Why, you need one?" he laughed.

Cohen nodded his head. "You better believe he does."

"I was just kidding," I mumbled. "The way I was acting, I didn't want you to think I was crazy or anything."

"Are you?"

FLASH! KA-LAP!

"No, Scott, I'm not. It's just that we don't see many civilians, from *The World*, that is."

"I understand. Anything you want to ask me about the States?"

"Boy! is there ever," Cohen and I said in unison.

We spent the next tantalizing half-hour just chewing the fat. And it was dee-licious! Eventually, Dr. Kingston and his companion had to leave.

"That was great," I said to Cohen as they disappeared into the foreboding blackness outside. "I'm goin' downstairs and tell Bohnny all about it."

"All right, Pinky. And on your way back, see if Mr. Blue's got any more ID-card blanks. Okay?"

"Yeah. Yeah. Sure," I said, already halfway out the door.

KA-LAP! FLASH! KA-LAP! KA-LAP! FLASH!

The rain pelted me as I descended the slick stairway, pouring down harder than a cow pissing on a flat rock. Thunder and lightning rivaled the best fireworks display I ever viewed. *So this is monsoon season, eh?* Once inside the dry safety of Team 4, I shook off buckets of water.

"God, Pinky, you look like a drowned rat," White said.

"Me? Nah. It's only drizzling out there."

Bohnny was just returning to his area from the rear of the office. I sloshed over to him, leaving a three-foot-wide puddle by White's desk.

"Guess what, Clyde?"

"What?" He looked up from his typewriter. "Don't you look dry as the Sahara?"

"Guess who the Coach and I were just talking to?"

"A civilian?" he beamed.

KA-LAP! FLASH!

"How'd you know?"

Bohnny shrugged his shoulders.

"Guess where he was from."

"Chicago?" Grin.

KA-LAP! FLASH! KA-LAP! KA-LAP!

"How'd you know that?"

Shrug.

"All right. Bet you can't tell me what the guy does for a living."

Shrug.

"Hah!" I said.

"Is he a doctor?" Smirk.

KA-LAP! KA-LAP!

"Now how the hell did you guess *that*?"

"I have psychic, mystical powers." He beamed like a lighthouse, then returned to his typing.

"Wait a minute, Clyde. Who told you?"

He looked up and laughed. "The Coach. He called right after you left Team 3."

"That rotten son of a bitch! I'll get his ass when I see him."

"Excuse me," a voice whispered. "Can I get an ID card?"

I spun around and saw a timid PFC.

"Sure, sit down," Bohnny said. "What's your name and unit?"

"Barney. Jim Barney. 3d Battalion, 24th Infantry."

"Back in a sec." Bohnny got up and headed for the file cabinets along the rear wall.

KA-LAP! FLASH! KA-LAP!

Barney's unit rang a familiar note (D sharp?) in my subconscious. 3d of the 24th . . . 3d of the 24th . . .

"Barney."

His eyes drifted to my nametag. "Yes, Specialist Papp?"

"Did you know a Lieutenant Maven?" Memories of the dead lieutenant who shared my birthday came forth from my subconscious. His floating 66 File mysteriously appeared before me. "Jonathan Maven?"

"Oh, sure, Specialist Papp. But he's dead," he smiled.

KA-LAP! FLASH! KA-LAP!

Ignoring the odd smile, I continued the interrogation.

"I know he's dead. I did an OER on him." I pictured Maven's wife cradling their two daughters when she was informed of her husband's death; the empty memories of the infants never knowing their father. "Do you know how he died?"

"Oh, sure, Specialist Papp." Bigger smile.

"Well?"

Bohnny eased himself into his chair, 201 File in hand. Seeing the expression on my face, and hearing the tail end of our conversation, he sat there with his mouth shut and his ears wide open.

"We pumped about thirty rounds into him," said Barney.

KA-LAP! FLASH! KA-LAP! KA-LAP! A gust of wind sent the forms in Bohnny's IN box swirling like a tornado.

"What?"

"I said we pumped—"

"I heard you. But why did you kill your own officer?"

"Do you really want to know?" His eyes twinkled.

KA-LAP! FLASH!

"Yes," Bohnny answered for me.

"Well, it was mostly due to his attitude around Christmas." Barney leaned closer to us. "We went on about half a dozen patrols the week before and after the holiday." He paused and carefully looked to the left. Then the right.

"And?" I prompted.

"Well, each time we went out—"

KA-LAP! FLASH! KA-LAP! KA-LAP!

"—we lost half of our squad. When we returned to our base camp," he repeated his cautious survey of the office, "Lieutenant Maven made piss-poor excuses to the captain. On his way out of HQ, Maven was heard to remark, 'Privates. We can always get more privates.' "

KA-LAP!

This time Bohnny prompted him: "And?"

"Well, after four or five times of this needless dying, we—the guys in my squad—decided enough was enough." His voice dropped to a whisper: "Next mission, New Year's Day, four of us opened up on him with our M16s and the M60." In a thunderous voice, he concluded: "We tore the fuckin' shit out of him. Sawed him right in half! Hah!"

KA-LAP! FLASH! KA-LAP! KA-LAP!

Bohnny and I stared at each other in total disbelief.

"See ya, Bohnny," I said, jumping to my feet. "Gotta see the Chief about something." I sped out of Team 4 into the welcome cleansing of the monsoon.

"Ah, Papp, you're just the person I wanted to see."

"About what, Mr. Blue?"

"We're getting hit with a severe amount of ID card requests."

"I know. I need more blanks—if you got in the new supply."

Totally ignoring me, he continued: "The men are losing too much time out of the field coming here for replacement cards."

Like they couldn't use the break for a few days?

"So we decided to have a PA clerk go out to several of the units and make the ID cards right in the field."

"You mean in the *middle* of the fighting?"

"You'll be leaving tomorrow at 0600. Meet PFC Holmes at the air field."

"But—"

"He'll be the photographer. These are the units you'll be visiting." Blue thrust two copies of the list at me. "See you in a few days, Papp."

"But—"

"You're dismissed, Specialist."

⊏══════▶

"Morning, Specialist Papp."

"Morning, Holmes." Nametags made introductions easy.

He grinned and stuck out his hand. "My first name is Steve. But everybody calls me Sherlock."

"You can call me Dennis. Or Pinky."

The torrential rain had stopped late last night, leaving sodden footprints all over the ground. Some that Big Foot would have been proud of.

A 1LT Wood walked up to us and waved off the salute. "Papp, Holmes, you're with me. Let's go."

"Come on, Sherlock," I said, "the game's afoot."

"Okay, Watson."

We grabbed our gear, including our empty M16s (*Why would they give us any bullets just because we're going to be in the midst of all the damned firefights?*), and climbed aboard the chopper.

⊏══════▶

First up on our agenda was Dong Tam. Two days there, and it was off to some place called Tan Tru. If we survived that stop, a quick chopper ride would return us to the security of Bearcat.

Wop-wop-wop. The massive blades spun overhead.

"Bearcat control," 1LT Wood barked, his two hands occupied with something on the left side of his seat and a stick that rose from the cockpit's floor between his legs, "this is Bearcat three-zero-niner."

I looked at PFC Holmes. He had duplicated Wood's handiwork by grabbing his butt with his left hand and his dick with his right. My impulse was to grab my knees and kiss my ass goodbye.

"Roger, Bearcat control. Three-zero-niner out."

Wood turned his head toward us and said, "We're clear for takeoff. Hold on."

Wop-wop-wop.

We swooped up off the security of the muddy ground and circled Bearcat. I memorized the scenery below, hoping to replay the view in a few days.

"Either of you ever been aboard one of these babies before?" Wood shouted.

"No," came two, dry responses.

"Guess you've never flown one either?" he smiled.

Echo the dry response.

"Well, there's nothing to it." He indicated the area by his left butt cheek. "This stick is the collective control. Basically raises and lowers us. I can get more throttle by twisting the grip."

He twisted his left wrist and we ate sky.

"To slow down, I just roll it off a little. Like this."

The effect was like putting your car in reverse while going 30 mph.

He nodded at his manhood. "This is the cyclic control stick. Lets you move in any horizontal direction."

He began playing with himself. The chopper went to the left; our stomachs flew to the right.

"The force that spins the main rotor clockwise also rotates the fuselage counterclockwise. This effect is called torque—"

That can't be right, because Eaton told me that torque was springing to your heels while trying to push a rock-hard dick toward the toilet bowl.

"—and your foot pedals counter that by controlling the pitch of the anti-torque rotor." Wood looked at two blank faces. "The little rotating blades on the tail boom."

We nodded with wide-open mouths.

"Got all that?"

We did our zombie impression again.

Wood gave up and headed south to Dong Tam.

Turning my attention to the passing view far below, I dug into my laundry bag and pulled out an imaginary folding wooden ruler. Sticking it outside, it continued to open. And open. I put our altitude at twelve hundred feet.

Wop-wop-wop. Wop-wop-wop.

The chopper sped like a bandit and made a sudden nose-dive as if we'd been hit by artillery.

"Oh, shit!" Wood screamed.

Yellow smoke belched out before us.

My ruler broke off—chunk by chunk. 1,000 feet. 800 feet. 500 feet.

I grabbed my knees in the kiss-the-ass-goodbye position.

200 feet. 100 feet.

Lieutenant Wood let out a thunderous laugh, and we were jerked skyward.

"Gotcha," he shouted.

When my internal organs regained their original positions, I said, "I thought we were hit."

"Nah."

"But I saw yellow smoke," I screamed.

"I set off a flare."

"I think I shit myself," Holmes confessed, gently touching his soiled pants. "I know I shit myself."

"Dong Tam control, this is Bearcat three-zero-niner."

Wood flipped a switch. "Listen in," he said to us. Evidently he was trying to make up for faking the plummet to our death.

A voice drifted out of the heavens: "Roger, Bearcat three-zero-niner. Go ahead."

"Dong Tam control, Bearcat three-zero-niner, five miles north for landing instructions."

"Roger, Bearcat three-zero-niner. Cleared for a straight-in approach north on row two. Follow your ground guides."

"Roger, Dong Tam control. Three-zero-niner out."

We began our descent to the awaiting arms of Dong Tam, which appeared similar to Bearcat in its size and fortifications. This time, my ruler collapsed only ten feet at a time.

"Hope you guys enjoyed the ride," Wood said, as Holmes and I made a hasty retreat from his death machine.

***

We set up shop in a conference room in the adjutant general's office. Within minutes, the parade of ID card seekers wore a path to us, and the monotony of typing, photographing, fingerprinting, assembling, sealing, and trimming hundreds of cards was underway.

Besides the cards, I had another important mission in Dong Tam: finding the status of my medic friend, Rick Rodriguez. A month ago, my last letter to him was returned, with a rubber-stamped *REFRAD*. (Released From Active Duty.) With each completed card, I asked the GI if he knew Rodriguez.

"Rick? Yeah, I remember him," a shaved-bald Spec 4 said. "He was pulling a wounded guy to the safety of cover so he could work on him. Then Rick got hit."

I dropped a half-assembled ID card. "Where was he shot?" I blurted out. "Was it bad?" *Was there a* good *way of being shot?*

"From what I heard, the bullet entered the bottom of his right foot and traveled upwards—until it came out his kneecap."

I shuddered, sharing Rick's pain.

"They sent him home to El Paso."

The medic wiped the top of his head with a green towel slung around his neck. Sweat, which resembled beaded-up rain on a well-waxed car hood, quickly disappeared.

"I don't know how to ask this," I tried to form the words with my hands, "but was he *all right*?"

"He'll walk with a heavy limp the rest of his life. Otherwise, he's okay."

"Thank God for that at least."

***

When we landed in Tan Tru, we were notified our mission had been cancelled due to an uprising in the nearby hamlets.

"You're free to go back to Bearcat," Sergeant First Class Baker said. "And I'd advise you do so ASAP."

The look in his eyes spelled trouble with a capital "O" for: We're gonna be *OVERRUN* by the VC. *Tonight!*

Holmes and I double-timed it to the helipad.

"Won't be another chopper out of here until 1400 hours tomorrow," a shirtless GI informed us.

"But we gotta get out today!" I shouted, and swallowed the "because you're gonna be overrun tonight."

"Sorry about them apples."

"We have strict orders to get back to Bearcat today," Holmes lied in his best military voice.

"Best I can do for you is put you on a deuce-and-a-half that leaves for Saigon in about three-zero minutes."

Holmes grabbed me aside and whispered: "That means we'd have to drive through the VC with our empty M16s. I don't like those odds."

Bullets. Bullets. My kingdom for some damned bullets.

"Would you rather stay here and have dinner with the VC?" I whispered back.

"We'll take that truck ride," Holmes shouted at the shirtless tour guide.

"Just wait over there," he pointed to a distant shack made out of sandbags and empty ammo boxes, "and tell the driver Smitty said you're part of the convoy to Saigon."

Convoy? I felt safer already.

A Jeep slowed as it approached us and stopped about ten feet past the shack.

"Wonder what he wants?" Holmes said.

I shrugged my shoulders.

"You the guys going to Saigon?" he asked.

"Yeah," I said, "we're waiting for the convoy."

"I'm it."

"You're a damned convoy?" Holmes' eyes flopped out and hung by his chin. "One little Jeep?"

"You expecting a stretch limo?"

"More like five or ten deuce-and-a-halves," I said.

"Sorry. You guys coming or not?"

Holmes and I stared at each other and mouthed the word *overrun*.

"We're coming," I answered, trying to beat Holmes to the flimsy transport.

"Name's Watson," the driver said. Holmes and I gawked at each other in utter disbelief. "Toss your gear in the front."

We flung our meager belongings on the front seat and jumped into the back, holding tight to our impotent M16s.

"I can't believe we're driving all the way to Saigon with fuckin' empty rifles," Holmes moaned.

"Thanks for reminding me."

As we left the gates of Tan Tru, I shoved a full clip of *fear* into my M16. If we met up with the VC, I could just point my gun at them and *scare 'em to death.*

Alternately shutting one eye then the other, I studied the landscape as we sped along on our perilous journey. The one-eye trick was less obvious than shielding my face with my hand, since I needed both hands to keep my heart from pounding out of my chest and hitting the driver. As I peeked at the jungle, things looked only half-bad. Until we neared a big bend in the road.

The treacherous curve boasted dense foliage within spitting range. At the edge of the road, a mortar hole yawned at us. Flashing red lights circled a billboard that read *ambush*. I swallowed my heart. My reflexes guided my trigger finger to the ready. My brain reminded me: no bullets, dummy.

The Jeep slowed to a crawl to navigate the horseshoe. Watson stiffened—noticeably. I shifted my weight on the seat, preparing for trouble. Holmes shadowed my movements.

A bush moved. Up jumped a gook. The Jeep sped up, taking the remainder of the curve on two wheels.

I buried myself in the seat and turned one eye at papa-san. He stepped closer to the road, pulled up his pants, and waved. A second later, a teenage girl rose from the same bush, buttoning her shirt. Watson caught the action and slowed enough to let the other two wheels touch the road.

"The old coot was just tearing off a piece," I said to Holmes, exhaling deeply.

Holmes stuck his head up and yelled: "Atta way to go, you old fart."

Kapow. Kapow.

Two shots whizzed over our heads. Holmes and I became a sandwich on the floor. Watson brought us to two-wheel drive again. When we finally slowed down, Holmes and I casually resumed our seats, making sure to straighten the creases in our fatigue pants.

"For a minute there," Watson said, "I thought you two were gonna need a shotgun wedding."

"Nah," Holmes smiled, "I was wearing a rubber."

Crowd noises and the trumpeting of impatient drivers brought me out of a trance. I popped open both eyes: We were in Saigon.

Bright, shiny-white buildings stood everywhere. Deep-green trees and multicolored flowers punctuated many of the structures. Slender Vietnamese women, clad in traditional colorful dresses called *ao dai*, paraded by us. The surroundings almost looked civilized.

Watson spun the wheel and darted down a narrow street. He took a quick right at the next intersection and stopped at an empty space by the curb.

"Here's where I drop you guys." he said, turning to face us. "If you go up another block or two," he pointed over his shoulder, "you'll come to a circle. You won't have any trouble hitching a ride to your final destination."

Acting like veteran travelers, we climbed out of the back seat, grabbed our gear from the front seat, and confidently trembled in the assigned direction.

We walked down a ten-lane-wide street. Divided in half by a twenty-foot-wide median comprised of open-air shops. Our half of the street was divided by another median, more like a walkway, about five feet wide.

"Come on," Holmes prompted, "let's take a look at what those shops have to offer."

Cars and motorbikes zoomed in, out, and around the medians, making crossing treacherous.

"I think we're safer where we are," I reasoned.

He dropped his head, exchanging his kid-in-a-candy-shop smile for a my-two-scoops-of-ice-cream-plopped-on-the-sidewalk frown.

A little girl came running across the median right at us. Her outstretched right hand held an icy, dripping bottle of Coke. Her left hand was concealed behind her back.

My first impulse was to rush up to her and accept the welcome refreshment. The hidden left hand made me cautious. Through her body, I could see a hand grenade. Minus the pin.

She stopped in front of me and offered the frosty bottle, lowering her left arm to her side. Missing were her hand and half of her forearm. Her misfortune made me ashamed for thinking she had a grenade hidden behind her.

Would I ever be able to trust anyone while I was in Vietnam?
Would this madness of not knowing who was my enemy or my friend
ever end?

"Fifty cents," she said.

I dug into my pockets and pulled out a soggy dollar. I handed her
the MPC note and told her to keep all of it.

She smiled and disappeared through the traffic.

"Here, Sherlock, take a swig."

He drained half the bottle and sheepishly handed it back to me.

Without even complaining about how much he emptied, I finished
it off.

"There's the circle," Holmes said with a beaming face, grateful we
were within spitting distance of Bearcat.

The landmark was on our half of the ten-lane thoroughfare. In the
center of a grassy "moat" stood a billboard and a fountain. Traffic con-
verged on the circle, making it difficult to cross.

A four-story white building occupied the opposite corner. The first
two floors were covered with signs of different company names and
products: SONY, ALFANA WATCHES, and others written in Vietnamese. People bustled in and out the swinging doors.

"Let's go over to that building," I pointed to the hub of activity,
"and try our luck."

We skirted between the swerving cars, M16s and laundry bags
flapping on our backs, as we searched the crowd until we found an MP
giving directions to a disheveled PFC.

"Excuse me, Sergeant," I said, tapping him on the back. "We're
trying to hitch a ride to Bearcat."

He stood there, rubbing his chin.

His puzzled expression made me add: "It's about 25 miles northeast of here. Headquarters for the 9th Infantry Division."

"Right. Right. Don't know about a chopper, but," his eyes pointed
through the fountain, "there's usually a few vehicles parked in front of
the two bars down the street."

"Thanks." Holmes smacked his lips. "We'll give it a try."

Holmes made a beeline for the door of the first bar. I grabbed his
arm and jerked him in the direction of the three vehicles parked at the
curb.

Eventually, we managed transport on a deuce-and-a-half headed in the direction of Bearcat. This time, we were fortunate enough to be accompanied by four infantrymen and a skyscraper of ammo.

Home (*home?*) was only twenty-five miles away.

Chapter 12

HOT SHOWERS, CLEAN SHEETS

"Hey, welcome back, Pinky," McGuire's voice boomed as he entered Team 3. "When did you return from ID-card duty?"

"Last night."

"Did you hear about the U.S.O. show we had the night you left?" He dropped into Cohen's chair and scratched his right ear.

I shook my head.

"The featured attraction was a French broad with the biggest set of hooters I'd ever seen. They had to be 50s. At *least.*"

Gulp.

"They were the perfect set to play 'Splat' with."

"Splat?"

He leaned closer. "You never heard of 'Splat,' Pinky?"

"No. But I'm sure you'll tell me," I tried for nonchalant, but ended up begging.

He stood and walked in circles around Cohen's chair.

"First," he said, sitting down again, "as I already mentioned, you need a woman with a big set of boobs. At least 40s." He held his hands ten inches apart, as though he were catching a football. "Ones like this. Then, of course, she has to be topless."

"40s. Topless. Of course," I hoped I sounded authoritative.

"Carefully place her left boob in her left armpit, making sure it's held firmly. Then the right one in the right armpit. It's important to check that they're snugly in place."

"Yeah, snugly," I groaned.

"Then you tenderly rest your face in the cavity you created between her breasts."

"Yum."

"Without moving your face, you tickle her sides. When she begins rocking with laughter, her boobs come flying out," he clapped his hands with delight, "and *splat!* your ears are crushed."

"Hey, Pinky," Eaton said, coming up behind me, "know what these are?"

He sat on the edge of my desk and waved a couple typed forms in my face.

"Stupid Department of the Army forms." I couldn't make out exactly which ones they were. And I didn't give a damn either. I still had bruised ears on my mind.

"Well, they're 31s, one for you and one for me."

"You mean *R&R* forms?" I beamed.

"Atsa Rog. For Vung Tau. Three days of hot showers and clean sheets."

"Hot damn! When do we leave?"

"This Saturday. The 18th." He waved the forms at me again, tantalizing me with their intoxicating aroma. "Just gotta get these babies signed, and we're in business."

"Well, go to it," I ordered. "Move it, Specialist. Move it!"

Eaton came to attention and saluted me. "Yes, sir!"

"Don't call me *sir*," I shouted, "I work for a living!"

"Goodbye, lifer," he called out, disappearing through the door.

Saturday. The 18th. R&R bound. My best day of being banned to Vietnam.

Eaton and I walked out of the orderly room with R&R forms in hand. Since it was only 0700 hours, we managed to get in and out before Sergeant First Class Smith staggered in for work. This was one event Top wasn't going to screw up for me.

We made the trip to Tan Son Nhut airbase with a convoy of GIs who were DEROSing. Their rapture took some of the thrill out of our R&R plans; but Eaton and I knew our freedom birds would someday soon reach the sky.

Arriving at Tan Son Nhut, we played a new game called "Run Around for an Hour Trying to Find the Right Fucking Airfield." Eaton coined it "Running Around Like a Fart in a Mitten."

When we finally got to what we thought was the right field, a disgruntled Air Force officer told us the next available plane for Vung Tau was on Monday. Today was Saturday.

"If you'll excuse my being frank, Sir," I pleaded with the officer, "we've been chasing our tails for nearly two hours, and we're ready to puke."

"Don't lay your problems on me, Specialist Papp. If Monday isn't good enough for you pleasure-seeking enlisted men," he spat the words, "then tough shit!"

Eaton gave me a look that asked how many years he would get for smashing an officer in the face.

"That's a hell of a way to run an airline," Eaton said as I dragged him out of the terminal.

"Couldn't help but hear your conversation inside," a voice echoed behind us.

We spun around. Another Air Force representative, a fellow enlisted man, was three steps behind us and gaining ground.

"You guys headed for a little R&R at Vung Tau, right?"

"Yeah."

"Just so you don't think the entire Air Force is a bunch of piss ants, how about letting me take you to the right terminal? One that has a plane leaving for Vung Tau within ten minutes."

We jumped into his Jeep and burned rubber, racing across one air strip after another.

"We want to get there *alive*," I shouted as we squeezed between two moving planes.

He laughed and drove faster.

Ska-reeech!

"Hey, Slats," our driver yelled, "two more for the 1100 to Vung Tau."

"Okay, Buz."

Looking our way, Slats gave us the hand signal for double-time-it. "We're boarding now, so move it."

"Thanks, Buz," Eaton shouted, raised his open left hand, and added in his soliloquy-from-Shakespeare voice, "Nobody better ever say anything bad about the Air Force while I'm around."

We climbed aboard the opened tail-end of the caribou, like walking in through the unbuttoned back flap on a pair of long johns. Twenty guys were seated *on* the belly of the plane. Moments before we took off, someone on the end of our row threw a strap across our laps to a waiting pair of hands at the other end. So much for fasten your seatbelts. We held onto the strap for dear life, literally, because the caribou took off with the back door yawning. We flew in that open-door position the entire trip.

Three rosaries later, and a change of underwear, we touched down in Vung Tau.

"Hey, Pinky," Eaton smiled, "did you notice the clean, crisp, white sheets on the bed?" His smile took over his entire face. "I mean they were whiter than white and brighter than bright."

"You sound like a TV commercial."

He continued smiling and added, "Let's get a few drinks and begin our R&R the right way."

"And lunch," I added over my growling stomach.

The bar was located in a bountiful patio. Selecting one of the dozen-plus circular metal tables, we ducked under the colorful striped umbrella, and plopped down in aluminum folding chairs. A Vietnamese waitress quickly appeared in front of us.

"I'll have a screwdriver."

"Dewars on the rocks for me," Eaton said. "And please bring us some pretzels and chips." He looked at me and added a single word of explanation: "Lunch."

The waitress departed gracefully with something between a curtsy and a bow.

I leaned back, rested my feet on the edge of the empty chair across from me, and relaxed for the first time since landing in Nam on New Year's Day.

In the corner, along the far wall, I noticed an empty platform. Six microphone stands waited for musicians and a singer or two. A circular fountain separated us from the bandstand.

"Wonder why there's a fence around the fountain," I said.

Three-foot-high poles, painted red and white, butted the circular cement curb that held the fountain's water. Each pole had two holes drilled through it: One about a foot from the top, where the white paint ended and the red began, the other six inches above the curb. A chain was strung through each of the holes, preventing easy access to the fountain and its supply of water.

"Keeps the drunks from falling in and drowning," he answered.

"Won't stop them from *peeing* in the pool."

The waitress returned, weighted down with a tray of drinks. Trying not to unbalance her load, she carefully selected the screwdriver for me and the scotch for Eaton. Bowls of chips and pretzels were placed between us.

I picked up my glass and drained it. Eaton stared at his.

"Aren't you gonna drink it?" I asked, bits of orange pulp sticking to the tip of my nose. My right hand dove into the pretzels.

"Oh, yeah." He came out of his trance. "I was just admiring how the tea-colored liquid sparkled on the light-blue table top."

"And its fruity bouquet was bold, yet subtle," I kidded, attacking the chips.

"Are you a connoisseur of spirits?" he asked intently.

"No. Are you?" I shoved more pretzels into my mouth.

"As a matter of fact," he said, sipping his drink, "I do know a thing or two. Especially about wine."

"Great! Then you can select the right beverage to accompany to-night's dinner."

"Fine with me," he responded, taking me seriously.

We ordered two more drinks, each, plus more munchies.

I emptied half of my second drink in one gulp and stared at the remainder in my glass. Even though I was enjoying the wonderful mixture of vodka and orange juice, it didn't feel right to be sitting in the middle of this war zone sucking up booze. Somewhere in Nam a GI just got wounded, or killed, while I was guzzling the nectar of the gods. While I'm celebrating my good fortune of being on R&R, an-other GI was mourning the loss of his buddy.

Was it wrong for me to be having a good time while others were dying? Should I be rejoicing while others suffered? Did I have the right to be happy at the same moment another GI was taking his last breath? Could I ever have a moment's peace or happiness while I was entombed in this patch of earth called Vietnam?

I finished the drink, trying not to feel sorry for myself. Exchanging it for the full glass, I made an orphan of it in one long swallow, and ordered another round plus the check.

"I can't believe it," I almost shouted, pushing our bar tab in Eaton's direction. "My four screwdrivers cost sixty cents. That's only 15 cents *each*."

Eaton looked at his meager half of the tab and said, "Boy! I'm looking forward to getting drunk here."

We both put two MPC dollars on the table and began our search for the perfect meal.

In spite of approaching twilight, GIs freely walked the streets of Vung Tau. Even the comfort of an impotent M16 wasn't necessary. After roaming around for the better part of an hour, Eaton came to a sudden stop in front of a brightly lit restaurant.

"This is the place," he said. "Look at the name."

I gazed up at a hand-painted red-and-blue sign on which four words of Vietnamese gibberish were emblazoned.

"Since when do you read Vietnamese?"

"I've been studying it the last two months."

"Well," I prompted, "what's it say?"

"The Chu Sum Twat Cafe."

I pushed him through the swinging blue doors.

An overweight papa-san dropped two food-stained menus in front of us. Before reviewing the bill of fare, I told the waiter to bring us two beers.

"Hey, these two items look good," Eaton prompted.

The selections he pointed to were Fuc Mi Slo and Sum Cum Goo.

"I kinda had #11 or #33 in mind."

He read aloud: "#11 . . . Sum Dum Fuc; #33 . . . Suc Mai Dik."

Papa-san dropped two frosty bottles in front of us, took our order of unpronounceable appetizers and unknown pork dishes with vegetables and white rice, and shuffled back to the kitchen to torture supper.

"So tell me how to select the right wine, Numbers."

Eaton settled back in his chair and put on a scholarly look.

"Well," he began, "you've often heard that white wine goes with fish and red with beef?"

Nod.

"Well, that's basically—"

Eaton continued his explanation, while my mind wandered to the other tables. My eyes focused across the room on what I presumed was a family of four. Seated facing me was the most beautiful Vietnamese woman I had ever seen. She was in her late teens or early twenties. As she ate, her dainty hands made the chopsticks dance from her plate to her full lips. When she turned her head to talk to her mother, her lustrous hair fell to the side, exposing the hint of a mole on her neck. A smile to her father made the ceiling lights twinkle.

A chopstick jabbed my left forearm.

"Do you have any questions?" Eaton pushed the chopstick deeper.

"Huh?"

"Were you listening to anything I said?"

"Yeah. Sure." I searched my gray cells for a question. "Glasses. Why are there so many different wine glasses?"

"Well, depending on which wine you select—"

Her meal completed, my Vietnamese goddess stood up to leave. The expectation of getting a closer look made the room temperature soar. Following her parents by a respectful distance, her face was hidden behind her mother's head. As a clear view became possible, our waiter chose that precise moment to come to our table and ask if we wanted more beer.

The moment's distraction was enough to enable the heavenly vision to disappear into the crowd outside. Frustrated at not seeing the girl's face up close, I picked up my chopsticks and stuffed my mouth with generous helpings of pork, vegetables, and white rice. After shoveling in another mouthful, I washed it down with the remainder of my beer.

By the time we finished supper, the table was laden with a stack of dirty dishes and more than a dozen empty beer bottles.

We paid the check and staggered to our feet.

"How about a nightcap?" I suggested.

Even though we'd already had enough, Eaton gave me an R&R "Sure. Why not?"

Two hours and a trail of MPC notes later, we stumbled up to the R&R center.

"Let me give you a hand to your bunk," I suggested. If it weren't for my supporting arm and his starched boxer shorts, Eaton would have still been playing "Hide and Go Seek" in a gutter.

"Thanks." Pause. "Pinky." Burp.

When we got to the second floor, he said, "Take me to the head. Fast."

Instead of dropping his drawers when he reached the toilet, he dropped to his knees and held onto the bowl. Myriad colors, unmatched by any rainbow or peacock, flowed forth. For the next half-hour, Eaton made love to the toilet . . . totally, passionately, giving of himself: his lunch, his supper, his nightcaps. He gave. And gave. And gave.

I looked at my watch. Mickey's big glove was standing straight up; the little one was on the 6. I turned over on the still-crisp white sheets, buried my head under my pillow, and slept.

My dreaming drifted from fast cars, to piles of money, well-stacked women . . . and someone tickling my wrist.

I lifted the pillow and opened one eye. The tickling wasn't a dream; it was the maid.

"Time for bleckfest, GI," she whispered.

"No. Sleep."

"No. Get up."

"No. Sleep," I repeated.

"No. Get up," she demanded, and, along with the lower sheet, she yanked me out of bed. "Time for bleckfest," she smiled through two missing teeth. "I make bed."

Having no choice, I got off the floor and plodded to the bathroom. There I took the most sensuous hot shower in my life. Preceded by a hot-water shave. Donning fresh civvies, I ambled over to Eaton's room.

"Good morning, Numbers," I bellowed.

"Morning, Pinky," he responded in a substantially lower decibel rating.

His crimson head was sticking out of a University of Michigan sweatshirt, and he was making a college try at getting his arms through. Unfortunately, the sleeves weren't taking the shape of his hugging-the-toilet-bowl arms.

I reached over and guided one arm through, then the other.

"Thanks," he smiled weakly.

"How 'bout some bleckfest?"

"You been long time dis country, Pinky?"

"Too long, Numbers. Way too long."

I tried not to enjoy breakfast too much, because I felt sorry for Eaton: He was struggling through the entire meal using his left hand to simultaneously cover his ear and prop his head until he could take a mouthful, release his fork from his right hand, and cover his right ear with his freed hand.

Two drinks after breakfast were the medicine Eaton needed to erase the pounding in his head and agree to a little romp on the beach.

"This water is as warm as pee," I complained, standing knee-deep in the South China Sea.

"Isn't is supposed to be? Never been in an ocean before. Just Lake Michigan."

"Well, I've been in the Atlantic, the Pacific, and the Gulf of Mexico. And none of them," I cupped my hands, letting the water dribble out, "felt like this."

"But it sure feels good to see those bikini-clad lovelies over there," he pointed.

I followed his lead and feasted upon two Vietnamese girls in their late teens sporting the skimpiest bikinis I'd ever seen.

"They might as well be wearing two Band-Aids and a cork," I gasped.

Eaton smiled and licked his lips.

"Trying to give Boomerang some competition?" I asked, pointing to his swollen manhood.

He knelt in the water, modestly covering himself above the waist, and gave me an "ooops" shrug of his shoulders.

"No," he grinned, pointing to the Naval arsenal anchored farther out at sea, "I'm the advance party for the fleet."

We began Monday with a sensible bleckfest—and made up for it by getting totally shit-faced in our favorite patio bar.

"You k-know w-what I w-wanna do?" Eaton stumbled through the question.

"Yeah." Pause. "Drink some more." I hoisted my arm, signaling the waitress to bring us another round.

"Yeah. No." Pause. "I w-wanna p-play p-pool."

"You wanna go in the pool?"

"Yeah." Pause. "No, P-pinky." He emptied his glass and grabbed the fresh drink. "I wanna play p-pool."

"Oh. You wanna play with yourself." I held up a drink in each hand and studied them in the sunlight. "Don't let me stop you." I smiled. "P-play pocket pool."

"No. I wanna—"

"Did you hear the latest in p-pocket pool, Numbers?"

"Huh?" Pause. "What?"

"Away games," I said, holding my pants pocket open for his hand.

As Eaton leaned over with his left hand, I opened my pocket wider. Instead of inserting his hand, he clumsily swung his right arm around and emptied his full glass into my pocket.

I jumped back in my seat, almost flipping over. "Damn, you." I extracted a handful of ice cubes and threw them at him.

Our one for the road was a cup of black coffee. Psychologically, we felt better. Enough so to rise gracefully from the table and walk the proverbial white line to downtown Vung Tau.

"Is it possible to sweat vodka?" I asked.

"Why?"

We jumped out of the way of two Vietnamese men bearing down on us with their bicycles.

"Because I suddenly feel clearheaded."

"Me, too, Pinky."

A Buddhist monk, garbed in a yellow sheet, stepped in front of us, slowing our pace. Eaton and I separated, sidestepped, and passed the monk.

"How many screwdrivers *did* I have?" I pondered out loud.

"Your share of the bill was $1.20. That means you had eight!"

"Thanks, Numbers." I patted him on the shoulder, gently. "That was a rhetorical question."

We crossed several streets, bravely avoiding bicycles and motor-bikes, and eventually found ourselves in the midst of a marketplace. Unwelcome odors attacked my senses from every possible direction.

"Look," I pointed for Eaton, "check out the meat."

Vendors were selling a variety of fruits, vegetables, meats, and fishes. A few plucked chickens hung from a short clothesline. Many of the selections, recognizable as beef and pork, were displayed on the filthy sidewalk. Handfuls of insects crawled over, around, and under the raw meat.

"Makes me wanna puke," Eaton gagged.

"Please don't use the 'P' word," I begged. "Not after all the drinks we downed."

We coaxed our feet to bypass the market and headed down a wide street. Again playing the role of a tour guide, I pointed to a sign partially attached to a two-story, bright-yellow structure.

When Eaton identified the "POOL HALL" on the sign, he threw his left arm around my neck and encouraged me to walk faster.

A smiling shoeshine boy blocked our entry. His right hand expertly held a lit cigarette. His left foot was planted on the box that held his tools of the trade.

"Shine, GI?"

I pointed to my sneaker-clad feet.

He smiled broader and repeated, "Shine, GI? One dollar."

The little entrepreneur straightened up, his chin coming up to my belly button.

"You crazy?"

He scratched his head enthusiastically, almost boring a hole in the shortest crew cut I ever saw.

"Don't call me *dinky dau*, GI." Another smile. "Want shine?"

"What's your name?" I asked.

On top of a torn T-shirt, he wore a faded blue shirt-jacket unbuttoned to the waist. The shirttail partially covered his hand-me-down pants. The cuffs were rolled up several times, exposing his well-shined sandals.

"Tom."

"*Tom*?" I looked at Eaton in disbelief. "I thought the Vietnamese named their kids by throwing a handful of silverware in the air."

Eaton stared at me.

"The sound the silverware makes when it hits the ground is the kid's name: *Ping, Dong, Ding, Pong . . .* "

"GI funny. Want shine? One dollar." Tom held up his shoeshine box and threatened me with it.

"No. GI want play pool," I repeated, lapsing into broken English.

"Tom good pool player. Play you for one dollar."

"How old are you?"

"Nine," he told me, sticking out his pathetically thin chest.

"I'm being hustled by a nine-year-old kid, Numbers."

"GI chicken shit?" Tom challenged.

"You're on, you little bastard."

Tom looked at me as though I had just uncovered a closely guarded family secret.

Tom dug a hand into a pocket and placed an MPC dollar on the edge of the pool table. He looked me squarely in the eyes and said what were probably the first two words he ever uttered: "Eight ball." His next eloquent stab at the English language was: "I bleak."

Eaton looked at me and smiled. "Well? You gonna take up the challenge? Or are you chicken shit, GI?"

I slammed a dollar on top of Tom's. The impact shook the table. "You're on, you little piss ant."

Eaton grabbed the loose balls and filled the rack. After alternating the stripes and solids the best he could, he placed the black sphere in the center, stuck a few of his fingers inside the base of the triangle to assure a tight rack, and slid the pyramid over the dot.

Tom searched his right shirt-jacket pocket and extracted a cube of blue chalk.

"Kid's got his own chalk," Eaton whispered in my ear. "You in deep shit, GI."

The little pool shark glided his cue stick back and forth like a well-oiled piston. With the force of a 105mm shell, he made contact with the cue ball. The rack exploded on impact, sending stripes and solids flying in one ricocheting blur.

Two balls flew into one of the corner pockets. Seconds later, the 8-ball headed for the side pocket where I was standing. Behind a tail of black smoke, the game-winner precariously perched on the rim of the pocket. Another quarter-rotation, and it fell with a solid *plunk*.

Tom folded my MPC note in half and put it in a back pocket. "Another game, GI?"

Eaton whooped with laughter.

"Shit. All the years I been playing pool," I said, "I've never seen anybody sink the 8-ball on the break."

I put another dollar on the table and racked the balls myself. After I positioned them on the dot, I gave the rack the Italian whammy with the index and little fingers of my left hand. Just like my sweet wife taught me.

Another explosive break, no 8-ball this time, awarded the low-balls to Vung Tau Slim. After an exchange of turns, we had two balls left. Not counting the two between my legs, which shrank to the size of BBs.

I sunk the 10-ball, then bounced the 13 off the rim of a far corner-pocket.

"Damn!" I moaned.

With a single shot, my brazen opponent sunk the 3-ball in one corner, kissing the 4-ball into another. His brilliant effort left him with a difficult shot on the 8-ball.

Applying a little right-handed (broken?) English to the cue ball, he banked the 8 off the side rail. With every rotation the *8* emblazoned on it mocked me as it headed for the pocket, falling in with a loud *plunk*.

Before Vung Tau Slim could take the wager from the pool table, I extracted another dollar from my wallet and handed it to him.

"What this for, GI?"

"It's for the shoeshine."

"You no get shine, GI."

"I know. But I've just been taken to the cleaners, and feel like you did the sneakers, too."

The diminutive hustler looked at Eaton and said, "GI want a shine, too?"

Eaton handed Tom a dollar and chased him away.

"329," a voice shouted.

"274," another echoed.

"What's going on?" I asked.

Eaton shook his head.

After enjoying a great supper, Numbers and I settled down in the patio bar determined to put a serious dent in the R&R center's liquor supply.

"Yelling out how many days they have left," a jubilant PFC told us from an adjoining table.

"142," I proudly bellowed.

"*69*," came the retort from a distant table.

Eaton laughed. "Eat, eat, eat. Doesn't anybody want to fuck anymore."

Our neighborly PFC put his palms on the table, pushed himself to a bending-standing position, and shouted: "Threeee. And a wake up." He grabbed his drink and triumphantly held it in the air. Carefully bringing it down to his mouth, he downed the golden contents in a single swallow. Proudly thrusting the empty glass high overhead, he screamed: "FTA!"

We helped the short-timer celebrate with a few more drinks. After inhaling my final one, I calculated I'd had a grand total of 26 screwdrivers today. Not a bad day of R&R!

Eaton and I were seated at Vung Tau International, waiting for a flight back to Bearcat. I was in a smiling trance, replaying the happy memories of the three-day R&R. A friendly tap on the shoulder made me turn around. Standing there was Spec 4 Ben Palk, a Fort Sill buddy who left for Nam a month before me.

Following the handshake and an emotional hug, I introduced him to Eaton.

"You're a long way from Pleiku," I said. Palk was a cook and had orders for the same unit as I originally did: the 309th Communications Battalion. "Here for some R&R?"

"Just got back," he smiled.

"Huh?"

"Went to Kuala Lumpur."

"Whatcha doing here?"

"The 309th is stationed here. At the R&R center."

I did my faint-in-your-chair impression.

"Didn't you know that?" he asked.

"You mean to tell me I would have ended up in Vung Tau? At the R&R center? *Not* in Pleiku?"

"Atsa Rog."

Poof!

Every day since the VC overran Pleiku during the Tet offensive, I thanked God that my orders had gotten screwed up and I had ended up with the 9th Infantry. In Bearcat. Instead of with the 309th. In Pleiku. Now I find out that *I* was the one who got screwed. Not my orders. The Army, in its devious methodology, had fucked me again.

"What's the matter, Papp? You look like I told you Santa Claus and the Easter Bunny just had a head-on collision."

"Worse," I spat the word. "FTA worse!"

Chapter 13

When we got back to The Pit, a pile of mail was waiting for me on my bunk. I needed something to get me out of the double-depression of: (1) learning I could have been stationed in Vung Tau, and (2) returning to the dismal surroundings of Bearcat. This collection of envelopes from *The World* could just do the trick.

Dropping my satchel and bags of souvenirs next to my bunk, I sat down and flipped through the mail. There were several letters from Annette, one from my father, one from Rick Rodriguez—postmarked *Dong Tam*—and a bright yellow envelope from Joyce and Sam Tarcza.

I grabbed the one from Rodriguez and tore it open. It was dated 12 *March*. The damned thing knocked around Nam for more than two months. Thank God Rick's wound wasn't fatal. It would have been spooky to read a letter from a *dead* friend.

> *I heard about Bearcat getting hit. Would you believe it if I told you that we were mortared eight times in two days? And I thought Dong Tam was going to be safer than being in the field.*
>
> *Well, tomorrow we go out for five days. From what I've heard, it shouldn't be too bad. Well, as good as going out on patrol can get. Anyway, every time before we leave, I always find me a quiet place,*

kneel down, and ask God to help me stay alive. So
many times I've gone out with the feeling that I'll
never return again . . . alive.

So far, Rick's letter wasn't doing a damned thing to relieve my
depression. It was having the opposite effect. Until I got to his closing
paragraphs.

Since I'm writing to you, all of a sudden I got
the urge to take a crap. Could it be your charming
personality that's making me feel this way? Guess I
better go to the latrine before I soil my bed.
Would you believe that I'm getting short?
                    A good friend always,
                    Rick

Putting Rick's letter aside with a smile, I dove into my father's.
After the usual I love and miss you, he closed by getting uncharacteris-
tically emotional about the present I should get him when I go to Tokyo
for R&R.

There are a lot of things I would like to have you
get me when you go to Tokyo. But the only thing I
really want is for October 16th to come and have my
Son Dennis say to me: "Hi, Pop. How are you?"
Man, the blue sky would open up, and the Sun
would shine like it never did before. And the whole
world would be alive and happy again.
That, and that alone, is all I want from Japan.
                    Love,
                    Pop

Chapter 14

"Hey, Pinky," Cohen said, wiping crumbs from his chin. "Aren't you going to lunch?"

"No, thanks," I mumbled.

While at The Academy, we had been warned that malaria tablets could enable healthy, frequent bowel movements. Well, I was on day three of Ho Chi Minh's revenge, and had been running like a three-time loser from a crime scene. My butt was so sore that I could hardly stand, let alone sit and work.

"But the Red Cross girls are serving the corn bread and cake," he encouraged. "Everybody's getting a piece. Hah!"

Food was the last thing on my mind. But a piece of ass from a Red Cross broad was especially distasteful. Even if it were for free, instead of the customary $40 a throw.

"I'll pass, thanks. My whole body aches. In fact," I stated with only mild exaggeration, "the only thing that doesn't hurt is my left shoe-string."

Hopefully I would feel well by the evening, because Mr. Blue was DEROSing in a few days, and tonight was his party. Whenever some-one in Personnel Actions DEROSed, Mr. Blue always footed the bill for the big bash. This time, everybody in PA chipped in a few bucks to give the Chief a proper send off.

"Have you gotten the leave forms from him yet?" Cohen asked. "We're running out of time if we want to go to Tokyo the end of June."

Cohen was married and shared a common disinterest in screwing his brains out when he went on R&R. Since neither of us wanted to hold somebody back from "having a good time," we decided to go on R&R together, taking in the sights, eating great food, and escaping from this cesspool, etc.

We ruled out Hawaii, to meet our wives, because it seemed a lot of trouble and expense to see someone you deeply loved, and then have to say goodbye in a few days. Just to return to this hellhole.

Our next choice was Australia. With the horny guys wanting to go there to screw *round*-eyed women, the waiting list was longer than Boomerang's best erection. Plus we had to be in Nam nine months before moving to the top of the list. By then, Cohen and I would have been on our way home. Hopefully.

Our first choice became Tokyo.

"No, I haven't gotten the forms yet. But—"

"Do you really think he's gonna let us both disappear at the same time? With *nobody* guarding Team 3?"

Could we guard anything with a typewriter and an impotent M16?

Since Cohen and I were on the same team, we had a hard time convincing Mr. Blue to let us go. The Team-1, -2 and -4 guys in PA said they'd cover for us. They even made up a rotating schedule of half-day intervals when someone would actually be sitting at our desks to help any GIs who came to Team 3 from the field.

Mr. Blue signed the forms, but wouldn't give them to us. He wanted to talk it over with his replacement, out of military courtesy. In order to get on Blue's good side, I wholeheartedly supported his decision whenever I spoke to him about anything.

"I think I can get my hands on them tonight," I assured him.

"How?"

"The guys in The Pit have worked out a game plan with me."

There was nothing remarkable about the plan. All it amounted to was getting the Chief's replacement drunk at the party, having him agree to the leave, and getting the forms from Blue. Tonight.

"What about getting *Blue* drunk?"

I gave Cohen my best don't-be-naive look. "Do you honestly think the Chief will need any help? It's *his* party, remember?"

"Are you dripping yet?" the Spec 4 asked.

The Specialist in question was seated behind a table serving as a check-in desk at the 9th Medical Battalion. Five guys patiently waited their turn in line. I took my place behind the last one, deciding to go on sick call after three-plus days of the runs.

Patient #1 nodded a "Yes."

"Are you allergic to penicillin?"

Patient #1 shook his head "No."

"Here, get this prescription filled. Take it according to the directions on the label. Next!"

Without even asking, the Spec 4 asked, "Are you dripping?"

"Yeah, man," the next GI answered. "And my cock feels like it's gonna explode when I take a piss."

"Are you allergic to penicillin?"

Patient #2 rattled his head.

"Here, get this prescription filled. Take it according to the directions on the label. Next!"

"Are you dripping yet?"

Patient #3: "Yes."

"Are you allergic to penicillin?"

"Fuck, no, man," #3 replied with all the eloquence he could muster.

"Here, get this prescription filled. Take it according to the directions on the label. Next!"

Patient #4 hobbled up to the Spec 4 on a right foot that was bandaged with a pillow case.

The Spec 4 looked him squarely in the eyes and said, "Are you dripping yet?"

Patient #4 pointed to the obvious and said, "It's my foot that's infected. Not my dick."

"Are you allergic to penicillin?"

"Are *you*?"

"What's it to you, wise-ass?"

"Nothing."

"Well if you're not," Spec 4 said, ripping off the top sheet from the pad of forms, "get this prescription filled. Take it according to the directions on the label. Next!"

When it was finally my turn, I remained standing where I was and shouted: "No, I'm not dripping. And my foot isn't infected. I've got the damned runs, three fuckin' days now. And, yes, I *am* allergic to penicillin. And I'm also allergic to sulfa drugs."

A round of applause broke out from the guys in line behind me and those seated along both walls.

"So what the hell are you going to do for me?" I demanded.

"Sit over there, please," he said, pointing to a few empty chairs, "and wait until the doctor calls your name."

While waiting for the doctor, I looked absently around the room, stopping when I saw a GI whose mouth was burned and blistered. Almost like he'd eaten napalm (a jellylike incendiary bomb).

"He looks like hell," I whispered to the PFC sitting next to me and pointed discretely. "That one."

The PFC repositioned his makeshift-bandaged left hand in his lap. Blood was oozing out of the area by his index finger.

"Know how he got like that?" he asked.

I shook my head.

"There was another guy just like him about forty-five minutes ago. From California. Turns out he was on R&R in Bangkok and ate out a whore who had the clap."

I looked for some place to puke, but couldn't find one.

"Appetizing thought, eh?" the PFC asked with a twinkle in his eyes.

"Don't tell me the guy with the pillow case-bandage stuck his foot in the same broad. Please, don't."

"I'm sure he didn't. But if he's like the dozens who come in here with a similar foot injury, then I know how he got the infection."

"You sound like you come here often."

"I'm a cook." He held up his left hand. "I get a little careless with a knife every so often."

I was about 10 percent successful in holding back a laugh. The cook smiled and courteously continued.

"When a GI wants to get out of the field for a few days, he cuts his foot, then sticks it in a muddy puddle." He moved his left hand, until he found a comfortable way to position it in his lap. "In a day or so, the germs do their magic, and *voilá*, the gash gets infected."

The thought of yellow-white pus gushing out of my foot made me feel worse than my bout with diarrhea.

"Why would anybody inflict an injury like that on himself?" I asked unconsciously aloud.

"Beats taking an AK-47 round between the eyes."

"PFC Barton," a Spec 5 shouted." The doctor will see you now."

"That's me," he said in my direction, and looked at his watch. "Not bad. Only waited an hour, this time."

I nodded a goodbye and thought, *He waited an hour for a serious hand wound? I'll be here the rest of the afternoon with my insignificant case of the shits.* So I exited the waiting area and decided to stop at The Pit for a Hungarian cure for diarrhea: a healthy shot of whiskey laced with a couple shakes of black pepper. Thank God I had a hidden stash of whiskey in my footlocker.

"Here's that drink you wanted, Mr. Taguiped," Moritoni offered.

"That's right—*hic*—neighborly of you, Specialist Moritoni," Taguiped said, accepting his fourth drink in the last hour.

Mr. Blue smiled at Moritoni's hospitality and said, "You can get one for me, too."

"Sure, Chief."

So far, our plan to get Taguiped drunk was working. As long as we weren't too obvious with our ass-kissing, we'd have no trouble getting Taguiped to agree to just about anything. Without an objection from Taguiped, Blue would approve the R&R for Cohen and me.

"Where you from, Mr. Taguiped?" I asked.

"Effingham, Illinois." Pause. "Aren't you—*hic*—drinking, Specialist Papp?"

"One was my limit, Sir. Got a #1 case of the runs. I'm really here out of friendship and respect for the Chief."

Mr. Blue gave me a look that almost shouted: I know what you're up to, Papp. When he tapped his back pocket, I could hear paper crackle. His next look said: R&R forms.

Returning my attention to Taguiped, I flashed him a smile, and quickly added: "And to meet you, of course, Sir."

"That's right—*hic*—neighborly of you." Pause. "Specialist Papp."

Cohen came up to us, with beer in hand, and introduced himself to the Chief's replacement. When Cohen stared at me, I gave my head a no-R&R-forms-yet shake, and he faded out as quickly as he had appeared.

"Why don't you—*hic*—throw caution to—*hic*—the wind, Specialist Papp, and at least have a watered-down drink?" Taguiped asked, spilling some of his booze on the ground.

"Well, Sir, maybe I'll just have a beer."

"That would—*hic*—be right neighborly of you." Drink dribbled down his chin. "Specialist Papp."

"Here we are, Mr. Blue," Moritoni said, handing the Chief a drink. "Hope I wasn't too long. And I got you a refill, Mr. Taguiped."

While Moritoni handed the warrant officers their drinks, I used the break in the conversation to excuse myself and grab a beer. Mr. Blue saw me glance at his back pocket and gave it another crackling tap.

Whenever we had a PA party, we managed to get hold of a big washtub, nearly the size of a bathtub, fill it with water and a stolen block of ice, and *voilá*, a great cooler for the beer and soda.

I stuck my left arm into the tub, up to my shoulder, and grabbed a brew. The ice-cold water dulled my senses and momentarily made me forget about the runs.

Bohnny smiled, pushed me aside and extracted a cold one.

"Ahh," he said, "the water is the right temperature for the dousing."

Near the end of a going-home party, it was customary to drop the guest of honor into the tub, as a way of bidding him a fond farewell.

"Not until I've got those leave forms."

"Yeah, right."

Cohen appeared out of nowhere. "Well?"

"Not yet, Coach. Just be patient."

"I DEROS in August, Pinky. I'd like to go to Tokyo before that."

"Have your freedom bird stop there on the way to *The World*," Bohnny suggested.

Cohen gave Bohnny a stare that even chicken soup couldn't cure and walked away without saying a word.

I searched the crowd for Blue. Moritoni was feeding him and Taguiped another drink. Both of the "misters" stood on half-folded legs. Atta boy, Face, keep up the good work.

"That's the last one," Eaton yelled, extracting a beer from the cooler. "It's time."

In unison, the PA clerks put down our drinks and food. As only a bunch of drunks could do it, we marched up to Mr. Blue and circled him, scaring the crap out of Mr. Taguiped.

"Do you have anything to say for yourself," a slurred voice asked. Hoffman's?

Blue put a reassuring hand on Taguiped's shoulder. The replacement immediately relaxed. Extracting some papers out of his back pocket and unfolding them, Blue said: "Yes, I've prepared a few parting remarks." Looking at the group of drunken clerks he'd commanded for the last year, he added: "I hope you don't mind if I read them."

"Shit," I mumbled. "The damned papers aren't the R&R forms after all."

"First, I want to say it's been a pleasure serving with you men. I'm only sorry our tour had to be in Vietnam."

He looked at me and smiled. Shuffling the papers, he purposely let a few smaller sheets fall to the ground.

"Would you pick those up for me, Specialist Papp? I've had a few too many drinks to bend over."

"Yes, Sir!" I bellowed.

I dove on the ground. After consuming every word on the fallen documents, I got to my knees and yelled: "It's them, Coach. We got the signed R&R forms!"

Cohen's "Yahoo!" was drowned out by the group's stampede to the cooler with Mr. Blue in tow, and the subsequent *SPLASH!*

"Oh, shit! That's cold!" screamed Blue.

Chapter 15

"What do you mean you know nothing about it?" I demanded. "I handed in the approved request two weeks ago!"

KA-LAP! FLASH! FLASH!

It was 13 June, three days before our scheduled departure to Tokyo. The Coach and I gave up our lunch to slosh through the monsoon and go to R&R Headquarters to pick up our long-awaited orders.

"I'm sorry, Specialist Papp," the clerk apologized, searching a typed list, "but there's no record of our getting the request from your orderly room."

This sounded like the deliberate work of our damned first sergeant, that worthless piece of shit. He knew every GI coveted an out-of-country R&R. An opportunity to get out of Nam was the next best thing to being in *The World*. Other than DEROSing, that R&R was what we lived for. Asshole Top was screwing me. Again. Somehow, some way, I would get revenge if I learned Top *were* responsible for this mix up.

"So what does that mean?" Cohen asked.

"It leaves two possibilities."

KA-LAP! FLASH! FLASH!

"Which are?" I urged.

He held up his thumb. "One, I'll personally see the orders are cut tomorrow, or Saturday at the latest. Then you'll go standby." He added the index finger to his upright thumb. "B, if you don't get on the plane on the 16th, we'll reissue the orders, and you can try again on the 23rd.

And again on the 25th if necessary."

I didn't like his "1 . . . B" method. And it wouldn't have been any better if it were the "A . . . 2" approach.

Cohen and I exchanged helpless expressions.

With my face turning a deeper shade of red, I asked: "Can't you do any better than that?"

"No."

KA-LAP! FLASH! FLASH!

"Why the hell not? Why—"

Cohen pulled me aside and verbally assaulted me. To the clerk, he calmly said, "Please excuse my friend. He can be a hot-headed Hungarian at times." Putting an extra measure of ass-kissing in his voice, he added: "Please do what you can. And thanks."

On our way back to Team 3, I suggested a side trip to our orderly room to booby-trap Top's chair and blow the fat fuck to Hanoi.

KA-LAP! FLASH! FLASH! KA-LAP!

When we again gave up lunch to go to R&R Headquarters, yesterday's clerk wasn't around.

"He's off duty," his replacement explained.

A flame was lit. My temper simmered.

We related yesterday's events.

The flame was turned up a notch. Simmer became boil.

"Oh," the clerk said. "Then you guys got a problem."

"Why?"

Boil went to overflow.

"Because he left for R&R to Hong Kong this morning."

Overflow went to explosion.

"He what?" I shouted.

"Went to Hong—"

"I know what the hell you said." My blood pressure skyrocketed higher than my weight. Pounding on the desk to vent my frustration, I fought back the taste of bile. "I can't believe the son of a bitch lied to us."

"Sorry. But so you guys don't think we're total screw-ups," clerk #2's voice took on a consoling tone, "I'll personally walk the orders through, and I *promise* to have them for you tomorrow."

"Where have we heard that before?" I fumed.

"Promise." He crossed his heart.

"You forgot to add the 'stick a red-hot needle in my eye and hope to die,' " I growled.

Visit #3. Clerk #3.

I felt my face go beet-red. Veins in my temples erupted like a volcano. Cohen wouldn't let me talk. He told our story. Again.

Clerk #3 opened folder after folder; investigated one mountain of paperwork after another. Ready to give up, he looked at my expression and kept on digging. After ten minutes, #3 finally stopped.

"Tell you what," he squeaked, "come back at 1600 hours. I'll walk another set through and have them waiting for you. Okay?"

I stared through him. I clenched and unclenched my hands.

"So help me God," clerk #3 said. I promise on my saintly mother's grave that I will."

At 1600 hours we returned, greeted by clerk #4.

I screamed one obscenity after another. First in English. Then in Hungarian.

Cohen pulled me aside and hid me behind him. Not an easy feat by any means.

"Where's your buddy?" he asked the clerk. "The one that was here a few hours ago."

The clerk looked at me as I broke free of Cohen's grasp. Wanting no part of what appeared to be a raving lunatic (me?), he disappeared quickly into a back office. Muffled words were exchanged. Clerk #4 reappeared with #3 in tow.

Again hidden behind Cohen, I stood on my toes and spoke over his shoulder. "We're ba-ack," I yelled.

"I can see that," #3 said. "Got some bad news for you guys."

"What!" I pushed Cohen aside and extended both hands in a strangle hold.

"Relax, Pinky." Cohen had me by both arms and refused to let go. "We'll work this out."

Trying to squirm free, I finally gave up. As pissed as I was, I still wasn't any match for Cohen's strength.

"Now, what's the problem?" Cohen calmly asked clerk #3.

The clerk brought his right arm out of hiding from behind his back and produced a file folder. Opening it up, he extracted a few sheets of paper.

"I can only give you three sets of orders each. Instead of the usual five."

His smile disappeared as he read my frustrated expression.

"Damn, I was only pulling your chain," he said.

With smoke pouring out of my ears, I looked him square in the eyes. "Private, I'm in no mood for humor right now." I grabbed a set of orders and waved them in his face. "You don't *ever* mess with anybody's fuckin' R&R orders. Got it?"

"Y-yes, S-specialist," he stammered, backing up.

"Easy, Pinky."

"Sorry, Coach, but I hate it when people screw around with your life. And right now going to Tokyo *is* my life." I slammed the orders on the desk. "It's the only thing keeping me from going crazy in this goddamned place."

Sunday, 16 June.

Clutching our R&R orders, Cohen and I joined a group of GIs roaming around like a herd of buffalo hungry for good grazing land. As we waited patiently for the convoy to Tan Son Nhut Air Force Base, my heart was full of anticipation of a week away from Vietnam. When Cohen and I eventually boarded a Jeep with the name "Annette" stenciled below its windshield, I was overcome with the premonition of being in Tokyo tomorrow. The omen evaporated at the Camp Alpha reception area when a clerk issued us sets of bed linen for the night.

"Just in case you don't make the flight," he said.

At 1600 hours, a tall, skinny sergeant called the roll for Tokyo. Name after name . . . no Cohen and Papp. In what seemed like an afterthought, we heard our names.

Remembering back to the chaos of in-processing on my arrival in Vietnam, the last dastardly deed was when we severed our final tie with civilization and exchanged our precious greenbacks for Military Payment Certificates. The finance clerks even gave us this second-rate paper money for denominations lower than a dollar. Gone were the familiar coins to jingle in our pockets—or flip into the air—to remind us of home. For that one time, though, the Army made sense: No jingling noise means no early warning to Charlie that we were parading through *his* jungle. Now that dastardly deed was about to make an about-face. *Smartly!*

"320, 340, 360," the finance clerk counted, exchanging my MPC for good old greenbacks. With each *real* dollar, the joy of leaving Vietnam for Tokyo mathematically increased. "There's your $400, Specialist Papp."

I smiled at the paper symbol of *The World*, carefully guiding each bill into my wallet, as I ran to catch up with the group at the boarding area.

"You guys got the last two seats on the plane," the stewardess informed Cohen and me when we entered the waiting Pan Am jet.

"No? Really?" I said.

She showed me the typed list. Sure as hell, *Specialist 5 Joel Cohen* and *Specialist 5 John D. Papp* were added in pencil. Below us were three names crossed out.

"Look at that!" I said to Cohen, pointing to the X's.

"Holy shit!" he rejoiced. "Oh, excuse me, ma'am." Putting his free arm around my shoulder and squeezing my neck, he added an "I don't believe it."

A big red X went through three names: *Major* John T. Brown, *Captain* Raymond R. Johnson, and *Colonel* George L. Konners.

We got on . . . three officers didn't.

"There *is* a God," I rejoiced. "Even in Vietnam."

"And," Cohen added, "He's an *enlisted man*."

With faces pressed against the bus's window, Cohen and I imitated hicks from the country, gawking at the passing buildings of downtown Tokyo. Lost in our excitement was the fact that we were traveling down the *left* side of the street.

"Hey, look," Joel pointed, as we stopped for a light. "It's General Westmoreland."

I stretched my neck to look in the direction indicated. "Where?"

"Over there, outside of that building, the . . . Imperial Hotel. He's in civvies."

"I see him. I see him," I rejoiced, as though I'd just caught a glimpse of Santa on Christmas Eve. The last time I saw Westy was at a ceremony in Bearcat on my first day in Personnel Actions. Six months ago. "He looks as impressive in civvies as he does in fatigues."

When we rode by the U.S.O. Club, I reminded Joel we could get guides there, for no charge. All we had to do was pay for their meals and expenses.

Stepping off the bus at the Nikko Hotel, I repeated my hick impression and took in the 100-foot-high structure. A slap to the back of my head brought me back to my senses.

"You're not in Mayberry, Opie."

"Sorry, Joel." I smiled and added: "Yesterday we were in Vietnam. Today we're in paradise. It's amazing what 24 hours can do."

My amazement increased when the bellhop opened the door to our generous-sized room. On each of the twin beds, two pillows reached as high as the top of the headboard. I dove on the closer bed and buried my head in the pillows, as though they were two succulent boobs. Rolling back and forth in sheer delight, I smothered myself until I flipped over one too many times and fell on the floor.

Look at this," Joel called from the bathroom. "A God-honest bathtub. Haven't seen one of them for an eternity."

I jumped to my feet, catching the bellhop recovering from a hearty laugh. Giving him a generous tip, I ushered him out of the room in the midst of his ceremonial bowing.

"And look," Joel shouted. "A sink with a real faucet. And here's a real toilet."

I stared at the tub. It looked almost as inviting as a naked woman. (*See what Vietnam could do to you?*) I turned the knobs. Water cascaded into the tub to the sounds of Joel flushing the toilet.

For the third time that day, I felt like a country bumpkin. Something as simple as running water and indoor plumbing rivaled the discovery of the wheel. Six months in Vietnam could turn the things we took for granted into momentous events.

***

"Would you two prefer men or two women?"

Joel and I were at the U.S.O. Club in search of two guides. I looked at him, trying to contain my lust-filled thoughts. Evidently Joel was of a chaste mind also.

"Women, of course!" our voices rang out.

"Give me a few minutes to go through my FEMALE list," the clerk said, "and see who's available. Why don't you grab a soda while you're waiting."

We walked over to an empty table with two Pepsis in hand.

This U.S.O. was more than I expected. I thought it would be one big room, like a dance floor or something. And have a bar tucked in one of its corners. Guess I'd seen too many old movies. It boasted several rooms, including a reception area, dance floor, bar/lounge, and gift shop.

Lost in our sodas, we relaxed, waiting for someone to show us this beautiful city.

"Look," Cohen whispered. He discreetly pointed. "The girl in the red blouse."

The young lady in question had a glass of milk before her.

Taking ice out of another glass, she added it to her milk, followed by a few shakes of salt and pepper. After stirring the concoction with a spoon, she began drinking it.

I pushed aside my half-full bottle of soda. "Let's see if our guides are ready," I suggested.

"Just in time, gentlemen." The clerk motioned to two girls in their late teens. "Ladies, these are the two GIs I was talking about."

Both had the classic good looks found in Japanese women. Especially their long, lustrous, black hair. Instead of kimonos, somehow I had expected *all* Japanese women to be dressed in them, they wore skirts and blouses.

"Hi. My name is Joel Cohen." He put his right hand on my shoulder. "This is Dennis Papp."

They smiled in return and told us their names. One was Mayumi, which was fairly easy to say. The second one sounded something like Juneko. After we made clumsy attempts at pronunciation, she told us to call her June. By mutual consent, the Mayumi became May. Joel and I became *Ichi-gatsu* and *Ni-gatsu*: January and February. Since June was the shorter of the two, and closer to my height, she volunteered to put up with me.

During our introductory small talk, May and June told us they were college students. Some day they wanted to be interpreters for the United Nations or a similar organization. Being guides was a good way for them to learn English from real Americans. They were especially interested in picking up our slang, something they couldn't learn in textbooks.

When we suggested going somewhere for a late lunch, they apologized that they couldn't be our guides today, but recommended the Belvedere atop the Sony building. Besides good food, it promised a great view. We all agreed to meet tomorrow at the U.S.O. at 9 a.m. Our goodbye was answered with *sayonara.*

Through clean living, pure thoughts, and a major stroke of good luck, we eventually found ourselves walking through the doors of the Sony building. Exiting on the seventh floor for the Belvedere, the elevator operator bid us an *arigato.* It felt funny to have someone say "thank you" just for riding his elevator.

Moments after we were seated at a small table in the center of the restaurant, a waitress placed two, steaming, rolled-up washcloths on our table.

I looked at Joel for help.

He shrugged his shoulders. "Beats me. Guess they know we're dirty."

We glanced at the other tables. People were wiping their hands with the cloths, but not their faces. When finished, they rolled up the washcloths and replaced them on the table in front of themselves, instead of simply tossing them in a used heap.

Like native-born Japanese, we picked up our steaming cloths and prepared ourselves for the meal.

"Look," I pointed at a distant window. "Isn't that building colorful?"

Joel strained his neck to take it in.

After a few minutes of stretching like a giraffe, the hostess came over and asked if we'd like to move to a window table.

"Yes, please," we nodded.

After we were seated, Joel said eloquently, *"Domo arigato."*

The hostess smiled and gave a slight bow.

I complimented my scholarly companion.

"I've been reading a few phrase books. Other than my 'thank you very much,' " he confided, "I can only ask 'how much,' and find out the location of the bathroom."

"So I shouldn't call the U.S.O. Club and cancel our guides?"

Behind the cover of his napkin, he raised his middle finger.

"So eloquently put," I complimented again and gave him a slight bow.

Not paying any attention to our meal, we continued to look out the windows. As promised, the view was impressive.

Atop one building, thousands of brilliantly lit bulbs created an animated billboard. Three colorful scenes repeated.

The first was two men juggling bowling pins. Periodically, they'd flip the pins to each other. Their performance reminded me of an act I'd seen on the "Ed Sullivan Show." As I thought about it, the act might even have been the same night I saw the Beatles for the first time.

After another ten seconds or so, the jugglers disappeared, and the Pepsi logo was emblazoned larger than I'd ever seen before.

The logo soon became the best scene of all.

The silhouette of a shapely female appeared in the lower left-hand corner. She began a seductive dance (*any* female movement was seductive to a horny GI), slowly undulating her way across the billboard. Missing was the rhythmic music that usually accompanied a virgin sacrifice. When my eyes finally drank in all they could consume, I focused them on a billboard below the animated display.

Triangular rotating vertical panels created different signs. One was a red background with unknown white Japanese script. Another view displayed several smaller advertising-type signs or cards. As the third one began forming, the undulating dancer reappeared on the billboard above, and my eyes coveted her every movement.

When I looked down at my plate, it was empty.

"I have no idea what I just ate, Joel, but it sure tasted good."

"Wipe off the drool on your chin, Den."

Getting up to leave, we worked our way to the other windows to study the view.

Acting like a kid in a candy store, I grabbed Joel's arm. "Look. There's a highway right over that building."

"I think that's the Nishi-Ginza department store," he said. "It looks like the roof is actually an overpass."

The highway, or street, continued around the other side of the Sony building. Viewing it from across the room, the elevated road fronted a large circular building. Atop this structure was a big sign that read Toshiba.

Once outside, Joel had an alarming suggestion. "Let's walk back to the hotel."

"What? We don't know where the hell it is."

He tugged at my sleeve. "It should only be a few blocks from here."

"Great," I mumbled.

"Relax. Japan is an island. How lost can we get?"

That was like saying Manhattan was just an island. Granted, a much smaller one. Still. . . .

Joel walked up to a group of Japanese businessmen. I made believe I didn't know him when he tapped one of them on the back, mumbled "Nikko Hotel?" and pointed to the left. The man smiled, nodded, and bowed all in one motion. Throwing caution to the wind, we headed down Sotobori-Dori Avenue in search of the Holy Grail.

"Come on, Den, we're gonna be late."

"You sure there's a House of Pancakes at the Imperial Hotel?" I asked, anxious for a big breakfast.

"That's what it says in this little red guidebook," Joel affirmed, holding the book in my face to validate his remark.

Well, the *little red guidebook* didn't prove correct. Although we scoured the entire hotel, we couldn't find the House of Pancakes. Settling for a handful of this and a cup of that at a coffee shop, we hurried to the U.S.O. Club. May and June were waiting for us when we stampeded through the door. After our gentlemanly apology, we let the ladies pick the agenda for the day.

Following a conference between them, May said, "Meiji Jingu Shrine? Okay?"

I gave Joel a blank look.

"It's supposed to be beautiful," he whispered to me. "I read about it."

"In the same little red guidebook," I whispered with a double dose of sarcasm and doubt, "that mentioned the House of Pancakes?" Putting a big smile on my face, I turned toward the ladies and said, "Sounds great. Where is it?"

"West of Tokyo," June said. "By the Olympic Stadium, from the 1964 Olympics."

"According to the map," Joel chimed in, "it's about eight inches from here."

Once outside, I looked for the telltale red color of a Tokyo cab. As

I was ready to give a New-York-City yell for an approaching red blur, June touched my elbow and said, "Wait for red light."

I looked skyward, but saw no traffic light.

She laughed. "Light is on—dashboard."

That's when I noticed the little lights through the passing wind-shields. Most were green. When a cab with a red light approached, May simply stuck up her arm, and the cab slowed down. No yelling or screaming like a maniac, nor shouting obscenities. And no waving of the arm till it fell out of the socket. "Watch out," June said, detaining us with an outstretched arm.

Joel and I stood our ground.

When the cab made a complete stop, the back door opened by itself.

"Control on dashboard," May explained.

Not only was this automatic device clever, it brought me to the reality that we were in a civilized country . . . free from the inhuman-ity of Vietnam. A smile blossomed on my face. In three more months, God willing, I would begin experiencing these commonplace joys the rest of my life.

We piled into the cab and headed west. During the ride, May and June put on their official tour guide hats and told us a brief history of the Shrine.

"It was built around 1920," June began, "in honor of Emperor Meiji and his Empress Shoken. He restored the Imperial power after the Sho-gun ruled for three centuries."

May pointed to our sneakers. "It is good you have comfortable shoes on. Because the Meiji Jingu Shrine covers more than 175 acres."

After Joel paid the driver, the four of us walked along a wide pebbled path until we came to a spectacular entrance. On either side of the trail stood a 40-foot-high cypress tree trunk.

"The trees are called a *torii* gateway," June informed the unknow-ing. "They are over 1,700 years old."

Two parallel horizontal timbers, about three feet apart, hung across and slightly below the two treetops, creating a majestic archway. Not only was the gateway formidable, it was beautiful in its simplicity.

"The *torii* is what makes a Shinto shrine different from a Buddhist temple," May explained. "The gateway separates the every day world from the spiritual world."

The landscaping on the way to the Shrine was magnificent. After viewing thousands of lush, green trees, we came upon the Iris Garden, where thousands of irises were in bloom. The magnificent blues, whites, lavenders, and yellows of these three-petaled flowers were in evidence wherever I looked. It was unbelievable how much beauty existed only a five-hour flight from the desolation of Vietnam.

A short distance before a building, several women were standing around a smoking cauldron. They were reverently waving the smoke toward themselves. Some even appeared to put handfuls into their clothing. June's explanation of the women's actions had something to do with keeping away the evil spirits.

"Come," June coaxed, tugging at my arm.

I followed her to a stone structure that stood a little higher than my waist. It resembled a square basin or water trough. Several streams of clear water flowed from a pipe.

Both May and June picked up long-handled dippers. Taking some water, they rinsed their mouths, then cleansed their hands.

"Here," June offered me her dipper, "purify your body before praying."

I took the dipper and repeated carefully her ritual. I felt awkward doing it, as though I were being sacrilegious to her faith or defying one of the tenets of mine.

June saw the hesitancy in my movements. "You are doing fine. Do not be embarrassed."

Her words comforted me, reaffirming there was *one* God, whatever name we used, Who watched over all of us. The one Who brought me to this lovely country . . . and would see me home safely in October.

We approached a reddish structure with green copper roofs. Both girls dropped a coin in a slot, bowed, clapped their hands three times, meditated, then bowed again.

June came over to me and smiled. She motioned for me to duplicate her ritual. Feeling hesitant, I didn't move.

She put a hand gently on my arm. "It is all right. Pray for something. Make a wish."

I looked at Joel, hoping he would go first. He immediately looked the other way, as though he didn't see me. Reluctantly, I stepped forward.

Without trying to exaggerate my movements, I dropped a coin into the box, bowed, and quietly clapped my hands thrice. Saying that I was grateful to have survived the last six months, I wished, *prayed*, I would make it home alive in October. Bowing again, I reverently backed up.

A solemn expression came over June's face. This time she placed a hand on my arm, slightly lowered her head, and whispered, *"Your wish will not come true."*

My heart dropped to my toes. How did she know what I wished for? I became more petrified than I'd been on New Year's Day when I stepped off the plane in Vietnam. I felt the blood drain from my face. I became stone cold.

"What? Why?" I pleaded.

With the slightest trace of a smile, she whispered, "Because he doesn't understand English."

As tears of relief came to my eyes, her smile broadened.

"Here," May said. "We will eat here."

Back in downtown Tokyo, our companions wanted to take us to a restaurant where they could cook dinner for us.

Upon entering the restaurant, we were instructed to take off our shoes. Given the choice of a "regular" table or a low one, the ladies chose the latter, which meant we sat on the floor. Repositioning my legs several times, I finally found a half-comfortable way to sit.

When the hot washcloths were placed before us, Joel and I immediately cleansed ourselves and rolled up the tiny towels. Our proper usage impressed our guests.

"I see you know how to use the *oshibori*," May said.

Not knowing what they were called, we still nodded recognition.

Soup, sukiyaki, and sake were the chosen fare.

June picked up a small ceramic vessel and poured some sake into tiny, handle less cups.

"What do you call that little jug, May?" Joel asked.

"A *tokkuri*. And the cup is *choko*."

Joel and I repeated each of the words.

The sake was lukewarm and tasted like bitter wine. With a little kick to it. Maybe more than a *little*.

June explained briefly that, from start to finish, it took fewer than two months to make sake. And it could be drunk after it was made, no aging was necessary. I was amazed to learn that the rice was polished to half its original size before the brewer's yeast and other ingredients were added.

While I sat and watched, May taught Joel the proper way to use chopsticks.

"The bottom chopstick is held motionless between the thumb and the hand." May positioned a chopstick in Joel's right hand, resting it on the top of his ring finger. "The top chopstick," she picked up another miniature spear, "is used to grasp the food and it moves freely." She positioned it while saying, "It is held by the thumb and index finger."

Joel easily maneuvered the utensils.

When it came to teaching me, June had a problem: I was left-handed. No matter what she did, I clumsily dropped them, because she couldn't position the sticks "backwards."

"Here, let me try," May said, while I continued laughing.

After a few minutes, May gave up. So did my laughter.

Feeling like I had the intelligence of an amoeba, I stuck the chopsticks in my left hand and started flapping away. With a little practice on my napkin and Joel's shirt collar, I slowly got the hang of it.

A waitress took in my awkward movements and smiled while placing cookware and sukiyaki fixings in front of the girls. She also gave each of us a bowl containing what looked like raw, beaten eggs.

May and June took turns sautéing the beef in a mixture of soy sauce and a sweet wine they called *mirin*. After pouring some broth into the skillet, they added a portion of each ingredient, careful not to mix them. While doing so, our chefs sounded out the Japanese name for each one.

May pointed to the beef, saying "*gyuniku*." She picked up some leeks, calling them "*negi*."

June added two kinds of mushrooms: *shiitake* and *enokitake*. She called the carrots "*ninjin*." The final ingredient looked like dandelion leaves or flat parsley stalks. Actually they were chrysanthemum leaves: *shungiku*.

After serving us, they served themselves.

June held up a piece of beef, said, "*Itadakimasu*," and dipped it into her bowl of raw egg.

"What did that word mean?" I asked. "And why did you dip the meat?"

She explained it meant "I receive," and was customary to say it before a meal. "The egg coating cooks on hot food. Tastes good. It also helps hot food not to burn mouth."

I decimated sukiyaki with my chopsticks and said, "*Itadakimasu*," butchering its pronunciation.

Joel and I froze in front of a noisy, brightly lit building. It resembled an arcade with its beehive of activity. I stuck my head against the plate-glass window to get a better view of the hundreds of people sitting on low-backed red stools playing "vertical" pinball.

"What are they playing, June?" I asked.

"It is called *pachinko*. Come." She pulled me inside the cacophony.

The walls and aisles were lined with dozens of game machines possessing bright, flashing lights. Teenagers and adults alike were pumping coins into the 2- by 3-foot machines, making steel marbles spin and ricochet behind the glassed enclosure.

Steel marbles shot out from the top in myriad directions. When a ball fell into a slot or short trough, it landed in a well below the red plastic base, like a slot machine paying off in balls instead of coins.

"Players turn balls in for prizes," June said, answering my thoughts before I could form them into a question.

Joel covered his ears and asked, "Why would people want to play such a noisy game?"

May laughed. "It is an inexpensive way to escape from the reality of daily life."

With his ears still camouflaged, Joel shouted, "I'd want to find a quieter way to do it."

I pushed back my empty breakfast dishes and gave Joel a thumbs-up sign, saying, "Today we buy out Tokyo."

Enjoying the pleasant weather that greeted us, we strolled down Sotobori-Dori Avenue and headed for the Ginza, the heart of the shopping district, the "Fifth Avenue" of Tokyo.

"This place is supposed to have everything," Joel said.

"What about kimonos, figurines, lacquer ware, and stuff like that?" I asked, anxious to spend my remaining 108,000 yen (about $300) on some genuine Japanese souvenirs.

"Let's see," he ran his finger down the department store's directory, "foodstuffs are in the basement."

I rubbed my ample stomach. "We can skip that."

"First floor has handbags, shoes, neckties, accessories, cosmetics,"

Joel's finger raced through the list. "Here we go. Floors five and six."

Taking the elevator to the proper floor (with another *arigato* as we got off), we began our search for the right kimonos for our wives.

A saleswoman explained to us that most Japanese married women don't wear the overly ornate kimonos usually seen on TV and in the lavish Hollywood productions.

"Most wear a *shibui*," she said, "which is more conservative." Holding up one that was colorful and festive, she added, "But Japanese companies know tourists want something like this, so they make kimono that is not so plain as *shibui*, but still tasteful." Helping us with the sizes, the saleswoman guaranteed the ones we picked would fit our wives. She also convinced us to buy an *obi* (the belt or sash worn around the waist) to go with the kimono. We turned down the *zori* (sandals).

"Now something for me," I said to Joel. "I want one of those *happi* coats. Over there," I pointed across the floor to a tasteful display.

While the salesman helped us try on different coats, he explained the background or meaning of this standard tourist garment.

"A real *happi* coat is hip-length. It is made of heavy dark-blue cotton, and is essentially a loose jacket." He refolded the one I had tried on. "But we make all kinds now for tourists."

I selected a black coat that had two red horizontal stripes across the shoulders and sleeves, and two white ones that encircled the coat below the waist.

"That's a fireman's jacket," the clerk said, running a hand over my shoulders to smooth out the heavy-weave material. "The crest or *mon* on the back says the name of the fire station."

Making believe I understood him, I smiled and nodded recognition when he said the fire station's name.

After we had sufficiently depleted our wallets, we hailed a taxi, and said: "Nikko Hotel."

"This is great. No matter where we are," Joel smiled, "all we have to do is get in a cab and say, 'Nikko Hotel.' And for 100 yen, we're found again."

"I wish I could get in a cab and say, '*The World*,'" I sighed. "I'd gladly pay a *million* yen."

It was time for two chaste GIs to sample the nightlife.

Paying special care to stay away from the infamous hostess bars—where you not only overpaid for your drinks and that of your hostess, but also forked over a hefty hourly fee just for her company and conversation—we found ourselves at a safe-looking place called the Albion Club. Sitting at the bar, vodka martinis in hand, we faced the crowd and let our eyes drink in the sights.

"Look over there," I said.

"Hey, that's neat."

One wall was covered with speakers that had dozens of tiny bulbs in them. As the music played, the lights correspondingly glowed to the tune and its volume. And the light show was in stereo.

Getting refills, we spied an empty table and walked over to it. A few minutes later, an attractive Japanese girl greeted us.

"May I sit?"

Eager for her company, we still were cautious.

"We're not interested in a hostess," I said politely.

"That's all right," she replied with a smile, "there is no charge." Holding up a glass, she added, "And I already have a drink."

With our objections taken care of, we had no reason to refuse her company.

We exchanged names, hers was Kay, and went through the usual small talk. Her expression saddened when we told her we were here on R&R from Vietnam.

"Maybe someday soon that war be over," she half-whispered.

We sipped our drinks and talked some more. She was especially fond of the design on Joel's wedding ring and, of all things, my dimples.

"You have nice smile," she said to me.

I thought that compliment would cost extra, but remembered this was all "no charge."

When we hit bottom on our drinks, we offered to buy Kay a refill, much to her reluctance. After the cocktail waitress took our order, Kay whispered something to her in Japanese. Her gibberish made me smile out loud.

"What is so funny?" she asked.

"When people speak their own language to each other, it always reminds me of my parents speaking Hungarian so that my brother and I wouldn't know what they said."

"I did not mean to be impolite."

"It's not that," I explained quickly. "I just found it amusing."

Kay smiled and said, "You won't find it funny when you get your bill."

Joel and I looked at each other with expressions that translated into: Oh, shit. This was gonna cost us. Big.

Halfway through her drink, Kay excused herself to join a friend at another table.

When the lights on the stereo speakers became one big blur, I suggested to Joel we call it a night.

Our bill gave us a surprise, as Kay had promised. But not the kind we expected. Instead of the regular price, which was crossed out, our drinks were substantially less. Although it wasn't the custom, we left a hefty tip, and asked the waitress to bring Kay another drink.

<hr>

"Let's get a little closer and listen," I suggested. Joel signified his agreement by leaving me where I was and melting into the back of the group.

We dedicated the morning to visiting the Imperial Palace. Like our White House, it is infused with history. Just the thought of seeing it made me feel closer to home. Walking along a wide gravel path, we came upon a bridge spanning a moat whose width was about the same as that of a football field's. Before us were a handful of British people on holiday, evident by their complimentary flight bags, being captivated by a tour guide reciting his history of this impressive site.

"In the 1600s," the guide barked, "the military government relocated to a town called Edo. The Edo Castle was the center of the Tokugawa Shogunate. Now," he pointed across bridges and moats to the majestic structure in the center, "Edo and its Castle are known as Tokyo and the Imperial Palace."

We followed the group across the bridge until halted by two armed guards protecting a gate. In the distance, partially hidden behind trees and shrubbery, was the Palace. Unlike the White House, this massive, whitish, multileveled edifice had curved/peaked roofs in evidence everywhere.

"The Imperial Palace," the guide continued in a monotone, "is surrounded by gardens and a system of moats on 450 acres of land." He looked to the back of the group and gave no evidence that two intruders had joined his clan. "It is further fortified by a 15-foot-thick wall that varies in height from 20 to 50 feet."

I tapped Joel's shoulder, trying to get his attention. His face remained glued to the viewfinder of his camera. If I counted correctly, he was on his third roll of 36-exposure film for the morning.

"The building you see in the background," the guide began another page of his script, "is the Fushimi Yagura."

Cameras clicked throughout the group. Lost in them was my R&R companion. The structure ate up the rest of his roll of film.

"It was built in the 17th century," the guide continued his statistical description, "and is the last of three surviving original watchtowers. Thank you. Now we will go to the Olympic Stadium, site of the 1964 Olympic games."

I searched the crowd for Joel, anxious to continue the palace tour on our own. When I finally spied him, he was furiously searching through his camera bag.

"Quick, Den," he pleaded, "we gotta find a store. I need more film."

Saturday, June 22. We were down to our last full day of R&R. Going through bags of souvenirs on my bed, I was struck by a thought.

"Hey, Joel, you know what's odd about the gifts we bought?"

He was changing into his sneakers, in anticipation of our four-block walk to the Sony building for lunch.

"No, but I know what's odd about you."

"Be serious for a minute."

He stood up and painted a stoic expression on his face. "Okay. I'm serious."

"Take a look at this stuff."

He picked up handfuls of figurines, jewelry, lacquer ware, and clothing.

"Looks like normal souvenirs to me."

"Take a look at the labels," I hinted.

He did as instructed, searching the bottoms of the figurines and similar objects.

"Well? What do you see?"

"Words."

I threw my fireman's *happi* coat at his head.

"Let me put it this way, Joel. When you buy something Japanese in Philadelphia, how do you know it's Japanese?"

"It says so right on the bottom, stupid."

"You mean the words 'Made in Japan' are printed on the label or stamped on the bottom," I prompted.

"Yeah, so . . . "

"Well, look at all this stuff. Not one 'Made in Japan' on it. And it all was made here."

Joel rummaged through all my gifts. Then he dumped his souvenirs on his bed and repeated the process.

"You're right. Not a single 'Made in Japan.'"

I knew it wasn't an earth-shaking discovery, but it just seemed so odd not to see those words on anything we bought. When I was in *The World* and bought anything, I usually checked to see if it were made in the States or some foreign place. Now that I wanted the people at home to *know* their souvenirs were authentic "made-in-Japan" ones, carefully selected while I was on R&R, the damned things didn't have squat on them. For all my family and friends knew, I could have gotten the "airport gifts" from Saigon International . . . never having set foot in Japan.

"Den."

"Yeah, Joel?"

"I think you need a double dose of sake."

Filing into the elevator at the Sony building, we were anxious to get to the seventh floor for another great meal at the Belvedere. When we reached the sixth floor, the crowd disgorged us with them. We turned to get back on the elevator, but the doors had already closed.

"Do you hear that, Den?"

"You mean the music?"

"Yeah. That and the crowd noise." He grabbed my arm. "Come on. Let's see what's going on."

We entered a room that must have measured at least 75 by 100 feet. It was overflowing with men. All with cameras.

"Must be a photography show," I guessed. Nothing like possessing a firm grasp of the obvious!

We worked our way through the crowd to the hub of activity. Two Japanese women, dressed in colorful kimonos, posed on pedestals. Words filled my head: gorgeous, beautiful, striking, stunning. None of them could do justice in describing the women's simple, quiet beauty.

Nor could rolls of film capture their radiance.

Like the two horny GIs we were, we elbowed our way to the front and snapped picture after picture. Thank God I remembered to load a fresh roll of film before leaving the hotel.

Five minutes later, the ladies bowed, stepped off the pedestals, and disappeared through a door.

"Boy! am I glad we got off that elevator," I said.

"So am I." Pointing to my camera, Joel added, "Wipe the drool off."

When we were within a few paces of the exit, the beehive behind buzzed again. Turning around, we saw the models re-enter the room and step onto their pedestals. This time they were wearing the skimpiest bikinis modesty permitted.

"Let's capture some more memories," I said.

"Great! Time for another *'Blue-Dot for a Sure-Shot.'*"

With our male hormones kicking into high gear, we shoved our way as close as possible.

On display were bodies standing, leaning, bending, kneeling, sitting, and stretching. These were just the men trying to get a better camera angle on the two models.

One Japanese man was flat on his back, his camera extended at arm's length, barely inches away from a bikini bottom. Without even looking through the viewfinder, he was clicking away. The guy standing next to him said something in Japanese, making those within earshot begin laughing. When the shutterbug responded, they laughed even harder. So did the model.

I asked the middle-aged Japanese man alongside me what caused the laughter.

He responded: "The first man said, 'You don't have any film left in your camera.' The photographer replied, 'I know, so what's your point?' "

Like a baseball team heading home after losing the final game of the World Series, Joel and I boarded our plane to return to the agony and danger of Vietnam. Looking out the window, I spied another group of GIs boarding their plane. They were laughing, smiling, and kidding around. There was only one explanation for their actions: They were reboarding their *freedom bird* after a stopover in Japan. Next stop, *The World.*

Chapter 16

With my right foot on the ground and the left perched on the bottom step of The Pit, I watched the second hand of my Timex make its final sweep of 1 July. *Tick. Tick.* Past the 7. *Tick. Tick.* The 8. *Tick. Tick.* When the second hand touched the 12, I cupped my hands around my mouth and let loose with a visceral yell: "s*ssshhhoooooooooooooo ooooooooorrrrrt*!"

Finally, I broke 100 AAWU. I was an official two-digit midget.

Taking the cap off a lukewarm beer I bought earlier in the day, I celebrated my short-timer status by downing the entire contents in one continuous swallow, followed by a burp that rivaled my Tarzan impression.

What better thing is there to do on Day One as a short-timer, but to get stuck on a detail?

"Okay, ladies," a skinny sergeant's squeaky voice commanded while standing next to the Mess Hall, "it's time to police the area. If it doesn't move, pick it up. If it moves, salute it."

Standard drivel from a lifer.

"Remember! All I want to see are assholes and elbows."

I never could envision that pose.

"E-5s and above," he squawked, "fall out to the rear of the formation and supervise."

Rank did have its privileges. Even for non-lifers like me. However, my supervising was short-lived, because asshole Top had other ideas.

"Papp," First Sergeant Smith mumbled, stepping out of the Mess Hall, chewing on his signature black cigar. Gee, the moron *could* do two things at once. "You got nothing better to do than walk around with your thumb up your ass?"

"No, First Sergeant," I offered, "I'm on police duty, supervising these troops."

"I have better use of your talents," he snorted like an overfed farm animal. "You just volunteered for a shit-burning detail. Report to 9th Admin H.Q. in three-zero minutes."

What better way to celebrate my having 99 AAWU than by being relegated to the menial task of burning shit? I had escaped my two earlier-scheduled shit-burning details by being on the ill-fated ID card trip and then going on R&R to Vung Tau. So I made a detour to The Pit to pick up a grenade earmarked as a gift for my favorite First Sergeant, wishful thinking, and got a few letters I planned to mail.

Not counting our wheel man, three others were on the detail: PFC Pete Murphy, Spec 4 Dan Foss, and PFC Ben Dover. Our mission: Visit the 27 latrines in our sector, and rid them of their vile collection of feces and urine.

Since I was ranking man, I was spared the tugging-pouring-replacing of the 55-gallon drum halves for the first two latrines we visited. Instead, with the assistance of Spec 4 Foss, my second in command, I held up the wooden back flap of the latrine while PFCs Murphy and Dover bent over, pulled out a full tub, and replaced it with one of the empties from the deuce-and-a-half truck. Whenever they came across a partially filled one, they emptied the contents into another tub until the mixture reached the handle holes of the drum. Then *that* drum was hoisted onto the truck. When we jumped out of the truck at latrine #3, Murphy and Dover graciously lifted the flap so Foss and I could do the emptying.

I made the first-timer's mistake of inhaling as I bent over to extract an overflowing drum. The acrid aroma of rotting feces mixed with stagnant urine spouted forth and attacked every fiber of my nasal passages. I straightened up, turned to my left, bent over again, and disgorged my breakfast.

"Atta way to go, Specialist," PFC Murphy said to a mixture of laughter and applause.

After calling myself an asshole, I wiped my chin with a new hankie and threw the besmirched rag into the drum.

Another round of applause, minus the laughter, followed my next attempt at drum-emptying, because it was letter-perfect. By the time we got to our eighth latrine, I was an experienced veteran.

Number nine was another disaster.

Murphy and I held up the flap, Spec 4 Dover reached in. Instead of a full drum, he came out with an "Oh! God. That's disgusting."

Dover backed away and emptied his breakfast on the ground, landing a few mouthfuls on Murphy's left boot, totally destroying a clerk's mandatory spit-shine.

"What is it?" Murphy asked, rubbing the toe of his boot on the ground to dismiss the vomit. His boot was actually cleaner than the ground.

"Don't ask," Dover said, using his right sleeve to erase the last of the evidence from his chin.

"Let me see. Let me see," Foss pleaded, like a little kid at a parade.

Pushing Dover aside, Foss's curiosity resulted in a "That's really gross," and a few dry heaves.

Bbblaah, came another mouthful from Dover. This one landed on his own left boot, much to Murphy's delight.

I dropped the flap and went over to the deuce-and-a-half to clear my head. The smell of a half-full truck of human waste drove me away.

"Who the hell would leave a mess like that?" Dover asked.

"Beats me," Foss answered, wiping spit from his lower lip with the back of his right hand.

"A better question," Murphy added, "is who the hell is going to clean it up?"

What we saw would have been better left unmentioned. But, I was sure we'd describe the scene in the minutest gory detail to everyone we saw for the next week. The best explanation for it was something out of a disgusting, low-budget horror movie. Only Hollywood could have come up with what I never thought I'd see in real life.

Between two drums sat an immense pile of shit that reached almost as high as the Tower of Babel. A yellow river ran throughout the pile. Floating in the river, and *out* of the actual pile, were hundreds of maggot-like insects acting like they were on a water ride at an amusement park. I could have sworn I even heard an occasional *wheeee!* as the slimy insects slid down one precipice after another.

"The only way to clean up that mess," Spec 4 Foss said, "is to burn down the damned latrine."

"All in favor of moving on to latrine #10," I said, "say aye."

Four "ayes" were yelled in unison as the voters jumped on the truck.

With 27 latrines completed (not including #9, of course), the only thing left was to take the full drums out the main gate of Bearcat to a dump where we would burn the waste. While we traveled down the road outside the post, my mind relived previous journeys when we left the protection of Bearcat grossly under armed. Sucking up my fear, and 400 gallons of aromatic shit, I prayed for our safety. Again, *with fear as my only weapon.*

A gust of wind traveled from a bend in the road right to our truck. My nose exploded a warning: We must be near the pit where earlier truckloads of Bearcat shit were burned. I held my breath longer than a pearl diver. Big mistake. As soon as I gasped for life, my lungs filled with the disgusting aroma.

A hundred yards around the bend, I discovered my nose again had betrayed me. Instead of a place to burn shit, we had reached the outskirts of Long Thanh. From a distance, it looked like a planned accident.

Several dilapidated huts, made of elephant grass, were mixed in with weathered corrugated metal lean-tos. A baby's incessant cry emanated from their midst. Off to the left, a pig (one of Top's relatives?) attempted to gain its freedom by pressing against the wall of a crude animal pen. A crippled old man feverishly chased a band of chickens that already had escaped the hastily made structure. Four ancient women were huddled around a makeshift fire, throwing handfuls of vegetables into a big pot.

The old man lunged at two chickens and missed. He shouted something in Vietnamese. Turning his scrawny head, he spied the smoldering pot. Evidently realizing it was big enough to hold him, he frantically got to his feet and quickened his race for the chickens.

Other than the chicken-chaser, no adult men were visible. A warning bell rang in my subconscious. *Here I am again with not even my impotent M16.* Carefully bypassing the village, our driver continued toward our predetermined destination.

The deuce-and-a-half stopped at the edge of what resembled an excavation pit. Charred remnants of previous burnings dotted the monument to waste removal.

Our driver unhooked the tailgate and said, "Okay, dump it."

We took turns carefully emptying one drum, then another. Gallon after gallon of human waste flowed into the pit, creating another pungent chocolate statue. When the last *plop* sounded, the driver doused the brown load with a 5-gallon can of diesel fuel. Lighting an entire pack of matches, he threw the blazing flame onto the soaked shit. Nothing happened. Another attempt produced the same negative results.

Taking a roll of toilet paper and a two-foot stick from the driver's seat, he shoved them together, constructing a crude torch. Squirting the toilet paper with a stream of lighter fluid, he ignited the torch with a single match and heaved it into the pit.

Whooosshh.

Bitter black smoke spewed forth from the burning pile. Cloud after ebony cloud rose to the sky, leaving our signature for everyone to see.

"God!" PFC Murphy coughed, covering his mouth and nose. "shit stinks even more when it's burning."

As if on cue, the sky opened and rain pelted us. We were clearly being punished for stinking-up the heavens.

Seconds after we rode past the sentries at the main gate, the rain stopped. I stood up in the truck and looked out toward the fading black pillars of smoke. Taking their place was the most vibrant rainbow I'd ever seen. It amazed me how this dichotomy of celestial fingerprints mirrored the emotional conflict we endured each day in Vietnam.

"You just got a phone call from the orderly room, Pinky," Cohen said. "You're 40 minutes late for CQ."

"I wasn't scheduled until tomorrow," I complained.

"All I know is Top said you're to report now. And he sounded pissed!"

"Damn! That's all I need."

"Relax, Pinky. Top will be gone in an hour, so you won't see him all night."

"Yeah, but I didn't want to spend the rest of my first day of being an official short-time by having Charge of Quarters."

"What difference does that make. One day is basically the same as the next around this damned place."

Even though Cohen was right, I was still pissed.

I walked on tiptoes into the orderly room. Top was leaned over, sneaking something into his bottom desk drawer. Staring at me were six long hairs plastered down against the grain in an attempt to cover his bald spot.

"Specialist Papp reporting as ordered, First Sergeant," I bellowed, with total military protocol.

He looked up with an evil smile. Straightening himself in his chair, he said, "Ahh, yes. Papp. My *favorite* specialist."

Translation: Welcome to my lair.

"Where the fuck have you been?" he demanded. "You're almost an hour late."

"According to the duty roster, First Sergeant, I wasn't scheduled for CQ until tomorrow."

"Bullshit, Papp."

"But—"

He opened the wooden box on his desk and took out one of his putrid cigars. Standing while lighting it, he walked to the front of his desk and sat on the edge. He took an extra-long drag and puffed a haze of smoke into my face.

"Did you look at the duty roster this morning?"

"No, I didn't, but—"

"Well, you sorry excuse for a soldier," another cloud engulfed me, "if you had, you would have seen your name listed for CQ."

Son of a bitch! The one day I don't look at the damned duty roster, it's changed. The look in Top's face said: Hah! Hah! I changed it and caught 'cha.

Trying to get on this fat asshole's good side, I said, "sorry I didn't have enough sense to double-check it this morning."

"No excuse, Papp!" he barked.

"Yes, First Sergeant!" I shouted.

"Good! Now here's what you're to do tonight . . . "

My mind drifted away from what he was saying, as I thought of ways to torture and dispose of this bastard.

"Got that, Papp?"

"Yes, First Sergeant!" I screamed, like any good lifer would do.

Without saying another word, the miserable prick parked his cap on his head and strutted out of the orderly room.

I sat at the company clerk's desk and resigned myself to staying awake while playing Army for the next 14 hours. CQ was no more fun than watching an ant crawl across the sidewalk.

When 1800 hours rolled around, I sent my CQ runner (PVT Williams) to procure supper, while I continued the letter to Annette that I started earlier.

> *Hi, I'm back.*
>
> *I'm on CQ now. Got switched to tonight by my favorite person: shithead Top.*
>
> *Wanted to mention something Bohnny said I <u>had</u> to tell you.*
>
> *I was working on a Compassionate Leave this morning. It made me realize a little more how very lucky I am to have such a wonderful woman for a wife.*
>
> *Let's call the guy who wanted the leave John, and his wife Mary. Seems like Mary left home with another man. Don't know where she is. A month ago, Mary was pregnant, and she took something to kill the baby. What makes this so devastating is John's been in Vietnam for <u>six</u> months, and Mary was pregnant for only <u>two</u> months. So guess who the father wasn't!*
>
> *Before Mary skipped town, she ran up big bills, took everything that wasn't nailed down, and beat up their five-year-old son.*
>
> *Swell, huh?*
>
> *When I was having John's orders run off, I saw Bohnny and told him the story. He said I was very fortunate to have a good woman for a wife. Very true. Very true.*

I stopped writing when two half-drunk GIs stumbled into the orderly room. They wanted to sign in from R&R and were having trouble getting the pen to write.

"Here," I showed them, "the pen works better when you push the little button on the top, making the point come out."

"Wow," drunk #1 said, "the mother's right."

"No—wonder—he's—a S-spec 5." Drunk #2 produced a shit-eating grin.

"Good night, guys." I gave them a friendly wave goodbye.

Drunk #1 smiled, hitting #2 in the face when he returned my good-bye wave.

Putting the finished letter aside, I took out a clean sheet of paper to try my hand at poetry. After filling the trash can with rejects, I finally came up with the following poem at 0200 hours.

FOR THE LAST TIME

> *The day to depart is close at hand,*
> *Soon I will leave this troubled land.*
> *The freedom bird flies high above,*
> *Soon it will take me to the one I love.*
>
> *Six months are gone, three more remain.*
> *Never will I leave my wife again.*
> *The days, the weeks, the months fly by,*
> *Faster than one can blink an eye.*
>
> *In a while I'll be home at last.*
> *Soon I'll live no more in the past.*
> *My days will be happy, happy and bright.*
> *The present, the future, will all be right.*
>
> *I'm waiting for the day in my life,*
> *When I can hold and kiss my sweet wife.*
> *I've missed her so much, since I've been away,*
> *Soon we'll be together, forever and a day.*

Admiring the poem one last time, I added a seven-word 'signature' to the bottom of the page: 98 days and a duffel bag drag.

At 0500 hours, I instructed PVT Williams, my trusty CQ runner, to wake the troops.

"Where's the extra bullhorn?" he asked.

"What for?"

"I overheard Top tell you to use it when you wake everyone up. So shouldn't I?"

"Forget it, Williams. Nobody's used the damned horn for weeks." I shot a thumb over my shoulder. "Now go wake up the guys like a good private."

"Whatever you say, Specialist Papp."

Straightening-out the top of the company clerk's desk in preparation of ending my sentence as CQ, I was distracted by feet-stomping and door-slamming as the First Sergeant invaded the orderly room.

"Papp!"

I jumped to my feet.

"Yes, First Sergeant!"

"It's 0630 hours. Half the company is still sound asleep." He threw his trusty bullhorn and clipboard on the company clerk's desk. The clipboard bounced and glanced off my left leg as I stood at attention. "I specifically gave you orders to use the extra bullhorn when you wake up the troops. Didn't I?"

I looked at PVT Williams, my faithful CQ runner. His I-told-you-so expression answered Top's question.

"Yes, First Sergeant!" I yelled.

"Then why the fuck didn't you?"

"No excuse, First Sergeant!" I swallowed the: Because nobody does any more, you dumb son of a bitch.

"Did you, or the runner, do the waking-up?"

"The runn—"

"I specifically gave you orders last night that *you* were to wake up the troops. Didn't I?"

"Yes, First Sergeant!"

"Then why the fuck didn't you?"

"No excuse, First Sergeant!" This time I swallowed the: Because the damned *runner* always wakes the company, not the CQ.

"Report back here at 0800 hours. With your runner. Both of you are going before Captain Oscar." He pulled a black rope out of his shirt pocket and lit it, filling the room with his disgusting habit. "I'm recommending an Article 15 for both of you. Now get the fuck out of my sight, you sorry excuse for a soldier. And take your fucking runner with you."

"What's with this Article 15 stuff?" Williams asked, when the orderly room door closed behind us.

"You never heard of an Article 15?"

"Not really, I've only been in the Army for about four months."

"You've heard of the UCMJ, the Uniform Code of Military Justice, haven't you?"

"Yeah," he replied timidly.

"Well, an Article 15 is part of the UCMJ, like a traffic ticket, or a misdemeanor," I explained.

"Oh."

"It's a reprimand. Not something severe, like a Court Marital offense."

"Oh!" he shuddered. "Then I won't get shot or anything like that?"

"No. More like extra duty and a small fine. Sometimes you lose a stripe."

"Oh."

"But don't worry Williams, I'll tell Caption Oscar it was all my fault. Not yours. So I'll get the Article 15. Not you."

"Thank you, Specialist Papp."

Seeing that the poor private was still concerned, I suggested we stop at the mess hall for a cup of coffee instead of going back to our tents. I didn't want the distraught trooper to be by himself for an hour, brooding over the inevitable . . . contemplating the firing squad.

"Yes, Specialist Papp. Whatever you say."

Williams and I stood stiff as toast in front of Sergeant First Class Smith. Since 0755 hours. He kept us waiting like that until 0830.

"Captain Oscar had to leave on important business," Smith began. "I spoke to him before he left." He stared at me and smiled. Then he gave his attention to Williams. "You're excused, Private Williams."

Williams stood frozen.

"Leave!" he yelled at the private.

"Yes, First Sergeant Smith. Whatever you say."

"As for you, Papp," he gave me another contemptible glance, "I've been instructed to inform you that you have two choices. Accept an

Article 15, or," his eyes opened wider, "appeal your gross misconduct to a higher authority."

"I—"

"You have 48 hours to decide, Specialist."

"I'll take the Article 15." I blurted out the words before Top could stop me.

"Very well, Specialist Papp," he said, pleased with himself. "Whatever you say. Report back here at 1700 hours."

<hr>

"Ah, Specialist Papp, you're on time," Smith said, reaching for a cigar. "Very good."

"Yes, First Sergeant!" God! Playing Army really sucks.

"Here," he thrust a handful of forms at me. "Sign these."

I took the multiple copies of the DA Form 2627-1: Record of Proceedings Under Article 15, UCMJ. Skimming through the name/rank information, I carefully read the charges against me.

> *It has been reported that, on or about 0500 hours 5 July 1968, at Camp Bearcat, RVN APO 96370, you were derelict in the performance of your duties in that you negligently failed to wake the K.P.'s for duty at the appropriate time and failed to wake the personnel of the 9th Admin Co at the appropriate time and in the appropriate manner as prescribed to you by the 1SG and the Charge of Quarters instructions. (This is in violation of Article 92 UCMJ MCM 1951.)*

Boy! I was in deep shit! There went my spotless military record. I could never be a lifer now. I would have to try making it on the outside. *Could I do that? Could I make it as a civilian?*

I unfolded the form. While reading Section II, my heart skipped a beat.

> *I acknowledge receipt of the foregoing communication. Trial by Court-Martial IS NOT demanded.*

When my hand stopped shaking, I continued with Section III.

> *The following punishments are hereby imposed:*
> *1. Forfeiture of fifty dollars ($50.00) for a period of one*

month, suspended for a period of one month.

2. Restriction to the company area for a period of fourteen (14) days.

3. Extra duty for a period of fourteen (14) days.

Signing the appropriate place indicating that I didn't appeal the punishment, I handed the copies back to Smith.

"Good," he gloated.

He sat on the edge of his desk, applied a match to his cigar, and spewed a disgusting cloud at my face.

"You can begin you extra duty by carrying the tire rims behind the orderly room to the motor pool. Then you're done for today."

That's it? This wouldn't be too bad.

"Yes, First Sergeant!"

I walked outside and circled the orderly room in search of a couple little tire rims. What I found were two rims from a *deuce-and-a-half truck.*

Putting my college education to use, I tugged on one rim until it was upright and attempted to roll it. The damned thing wouldn't budge. For God only knew what reason, the son of a bitch wouldn't roll. I felt like the caveman who discovered the *square* wheel.

It took me 30 minutes to drag, push, and cajole the damned rim the 200-odd yards to the motor pool. Sweaty, tired, and bent on revenge, it required 45 minutes to get the second rim to the assigned destination. Totally exhausted, I crept back to The Pit with my tail between my legs.

The next three days of extra duty were spent building a new bunker by the orderly room. *Four* hours each day.

The balance of Week #1 consisted of planting six palm trees. Two each in three places: outside the new bunker of the orderly room, in front of Captain Oscar's hooch, and, not to be outdone, next to the palatial mansion of Sergeant First Class Smith.

In addition to the planting, I fed the palm trees with 15 gallons of water. Each. Every day. Pouring the last few drops on tree #6, I made the mistake of calculating the weight of the water I lugged around.

I managed two 5-gallon cans per trip, which amounted to 40-plus pounds. Each trip was at least 100 yards from the water supply. Adding it all up, it came to almost 750 pounds of water carried halfway around the world. Every damned day!

Week Two of my punishment sounded like something out of "Clean Up, Fix Up, Paint Up Week."

Not only did I water the palm trees by the private property of my commanding officer and first sergeant, I fortified their bunkers, policed the ditches along their roadways, swept their boardwalks, and spruced up the exterior of their dwellings and their showers. All of this increased their property values quite handsomely.

If my body wasn't bruised badly enough during those fourteen days of extra duty, my ego was. For not one, single, fucking day during those two weeks did the CQ or his runner wake the troops with the coveted bullhorn.

And not one CQ, or his runner, joined me on extra duty after they violated that sacred rule.

Not . . . one . . . fucking . . . CQ!

Chapter 17

AN AGREEMENT WITH THE ENEMY

August was a bittersweet month, the time to say goodbye to several friends, and one dickhead, as they took freedom birds back to that wonderful place known as *The World.* It also marked Charlie's best effort to blow Bearcat to smithereens.

The attempted destruction of our camp began innocuously on 2 August, when there was a change of command with the 9th Infantry Division. One general DEROSed, and a new one took his place. Unknown to most of us, the outgoing general had a secret pact with the local VC high command.

There was a VC radio tower outside of Bearcat that transmitted routine, harmless information. One member of the general's staff was overheard to compare the communications to something as frivolous as baseball scores. Our general agreed the 9th Infantry wouldn't destroy the tower if the VC didn't hit Bearcat. Everything went smoothly until the incoming general decided he would not tolerate any agreements with the enemy.

Boom! went the radio tower. Echo after echo hit Bearcat.

At 2200 hours on the faithful night of 6 August, a warning siren woke me.

"Let's go, Pinky," Eaton kicked my cot. "Red alert!"

I grabbed my M16 and steel pot, stepped into my flip-flops, and tossed on my flak jacket. Then I raced Eaton and Hoffman to the bunker. I nearly climbed up their butts as I flew out the door. Without having to be told, I headed for the closest bunker, the one next to Bohnny's tent. Once inside the protection of the musty sandbag fortress, I squinted in the darkness, seeking my bearings.

"Back here, Papp. Follow the wall about ten feet," Bohnny instructed.

Grateful that he was there to guide me, I placed a tentative left hand on the soggy sandbags and let the wall steer me to him. My fingers touched something furry. It moved. I instinctively pulled my hand away and rushed to the back of the bunker, not caring if I ran into or over anyone or anything.

"What's the matter?" Bohnny asked.

"Something furry on the wall. I touched it." An icy ripple chilled my spine.

"Probably a giant spider," he kidded.

"Damn." Another icicle.

"Don't worry, it won't bite," he laughed.

When I finally rid my mind of spiders, the reality of the red alert returned. *Was this more than a mortar attack? Is this how I would die? In a spider-infested, musty pile of sandbags?*

I slammed shut my eyes and opened my ears wide as possible. No *whiz . . . bang!* Nothing. Relieved, I mistakenly took a deep breath. I quickly exhaled and spit out the putrid aroma.

With noticeable hesitation, I whispered, "I don't hear anything."

"Nothing yet, anyway," Bohnny warned.

Minutes dragged by. Thoughts of direct hits bounced through my mind.

How secure was this bunker? Why me, God? Why Vietnam? What had I done wrong to deserve being shipped halfway around the world to die in this hellhole?

Now I understood why some guys prayed that if they *had* to die in Vietnam, they would get wiped out their first week, so they wouldn't have to endure the indignity of this desolate patch of earth for one minute longer than necessary.

Something danced across my feet. *Was this a spider attack, or a mortar attack?*

"What was that, Boomerang?" Eaton asked.

"I said I was gonna get even with our new general for blowing up that damned radio tower," Boomerang fumed. "This is the third night in a row that we've been hit. So far," he counted off on fingers silhouetted against the dim back-lighting of the bunker's entrance, "they blew a 10-foot by 15-foot hole within arm's reach of bunker 39A, got a direct hit on an officer's club, hit the airfield, destroying one chopper, blew the door off the orderly room of the 9th S&T, ripped apart the mess hall at The Academy." He paused to take a deep breath, stuck up the thumb on his left hand and continued. "Then they—"

"That's enough, Boomerang," I cut in. "You've convinced me that Charlie means business." As though I needed convincing.

KABOOM! KABOOM!

We sat down, hoping to make ourselves smaller targets, and huddled close together.

KABOOM!

And closer.

"Did Moritoni tell you what happened last night?" Eaton whispered. Without waiting for an answer, he went on: "On guard, bunker 39A. Same one as on the night of Tet. It was a little after midnight, quieter than a sneaker-clad flea walking over an elephant's balls. Face saw three VC—"

"I know," I interrupted him. "And just like during Tet, the damned O.D. wouldn't let Moritoni shoot 'em. And the asshole O.D. was a *captain*," I hissed, "not a fuckin' know-nothing brown bar lieutenant like the last time."

"What time is it?" Hoffman asked.

I held my watch closer to a gun port opening. "Can't tell."

"Here," Hoffman lit a match and held it in my direction.

"A little after 11."

KABOOM!

Hoffman blew out the match.

We sat in silence, fearful the sound of our whispering would give us away. Three rosaries later, I heard sounds of approaching footsteps. My left index finger instinctively found the trigger of my M16. The finger relaxed when my brain reminded it that, even after all the nights we've been getting hit, the rifle was empty. Still no bullets for the *dum' clerks*.

A flashlight beam swept the inside of our bunker, searching for bodies. Tire tracks lined my shorts. I pulled my lower lip over my head and swallowed.

"Who's in there?"

"We are," Hoffman answered.

"Who's *we*?" the voice demanded.

"Specialists Hoffman, Papp, Bohnny and Eaton."

"He want serial numbers, too?" Eaton whispered.

"Papp!" the now-familiar voice growled. "Is that you, *Papp*?" it demanded.

"Y-yes."

"Get out here," the voice barked the ultimatum.

I crawled to the doorway and looked up at our beloved First Sergeant Smith. The damned son of a bitch could find me anywhere. Even if I were hiding up my asshole.

"Stand up, Papp!"

I got off my hands and knees, my left finger finding the trigger on my M16. *Bullets, my kingdom for a handful of bullets.*

"Where the hell are your pants and boots?" Smith spat the words.

"They're in The Pit. My tent."

"Well, get back to your pit, and put them on."

A sudden vision of an overweight typewriter jockey running between exploding rockets and mortars flashed before me.

Mrs. Papp, how did your husband lose his life in Vietnam? It happened during a mortar attack. He was on the way back to his tent to finish getting dressed . . .

"You've gotta be crazy," I screamed into Smith's face, making him swallow his cigar stub.

"What?"

"I said no!"

"Listen, you mother fucker," Smith shouted, the veins at his bald temples erupting, "I gave you a direct order. Now move it!"

"No, *you* listen, you son of a bitch!" I screamed even louder, my adrenalin flowing like the mighty Mississippi. "I don't like you. I never did. And I never will. I—"

Eaton grabbed my left arm, trying to pull me away from Smith. I flung away the attempt to silence six months' pent-up hatred and took a step closer to Smith.

"You can't talk to me like th—"

"Don't interrupt me, you sorry excuse for a soldier," I screamed loud enough to kill the VC with my decibel rating. "We're in the middle of a damned red alert, and you want me to go back to my tent and finish getting dressed?" I pointed my impotent M16 at him. "Get your drunken head out of your ass, and smell the goddamned roses, you fucking idiot!"

"I'll have you on report for—"

"You'll do no such thing, First Sergeant Shit-For-Brains." My heart pounded, almost drowning out the sound of my voice. "If you don't get the hell out of here, NOW, I'll have *your* fat ass on report for calling me a mother fucker in front of three witnesses."

Smith looked me square in the eyes, his mouth frozen open.

"Don't you understand the English language, Top?" I yelled. "I said get the fuck out of here, you dumb-shit lifer."

Shutting off his flashlight, he melted away into the darkness.

Eaton slapped me on the back so hard my lungs almost flew out of my mouth. "Atta way to go, Pinky," he said. "Had me scared for a minute. Thought you were gonna kill the son of a bitch."

"The thought *never* entered my mind. Let's get back in the bunker until the all-clear sounds."

The next day, Personnel Actions was buzzing with the reports of my confrontation with Top. Make that all of the 9th Admin, not just PA. The endless pats on the back and handshakes made me feel like a politician campaigning.

"Can I interrupt the festivities to get an ID card?" a Spec 5 asked, seating himself in front of my desk.

"Sure, sorry."

While going through the formality of the paperwork, the specialist told an interesting story of his own.

"Yep, G-2 confirmed that four rounds landed inside the berm last night. Two mortars," he held up the appropriate fingers on his right hand, "and two rockets," then the left hand.

I nodded as I typed.

"One landed 50 yards from our bunker. Scared the shit out of me—almost as much as that time two weeks ago."

I stopped typing and searched my memory.

"We didn't get hit two weeks ago."

"I know. But I was talking about what happened to me at work."

"What do you do?" My fingers froze over the typewriter keys.

"I work in S-4, Graves Registration. Clean the bodies and put them in the bags to send home." Realizing he had captured my undivided attention, he paused for effect. "One day, two weeks ago, a bag moved."

"Postmortem reflex reaction, huh?" I shuddered.

"That's what I thought at first." His hands shook. "But when I undid the bag, the guy's eyes popped open!"

My left hand fell to the keyboard. My right covered my mouth to hold back my lunch. "No?" I mumbled through my fingers.

"Yeah. Scared the living shit out of me." He leaned over, so that our noses almost touched. "Turned out the guy was still alive, after being shot almost *20* times." Leaning back a little, he added: "Doctor had even signed the guy's death certificate."

My expression evidently showed my disbelief.

"No shit, Sherlock." He crossed his heart. "Swear on my mother's grave."

Before he could tell any more stories, I handed him his completed ID card and ran for the latrine.

"Here, Pinky," Cohen said, throwing a flimsy gun case on my desk. "And here's your change." He dropped the soggy MPC notes on top of the black plastic case.

"Thanks, Coach."

"Second one in a month," Cohen added.

"If they didn't make them out of cheap plastic," I held the case up to the light, "the damned things would last a little longer. Look. It's almost transparent."

Due to the recent enemy activity, all clerks were required to keep their impotent M16s spotless. Even though we had no ammo for them, the M16s had to be squeaky clean. We were subjected to two daily inspections to verify their pristine condition. Thus the worthless plastic sleeves to keep the dust out. Somebody in HQ had to be getting a kickback from the gooks who sold the gun cases at their little store by the PX.

"Got the next supply ready for the cremation?" Cohen asked.

Ah, yes, the sacrificial burning.

As further evidence of the paranoia circulating throughout Bearcat, we had the paper witch hunt. So that the VC wouldn't know what was going on within our camp, all incoming mail had to be burned after we read it. We also incinerated used carbon paper and typewriter ribbons so Charlie couldn't read them. Although there was some logic to it, the genius who thought of burning the ribbons and carbon paper never considered that we were so short of supplies, we used the ribbons until they were threadbare, and the carbon paper until it was so worn and full of holes, it could be used as a sieve.

"See, ya," Cohen said, taking the traitorous contents to their death.

Specialist 4th Class Tony Moritoni said his last goodbye on 10 August. As with every farewell, we promised to keep in touch. When The Face left Bearcat to board his freedom bird and return to the glamorous women in Gotham City, a part of me accompanied him.

A week later, it was the Coach's turn to fly to the waiting arms of his wife in the City of Brotherly Love.

"See ya soon," I said.

He nodded.

Sergeant First Class Smith said goodbye to Vietnam on 18 August: my wife's birthday. What a present that was!

Two weeks before the asshole DEROSed, I was on my way to the orderly room to get some papers signed. Top was maneuvering his bulk out the door and down the walkway, leaving his cave unguarded. Planted on his desk was his infamous clipboard. Emblazoned on it in red was the word SHORT. Hearing no one approaching, I picked up a wide black marker from his desk, crossed out the SHORT, and wrote in larger letters: MAYBE! During the following days, I enjoyed the turmoil caused by that single word, as Top grilled everyone in an attempt to determine its author.

SSG Dickson, the Chief's faithful second in command, departed on 22 August for his hometown of Louisville, for a month's leave before his next assignment in neighboring Fort Knox.

"Maybe we'll run into each other some day," he said, as we shook hands for the last time.

One by one, friends (minus Smith, of course) left me to return to their families. Each departure left me feeling I had attended a funeral. Even though the "farewell" was accompanied with the solemn vow to keep in touch, it was a hollow promise that had little likelihood of being kept.

The last farewell for August finally arrived. Specialist 4th Class Dennis Bohnny was heading for his hometown of Hamilton, Ohio. To be a civilian once more. Bohnny, the friend who had taught me everything about Personnel Actions, was cutting the cord one last time.

I walked to his tent at 0600 hours to say goodbye. He was in the middle of bidding his tent mates farewell. I waited on the front steps, vividly remembering the 70-hour weeks we worked side-by-side to get the overflowing stack of Team 4 paperwork caught up. They were some of the best weeks of the last eight months.

Bohnny picked up his few remaining possessions and walked toward me. I retreated so we could say our final words on solid ground, rather than on the awkward steps of his tent.

We shook hands and gave each other a brotherly hug.

As I pushed up on the bridge of his glasses, saving him the trouble, all of August's farewells and promises to keep in touch flashed through my head.

I looked at Bohnny's gentle face one last time. With tears running down my cheeks, I put my hands on his shoulders and said, "Goodbye, Clyde. *I'll probably never see you again.*"

Chapter 18

With LTC Murphy long gone, Saturday inspections were a thing of the past. His replacement, COL Hill, stopped by occasionally, but didn't chew ass when he did. One day, in the middle of the week, Hill came through while I was in Team 4 straightening out paperwork with Spec 5 White.

When the colonel walked up to me, I stiffened in true military fashion. Next to him was a man dressed in a mixture of civvies and fatigues. After exchanging cordial hellos, Hill explained that the gentleman with him was Tom Horan, a wire service correspondent. I shook Horan's hand, happy to touch a civilian of such note.

"Dennis Papp," I stated proudly.

"I'm from Nebraska. Where are you from, Dennis?"

"New Jersey."

"Jersey, eh?" Horan smiled and rubbed his chin. "Got some good news for you."

"Oh?"

"When you leave, the Army is going to let you take your mosquito net home with you."

I aborted a laugh.

"The mosquito *is* the state bird for New Jersey, isn't it?"

Much to my surprise, COL Hill grinned, proving some lifers were almost human.

"State bird, eh, Specialist Papp?" Hill kidded. "You must grow 'em big in the swamps."

"Sure do, Sir!"

Why couldn't Hill have been our Adjutant General all along, instead of that asshole Murphy? The last six-plus months might have been more bearable with Hill.

"You wanted to see me, Mr. Taguiped?"

"Right neighborly of you to stop by," the Chief began the same as ever. "I want you to take the rest of the day off—"

"Hot damn!" I blurted. A day off. This sounded too good to be true. *Was this a reward for working so diligently the past months?* If it were, I sure as hell deserved it. And appreciated it! Boy! Mr. Blue's replacement was a great guy.

"—and get your gear in order. You're going to Dong Tam with the forward party."

"What?" My mouth fell open, hitting my left knee.

Didn't this moron know I'd be going home in six weeks? The thought of moving to Dong Tam, deep in the more-dangerous Mekong Delta, was scary enough. But being one of the first to go made me feel like a point man. I just broke 40 AAWU, and even though I was short, I'd feel like a redwood tree leading the saplings to the saw mill.

"You leave tomorrow at 0700."

"But why me, Sir?" *Yeah, why me? I'm too short for this shit. Ain't I?*

"Because you're the most-qualified clerk I've got."

And for that he wanted to get me killed?

"I need someone to do emergency leaves while the rest of us pack and move down with the convoy."

"But—"

"Plus," he cut me off, "I need somebody I can trust to get the new area organized, so we can move in smoothly when we arrive."

"Sir, don't you think it's better to keep me here to make sure my wealth of experience is used to guarantee a fluid organization of the packing schedule for the peregrination?" *How's that for Army bullshit?*

"Huh?"

"Sir, don't you think—"

"Specialist Papp, I *think* it would be right neighborly of you to do as you're ordered."

"Throw in another bag of gravel," Sergeant Mattei ordered.

"Got it," I said.

Staggering over to the stacked bags, I wiped my drenched face on my soggy fatigue shirt. *Was it possible that Dong Tam was hotter than Bearcat?* Every pore in my body discharged fluid. Even my eyeballs were sweating.

I grabbed a 50-odd-pound bag of crushed stones, carried it the 20 feet to the mixer, ripped open the top of the bag, and dumped it in.

Mattei waited for it to blend in. "Sand," he ordered. "And a little more water."

The new ingredients were added.

"Okay," the sergeant said, "looks good to me. Pour it."

We jettisoned the oatmeal-like mixture into the forms. After baking in the broiling sun for a week or so, the foundation for another doppleganger hooch would be ready.

"Okay," the sergeant droned, "that's enough for this morning. Take a 20-minute break for lunch. Enjoy your C-rations, while I make sure everything is okay at the NCO Club."

It was time for that rare treat: eating C-rations. I chose Beans and Franks. How could anyone screw up such an all-American meal? Leave it to the military.

I dug into my right-front pants pocket and took out the Army's answer to a miniaturized can opener: the trusty P-38. I tore away the lid of the can. One taste was all it took to tell me I'd made a big mistake. The franks were blander than sand and almost as gritty. The beans wouldn't have made a cowboy fart. Putting that can aside, I selected the Beef and Potatoes. One mouthful was my limit.

Taking out my canteen, and wishing I had a packet of Kool-Aid to make it a better-tasting beverage, I downed half of its contents. Wondering if the sergeant was enjoying C-rats and Kool-Aid at the NCO Club, I put away my canteen and waited for the old fart to return.

"Gravel," the sergeant barked. "Three bags of cement mix. Sand," he continued with the ingredients. "Easy on the water, Private," he ordered to the new recruit in our work party.

My first three days in delightful downtown Dong Tam, bag after bag was toted, opened, dumped, mixed, and poured. By the end of each day, I felt we'd built a six-lane highway to Saigon instead of mixing and pouring concrete for the foundations of new hooches. Had it been necessary for me to do an emergency leave, the purpose of my being in the forward party, my blistered hands wouldn't have been able to manipulate the typewriter keys.

Each day at 1700 hours, our work detail gratefully ended. Some headed to the mess hall for nourishment (*hah!*) and relaxation. Mess hall food instead of C-rations, wow! Being a more-intelligent member of the species, I was a Spec 5 after all, I had started the day with a bigger-than-normal breakfast. That way I had stuff that was less disgusting than what passed for the evening meal, and thus left me free to head for the showers to remove crusted cement.

The days were physically draining; the nights, emotionally so.

My first night in Dong Tam, I suffered the rude awakening I expected. Three red alerts introduced two mortar and rocket attacks. Each time the siren wailed, I grabbed my protective equipment and raced hell-bent for the closest bunker.

Why are you doing this to me, God? Haven't I suffered enough? Granted, I'm not going out on firefights every day like thousands of GIs . . . but does that mean You have to lull me into a state of reasonable security, just to pull the rug out from under me and drop me into a more-imminent war zone?

There was only one red alert the second night, from 0100 hours to 0400 hours. The 180 agonizing minutes were punctuated with sporadic incoming rounds.

After those three frustrating hours, I was too wound up to sleep. So I grabbed some stationery and decided to vent.

> *Dong Tam, Vietnam*
>
> *My darling Wife,*
> *Don't know how well you'll be able to read this letter, because my hands are swollen and sore from mixing concrete for building foundations. I hurt in places I didn't know I had skin, let alone muscle.*

*There's something I want to ask. I don't think it's
necessary to mention, but at the present time I'm
completely disgusted and about ready for a nervous
breakdown. After the first day or two when I get
home to your waiting arms, and we do our "mandatory" family visiting, I want to do ABSOLUTELY
nothing for the next two or three days. I just want to
stay in our apartment, relax, and be alone with you.*

*Annette, I am a physical and mental wreck. I may
not risk my life every day in the field, but Vietnam is
definitely showing its effects on me. At times, I think
I'll never make it out of here without going crazy.
Some nights I cry myself to sleep because I'm so
lonely and miserable. I feel like it's the end of the
world.*

*Forget the fact that there are days in a row that I
don't get a shower, that I can't wear clean clothes,
that I can't stand to inhale the stench of my own
body, that I can't stay clean for five minutes, or eat
decent food, or drink clean water.*

*I want to forget this madness ever existed, or that
I was ever here. Please try to understand what I'm
saying . . . and honor this one important request.*

> *I miss you,*
> *Denny*

When the siren went off at 2330 hours of my third night, I grabbed
my empty M16 and raced barefoot to the bunker. The Dong Tam vet-
erans I shared the hooch with were so used to the mortar attacks that
their trip to the bunker resembled little more than a cautious Sunday
stroll in the country.

After the all-clear sounded, I realized I was dressed in only a
T-shirt and boxer shorts. Thank God Sergeant First Class Smith had
DEROSed. He would have made me go back to my hooch and get on
my pants and boots.

I rested the M16 against the wall and flopped on my cot, waiting
for the next piercing warning. Minutes passed and things were quiet. I
figured the red alerts were over, and I could sleep. Standing up to get

my fatigues and hang them in the locker (otherwise they'd be limp and soggy in the morning), I realized my pants were nowhere to be found.

Some son of a bitch stole my damned pants during the red alert!

I didn't mind the 35 bucks in damned MPC notes that were in the wallet. Or the bullshit Army papers. The few memories of home were gone forever: my New Jersey driver's license, pictures of Annette with my folks, a snapshot of our dog, and worst of all, the $5-bill that was my birthday present from Aunt Betty.

Things were bad enough in Vietnam without having fellow GIs act like common thieves, stealing the precious memories of home that kept us going every damned day we were in this hellhole.

When would this insanity stop?

Chapter 19

VUNG TAU REVISITED

"Mr. Taguiped wants to see you, Pinky," PFC Horvath said through a cloud of smoke.

Horvath was Cohen's replacement, and he smoked more than an 1800s steam locomotive. When I first met him, he had two butts stuck in his mouth, resembling tusks. That mighty feat earned him his nickname.

"Do you know what the Chief wanted, *Walrus*?" I asked, dropping in my chair.

Every time Mr. Blue's replacement wanted me, I ended up on the short end of the stick. Like the last time, when he nominated me to be PA's representative on the forward party for our move from Bearcat to Dong Tam. I was considering a plot of revenge for that one.

Horvath answered with a *puff, puff.* That meant, "No, I don't know what Taguiped wants."

Pelted by quarter-sized raindrops, I plodded the worn path from Team 3 to PA Headquarters. Like the great Houdini, I appeared mysteriously in front of Taguiped, startling him. We began our conversation the same as always.

"You wanted to see me, Mr. Taguiped?"

"Right neighborly of you to stop by, Specialist Papp."

Standing next to Taguiped was a PFC with fire-red hair and peach fuzz for a beard. His two shaky hands were mauling the life out of a brand-new jungle hat.

"Papp, I want you to meet PFC Donald Wright."

Looking eyeball to eyeball with Wright, he was two inches taller than me. About twenty pounds lighter.

"Hello, Wright," I said politely, accepting the right hand he reluctantly unglued from his hat.

"He's your replacement, Papp."

"Well, *hel-lo*, Private First Class Wright," I beamed, pumping his hand. "Right neighborly of you to stop by."

"Thank you, Specialist Papp."

I held my breath and hesitated, "Does this mean you'll approve my R&R to Vung Tau, Mr. Taguiped?"

"Well, Papp." He paused. "Since your replacement is here, there's no reason to hold back my approval. But," he cautioned, "you have two weeks to get PFC Wright trained. Otherwise, no R&R. Understood?"

"Yes, *Sir*!"

"Dismissed."

"Where you from, Wright?"

"Idaho, Specialist Papp."

"Must be pretty there."

"It sure is, Specialist Papp. When it's dawn in the high country," he became exuberant, "the peaks of the Rockies shine like gems in the sunrise."

"And here I thought Idaho looked like a potato."

His brown eyes took on a thunderbolt-like appearance. "Not you, too."

"Relax, Wright, I was only kidding."

I had a spring to my step while we climbed the stairs to Team 3. I couldn't wait to show off my replacement. *My replacement.* Damn! those two words sounded great.

"Sorry, Specialist Papp. I get a little pissed when people only think of potatoes when they talk about Idaho."

"Tell you what," I put a fatherly hand on his shoulder, "if anybody talks like that about Idaho, I'll personally *mash* 'em."

He replied by smiling. And slamming the screen door on my ass.

"Smiles, I want you to meet Donald Wright. He's my replacement," I beamed.

McGuire offered his hand. "Chris McGuire at your service."

While shaking hands, McGuire studied the newbie. After completing his survey, he flashed one of his patented smiles. "That blond fuzz on your cheeks isn't an attempt at a beard, is it, *Peaches*?"

Wright rubbed his face, puzzled at the name. Then the light bulb over his head went to full power: "Oh, I get it. *peach* fuzz."

"Got some good news, Smiles," I said.

"What?"

"Now that Peaches is here, Mr. Taguiped said he'd approve our R&R to Vung Tau. That means we'll be out of here in two weeks."

McGuire and one of his buddies from another unit would join me to the shores of Vung Tau. This time I planned on doing it right: We'd check into a hotel the first day in Vung Tau, rather than the R&R center. By spending the first day in a hotel, we'd get an extra night of R&R, since our three days of leave didn't officially begin until we checked into the R&R center.

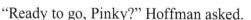

"Ready to go, Pinky?" Hoffman asked.

It was Sunday, 8 September. I got up from my cot, beaming like a peacock. I was down to 31 AAWU. Tomorrow, I'd be authorized to carry a short-timer's stick: the outward sign of a true Vietnam short-timer. Today, I would buy the prized symbol.

"Let's do it," I ordered.

"Hey, fart faces," Hoffman called out to Eaton and Grabowski, "we're leaving."

"Wait! I'm coming," Grabowski shouted when we were halfway to the door of our wooden hooch.

Weren't the spacious new accommodations at Dong Tam simply wonderful? Although not luxurious, they certainly were better than living in a smelly old tent.

The four of us, whose friendship went back to The Pit in Bearcat, exited the hooch and headed for the gook shop by the PX. It was renowned for its selection of short-timer's sticks.

"How about this one, Pinky?" Eaton asked.

"Not what I had in mind."

Grabowski held up a more intricately carved one. "This?"

"Getting closer."

Hoffman tried one.

I shook my head.

Stick after stick was offered and rejected. Then Hoffman held up one that was a deep, rich mahogany. The handle had a dragon's head carved into it.

"Yes!" I shouted, taking it from him.

The dragon's mouth was agape, exposing vicious teeth. A goatee hung from its chin. Two lustrous pearl eyes stood in stark contrast to the reddish-brown wood. I ran my fingers over the seven ribbed sections, each measuring two inches, beginning below the head. A circular notch separated each of the sections. The tip was covered with a brilliant half-inch brass cap. Yes, this 21 inches of solid mahogany was *my* short-timer's stick.

"How much?" I asked the shopkeeper.

We played seesaw until I finally agreed to his last offer. Half the original price.

I took the package from the shopkeeper and placed it in my left armpit. Like a general posing with this swagger stick, I marched out of the shop. My admiring trio followed a respectful distance behind.

"*Ssshhhoooooooorrrtt!*" I yelled, repeating my primeval Tarzan yell from two-plus months ago.

"Good morning, Pinky," Eaton said from across the hooch.

"Morning, Numbers. I'm so short, when I jumped out of bed earlier this morning, it took fifteen minutes for my feet to hit the floor."

Eaton threw a boot my way, accompanied by a "Go to hell, Pinky."

I picked up his boot and tossed it underhand to him.

"Do me a favor, Numbers."

"What?"

"Let Wright and Horvath know that I'll be a little late this morning."

"Why?"

"I'll need some extra time getting dressed. I have to roll up my sleeves and pants legs so my fatigues will fit, cuz I'm so *ssshort!*" I laughed.

The same boot came thundering my way again.

Not only was PFC Wright a fast learner, he showed an interest in the work and a willingness to learn, as if he were a reassigned infantryman given the chance to spend the rest of his tour as a clerk. Based on the progress that Wright had already shown, my final R&R to Vung Tau was in the bag.

"I'm gonna get some lunch," I told him, tucking my short-timer's stick under my arm. "Be back in an *hour.*" Might as well take advantage of his enthusiasm and my short-timer's attitude and extend the afternoon repast to double its authorized length.

"Okay," Wright said, fingers dancing over his typewriter keys.

The line of waiting GIs extended well outside the closed front door of the mess hall. Now was my first opportunity to make use of one of the privileges of being short. I held up my stick and smiled. Like Moses at the Red Sea, the line parted, and I walked in.

Standing by the trays was a PFC who towered a foot above me.

"Excuse me," I said to his back.

He turned around, lowered his eyes, snarled, and faced his original position.

"Excuse me," I repeated.

He looked down on me again. This time he grunted: "You want something?"

I held up my short-timer's symbol. And beamed.

"Oh, excuse me, Specialist." He gave me his tray and silverware, placed his immense paws on the shoulders of the two GIs in front of him, and growled, "Step aside. Short-timer comin' through."

God! being short was great. It was almost worth spending time in Nam to get this peer worship. A very *slight* almost.

Besides improving Wright's skills over the course of the next few days, I helped Horvath, our one-month veteran, whenever he had a problem. This double-duty made week two zip by faster than the previous one.

The day before I was scheduled to leave for Vung Tau, I had a long talk with Mr. Taguiped. He agreed Wright and Horvath could be left alone for the short time I'd be away.

"That's right neighborly of you, Mr. Taguiped," I smiled.

He accepted the barb without realizing its intention, and simply uttered: "Dismissed."

Using the influence of my short-timer's status, I got the three of us on an afternoon caribou that went directly from Dong Tam to Vung Tau. No side trips. No layovers. This impressed the hell out of McGuire and his buddy, Harold Bell. They continued to extol my virtues until distracted with the sights.

Every female we rode past on the trip from the airport to downtown Vung Tau got a hoot! and a holler! from my two horny traveling companions.

"Calm down, guys," I laughed. "You'll have time enough to enjoy yourselves."

"Vung Tau is great!" McGuire bellowed. Then he began chanting: "I'm gonna get laid tonight. I'm gonna get laid tonight."

"Me, too," Bell chimed in.

Over and over.

"Easy," I cautioned, "you're gonna cum in your pants before you've had the chance to drop 'em."

"Sign here, GI," the desk clerk at the Grand Hotel instructed.

I took the pen and wrote *J. Dennis Papp.* For the date I put *September 16, 1968.* It was time to start doing things the *civilian* way. Yahoo!

The sight of our hotel room kept me in a civilian frame of mind, since it in no way resembled the inside of the two-story wooden hooches in Dong Tam. It consisted of one enormous room, measuring at least 20 feet by 25 feet, with an adjoining bathroom. Most of the plaster, not wooden, walls were painted white, intensifying the room's generous dimensions. A 12-foot ceiling accomplished the impossible by making the room seem more overwhelming. Two ceiling fans spun slowly, providing modest relief from the moist air.

Full-sized beds, not Army cots, occupied three of the four corners. I threw my satchel on the bed nearest the door, leaving McGuire and Bell to select from the remaining ones.

When the three of us walked into the bathroom, there was room to spare, even with the oversized shower and double porcelain sink. I was amazed that such luxurious indoor plumbing existed in an *ordinary* hotel, let alone *anywhere* in Vietnam. If only the other "creature comforts" were as civilized, the inhumanity of being dropped in this country would have been more tolerable.

"We could get lost in here," McGuire said.

"You get lost when you stick you hand in your pants," Bell kidded.

"Speaking of personal entertainment, let's go get some booze and pussy," McGuire smiled.

Instead, I took them to the Chu Sum Twat Cafe, site of my delicious home-cooked meal when I visited Vung Tau with Eaton. They wanted to eat every item on the menu, and every woman in the place.

We already were half-drunk from the dozen or so beers we collectively consumed with dinner, when we visited a nearby bar. The alcohol apparently had no effect on the eyesight of my two companions, for they immediately spied two young ladies seated in a dark corner.

"Let's sit with them," McGuire pointed with his erection.

We took the empty chairs, and McGuire went to work on the taller of the two lovelies.

"That's a stunning red dress," McGuire blubbered while his eyes coveted the visible young flesh. Her skintight *ao dai* was bright red and featured a heart-shaped cutout in its bodice. Exposed was just the right amount of cleavage to make McGuire's mouth water.

She smiled in return and held up her near-empty glass. McGuire took the hint and ordered a round of drinks for the table. While Bell went to work on the remaining nubile teenager, McGuire's fingers anxiously examined the open spaces of the red dress.

As with my other R&R's, I had already warned my companions that I intended to practice safe sex by remaining celibate. Besides loving my wife, I didn't want to end up with Captain Ahab's disease: *Moby Dick.* So, not interested in seducing the local talent, I exchanged my empty glass for McGuire's full one, and eventually repeated the process with Bell's.

"How about another round, Smiles?" I urged.

Without even looking at his glass, or removing his fingers from paradise, McGuire yelled for the waitress and ordered a full set of refills. Moments after the drinks were placed before us, my companions' companions were ready for entertainment.

The five of us stumbled back to the Grand Hotel. As we walked past the manager, he said, "500 P more. For each lady."

It was amazing how the oldest profession benefited everyone's pocketbook, except the John's, of course.

Two anxious GIs dug into their near-empty pockets and hastily placed the required fee on the desk. Turning to leave for our room, the same GIs fed the outstretched palms of their ladies.

I pulled McGuire aside as he stuck the key in the door.

"I'm gonna wait out here," I pointed to a small bench a few feet from our door. "When you're done, send 'em out, and I'll come in. Okay?"

"You sure, Pinky?"

"I'm sure."

Four entered the room; one stood guard by the door.

I busied myself counting the colored tiles on the floor. When I got up to six *million*, I shifted my position on the bench.

The manager walked up to me and asked, "GI want companion?"

"No."

"Only 1,000 P."

"No." Not for 1 P.

"Okay, GI." He shuffled away on noisy sandals.

McGuire stuck his head out the door. "You okay?"

"Sure."

"These broads are great," he smiled and disappeared inside.

Amidst the sounds of giggling and noisy springs, I went back to counting the tiles.

"GI want companion? 750 P."

The manager must have figured rush hour was over, and it was bargaining time.

"No."

"600 P?"

"No!"

He lowered his head and reluctantly returned to his desk.

Now the sounds of our shower filled the night, with a "Let me wash that, GI," thrown in every so often. Moments later McGuire reappeared at the door.

"These broads are great. They even insisted on showering, between courses."

More running water and giggling.

"Hey, Pinky." McGuire came halfway out of the room draped in a towel. "They want to spend the night. No extra charge," he quickly added.

"Great. What do I do now?"

"We got it all worked out. I called the manager."

"Huh?"

Just then the manager walked by me carrying a folded room divider. Through a somewhat-toothless smile, he said, "Put around GI's bed. So he no see the boom-boom."

"Forget it!" I shouted. "Take the damned screen away."

"This give GI privacy."

"*Didi*," I yelled louder. "*Didi mau.* Get the hell out of here before I wrap that thing around *you*."

McGuire looked at me like I had burst a vein in my head. "Relax, Pinky, we—"

I started laughing. The tension melted away.

"I'm okay. I just didn't want that divider around my bed. I'd feel like a damned fool."

"We could—"

"Tell you what, Smiles," I interrupted again. "Why don't you join the ladies, get your rocks off one more time, put out the lights, and I'll come in. Okay?"

"You sure you won't mind them being in the room?" he asked, readjusting his towel.

"I'm sure."

Thirty minutes later, the lights went out, and I entered the debauchery. Stumbling over a pile of wet towels, I banged my left knee on my bed, causing me to verbalize a few, choice Hungarian cuss words.

Grateful for the modesty the darkened room provided, I stripped to my shorts and climbed between the sheets.

To a background of female giggling, McGuire, Bell and I began talking about checking into the R&R center in the morning and how to spend the rest of the day. Occasional groaning and the sounds of over-worked bedsprings punctuated our conversation. McGuire's voice became suddenly quiet, and the *boing! boing! boing!* intensified. Bell and I continued talking as though nothing were happening.

McGuire's rhythm increased to a fevered pitch, as he began chanting, "One, two, screw you. One, two, screw you."

The moaning escalated.

Boing! Boing!

Bell and I continued talking, ignoring the sounds of ecstasy coming from McGuire's bed.

A "Yahoo!" mixed with a few shouts of "GI number one" translated into an obvious simultaneous orgasm.

Then, as though nothing had taken place the past 15 minutes, McGuire picked up the conversation with us.

"Like I was saying, Pinky, Vung Tau is fantastic."

Bell joined me in boisterous laughter.

"What's so funny?" McGuire asked.

"Nothing," I cried.

Boing! went Bell's bed. Shortly, the level of activity in his corner quickly rose, and his bed inched its way across the room.

Boing! Boing! Boing!

He picked up on McGuire's chant of "One, two, screw you," and pumped faster to keep pace with his partner's groaning. Even in the darkness, I saw the top sheet fly off his bed, and smoke hover over the carnal bedlam.

"Yes! Yes!"

Boing! Boing!

"GI number one."

"Yes! Yes!"

"Number one. Number one."

"Yes! Yes!"

Boing! Boing! Yes! *Boing! Boing! Boing!* Number one!

"Yyyeessss!"

Boing!

"What time are we checking into the R&R center?" Bell asked, matching McGuire's previous undaunted tone.

McGuire's raucous laughter erupted, easily drowning out mine.

The erotic scene replayed itself twice before I finally drifted off to sleep.

"Morning, Pinky," came McGuire's greeting.

I cautiously pushed myself up on my left elbow and gradually sat up, my brain telling me to avoid quick movements until my head cleared. *How many drinks did I have last night?*

"Morning," I mumbled, looking around the room and seeing only

McGuire. "Where's Bell? And your ladies?"

"I'm in here," Bell yelled from the bathroom.

"And the *ladies* left an hour ago," McGuire added.

As I leaned over to get a clean set of clothing out of my satchel, I again was reminded to curtail my movements and, at all costs, avoid bending over.

"Guess what?" McGuire asked.

"What?" I mumbled. *Was it too late to seek revenge on the person who discovered alcoholic beverages?*

"My escort felt sorry you were alone last night. She asked if I'd mind her getting in bed with you and doing it."

The thought of warm, willing flesh excited me. It quickly put another story on my morning's erection, causing both of my heads to ache. Then the vision of my dick turning green and falling off brought that swollen member to ground level.

"What did you tell her?"

"Said it was fine with me. But you'd probably kick her out, or kill her."

"You were right."

"I figured as much." He tossed his dirty clothes in a separate section of his satchel. "Then she offered to give you a blow job."

My erection again surfaced. Next stop, the roof!

"But I told her you'd still react the same way."

"Yeah. Right. Sure."

Gulp.

After checking into the R&R Center, I wanted to shop for a Zenith lighter a guy in our hooch possessed. It was windproof and designed especially for pipes. Back in The World I enjoyed a pipe or two each day. What made this lighter unique was the intricate figure engraved on one side and the thirty-odd words on the other. McGuire and Bell had other things in mind: drinking and perusing the local talent. So we agreed to meet up for dinner, then have a few drinks.

"So where's the special lighter you had to get?" asked McGuire, shoveling in another mouthful of vegetables and rice.

I handed over my prized purchase.

After a quick look he mumbled, "It's got some words on one side, and a broad holding a bird in an outstretched hand. Big deal."

"Read the words," I prompted.

"Says *VIETNAM. VUNG TAU. 68-69.* And, *YEA THOUGH I WALK THROUGH THE VALLEY OF THE SHADOW OF DEATH, I WILL FEAR NO EVIL, FOR I AM THE EVILEST SON OF A BITCH IN THE VALLEY.* So?"

"Now flip it over and take a close look at the picture."

"Woman holding a bird. So?"

"Turn it upside down and flip open the lid," I instructed.

"Fuckin'-A, man. She's grabbing herself. That's cool."

When held that way, the woman's head and outstretched hand-holding bird disappeared, leaving her remaining hand placed between what now became her legs.

Our three days at the R&R center passed quickly. My horny companions got their fill of women and booze, while I concentrated on food and booze. Even though we were scheduled to get up at 4:30 to return to Dong Tam, we decided to get shit-faced our last night in Vung Tau.

Holding onto each other for support, we stumbled into the R&R center, after parting with handfuls of MPC at a variety of local bars. We made our way to the patio. A Vietnamese band was playing to a packed house. We snaked our way through the mob and slid into the few remaining empty chairs.

The vocalist was an attractive teenager, much to the enjoyment of my drunken accomplices. Her command of the English language was excellent. Despite my being plastered, it was difficult to discern a Vietnamese accent as she crooned one tune after another. When the band stopped for a minute to change sheet music, a GI rose and shouted: "324!"

Amidst laughter, came a "278."

The countdown had begun.

"211" was followed by "192," then "168." A hush came over the drunken crowd when a "66!" rang out.

A GI from the table adjoining ours extended his full six-and-a-half-foot frame. With a single glance, he convinced the percussionist to begin a drum roll. Stretching himself a few extra inches, the GI restarted bedlam with a resounding "38."

I got to my feet. Slowly. My lack of speed was as much for effect as the inability to move my numb limbs any faster. Since my height missed the six-foot-six mark of the neighboring short-timer by more than a handful of inches, I carefully stood on my chair, making full use of McGuire and Bell for support, then stepped onto the table. As I perched myself on the slippery surface, the crowd became tranquil. I stared at the band. The drum roll restarted. When it was at the peak of its crescendo, I yelled: "20!"

The proverbial pin bounced on the floor.

My glance danced around the crowd, challenging a rebuttal. When none came, I screamed: "And a fuckin' wake up!" Tears filled my eyes as I jumped down, without any help from McGuire or Bell, and retook my seat.

The chaos that ensued would have made an artillery explosion sound like a cap pistol. Through the band's next number, the noise continued. When the vocalist took the microphone out of its stand and held it reverently in both hands, the crowd became quieter than a tomb as she tenderly went into a song that every short-timer held in reverence.

> *When you're goin' to San Francisco,*
> *Be sure to wear some flowers in your hair.*

Dozens of lips began whispering the words. Table after table joined in, longing to be in the City by the Bay, DEROSing out of Nam. The band picked up on our emotion and played louder. Every GI got to his feet. Tears ran down cheeks as the intensity of our voices overshadowed the band.

> *All across the nation, such a strange vibration.*
> *People in motion.*
> *There's a whole generation, with a new—*

The unmistakable roar of a *freedom bird* sounded as it flew overhead. Every face riveted skyward, searching out the idol above. Voices crackled as we choked on the song's words. Unable to continue, I lip-synched while the final words drifted to the sky, embracing the symbol of our dreams.

Chapter 20

Now that I almost was a civilian again, I wrote *September 21*, not 21 September, when I began today's entry in my diary. Other than saying I was back in Dong Tam after a great R&R in Vung Tau, my only comment was I'd break 100 AAWU tomorrow if my tour had been for a full year.

Those extra three months was a depressing thought. Almost as bad as the ones running through my head: freak accidents killing guys who were short. I still had the short-timer's paranoia of dying the last few weeks of my tour.

"Here, Pinky," McGuire said, "this has got to be better than reading your journal." He straddled the chair in front of me, placing folded arms on its back. "It came with a letter from my brother. The poem's better if you read it out loud." He smiled, resting his chin on his wrist.

I picked up the slip of paper he dropped before me. The poem was untitled. I cleared my throat with a pronounced *ahem!* and respectfully recited the three stanzas.

> *As I awoke this morning,*
> *When all sweet things are born.*
> *A robin perched upon my sill,*
> *To signal the coming dawn.*

> *The bird was fragile, young and gay,*
> *And sweetly did it sing.*
> *The thoughts of happiness and joy,*
> *Into my heart did it bring.*
>
> *I smiled softly at the cheery song.*
> *There as it paused, a moment's lull,*
> *I gently closed the window,*
> *And crushed its fucking skull.*

I let out a hearty laugh, barely drowning out McGuire's.

"Thanks, Smiles, just what I needed."

"I've got something else you'll need, Pinky," Eaton said, waving a stack of papers inches from my face.

"What's that, Numbers?"

Clearing his throat with a double *ahem!*, he eloquently proclaimed: "This is an official document for PAPP, JOHN D., SP5 E5, US5268—"

"I know my service number," I said, anxious for him to get to the point.

"Ahem! This port call—"

"Yahoo! My port call. My port call." I jumped out of my chair. "Give it to me. Give it to me."

"No, Specialist Papp, I shall continue to read it to you." He pushed me back in my chair. "As I was saying, you are to get your shit together, because this port call constitutes an amendment to your orders. You are directed to report to the 90th Replacement Battalion, Long Binh, Vietnam, for transportation aboard flight number G2B4 at 1100 hours *on*—are you ready for this, Pinky?"

"Yes, goddammit! Tell me! Tell me!"

"On . . . a little drum roll please, Smiles."

"Brrrrrrrrrrrrr," McGuire chimed in.

"—ooonn . . . *2 October 68.*"

"Yahoo! I got my drop! I got my drop!"

McGuire slapped my face to calm me down. When I let out a "Ya—" another good slap shut me up.

"Furthermore, Specialist Papp," Eaton continued in a military tone, "you are directed to report to AG Section in Dong Tam on 28 September 68 NLT 0800 hours to begin your out-processing."

"Ya—"

Slap!

"That means today's my last day in the office. I pick up my clearance papers tomorrow. Ya—"

Slap!

"Atsa Rog, Pinky," Eaton said. "And tomorrow night's your party."

"Yahoo!" With my right hand, I blocked McGuire's attempt at another slap. "I'm so short, I belong on top of a wedding cake!"

I grappled the Port Call from Eaton, and along with it, the rest of the papers he held.

"What's this, Numbers?"

"You took the letter from my mom."

"I don't mean the letter. I'm talking about the newspaper article attached to it."

Eaton grabbed the letter and clipping out of my hand. "It's just some bullshit about one of the senators from Indiana."

"Well, what about him?"

"The paper wrote a big exposé on him for pulling strings to avoid the draft and get in to the Indiana National Guard. And circumvent ending up here."

"Let me see that," I said, regaining possession of the document.

I raced through the article. It quoted the senator as saying, "I broke no rules . . . I got in fairly . . . I admit that a family friend probably made a few phone calls on my behalf . . . "

"That damned peace-loving dove," McGuire scoffed.

"Oh, no, Smiles. The senator is from a very wealthy family," Eaton continued. "He's too rich to be a dove." Eaton's expression took on a disgusted aura, and he spoke in a tone that reeked sarcasm. "He's more like a *quail*."

"Well, I can't worry about that shit," I smiled, handing back his clipping. "Because I'm officially down to 7 AAWU."

That evening, I fell asleep to the sound of out-going artillery rounds. With each *bang!* I flew a few inches into the air, sounding a *bang!* of my own when I landed in my bunk. In between rounds, my thoughts drifted to the freak accidents that killed short-timers. One week to go, and I couldn't focus on the enjoyment of being short. Question after question invaded my thoughts.

What accident would happen to me? What did Charlie have in store for me? What kind of send-off would he give me? Would I live through it?

I had guzzled two drinks within the first half-hour of my party. While awaiting another refill from McGuire, I was explaining to Eaton that I spent most of the morning forcing my way out of my helmet.

"Whaddaya mean?"

"Accidentally fell in it when I got out of bed—cuz I'm so short!" I punched him in the arm. "Hah!"

He switched his drink to his left hand, took a black marking pen out of his back pocket, and wrote P-I-N-K-Y on my shirt.

McGuire handed me my screwdriver. After swallowing half of the drink, I graciously thanked him by grabbing the marker from Eaton and scrawling S-M-I-L-E-S on McGuire's bright white T-shirt. Followed by a N-U-M-B-E-R-S on Eaton's.

"If you're so smart, Numbers," I returned to my short-timer's diatribe, "can you explain how some guy had 8,965 AAWU?"

"No." He finished his drink with an annoyed gulp.

"Because he was *Vietnamese*."

McGuire laughed, slapping me on the back so hard, he splashed the rest of my drink.

I gave him a dirty look. "You know, spilling even one drop of liquor is a mortal sin according to my father-in-law."

McGuire stared at my empty glass. "Well," he said, "I guess you're going straight to hell now." Then he grabbed it to get me another refill, bumping into an already-tipsy Mr. Taguiped along the way.

"Right neighborly of you to stop by, Mr. Taguiped," I said.

He smiled and held up his drink.

"To you, Specialist Papp."

"Thank you, Sir." Getting out the marker, I smiled and said, "And to you," while writing e-M-p-T-y on his military-green T-shirt.

He grabbed the bottom of his shirt and pulled it away from his body so he could read the inscription.

"But I'm not *empty*," he said.

I drew a line through the three lower-case letters. Pointing to the remaining two, I said, "I know you're full of it, Sir, but you're still M-T to us, Mr. Taguiped."

"Oh, I get it." He finished his drink, held it toward me, and said,

"Look. My drink is M-T." Then he broke out in a shit-eating grin and laughed himself silly.

"Steaks will be ready in five minutes," Grabowski yelled. Pouring half a bottle of vodka into the bubbling pot next to him, he stirred it and asked, "Who's gonna put the finishing touch on the steak sauce?"

"I will," Eaton shouted.

"Me, too," came my echo.

Eaton and I put an arm around each other's shoulder. Staring at the ground, we began a purposeful walk around the area. Occasionally stopping and shaking our heads "no," we continued our important mission. Two minutes later, we stopped before a rock the size of a baseball. Nodding agreement to each other, we took out our manhood and drizzled all over the small boulder. Replacing our organs, we picked up the violated sphere, and with our heads held high, ceremoniously carried it back to the steak sauce. With a loud *plop!* the rock sank to the bottom of the pot.

"Now the sauce is ready," Grabowski proclaimed proudly. "And so are the steaks."

Like a herd of hungry elephants, we daintily took our food and ate it in textbook Emily Post fashion.

Shortly thereafter, PFC Horvath's face took on a green hue when he lit up yet another butt. I extracted the cigarette from his mouth and tossed it on the ground. Gently taking him by the arm, I walked him around in an attempt to sober him up. Like a bee drawn to a flower, Horvath's feet found every pebble we came across—and tripped over it. After claiming he felt a *lot* better, he took three more steps, then disgorged his supper all over his pants and boots.

"Come on, let's get you cleaned up."

Fortunately, we were within twenty paces of a water trailer. I held my breath, so I wouldn't inhale his ripe essence, and steered him in that direction. Bending him in half at the waist, I opened the valve over his head. As I saw the water cascading over him, my paranoid mind immediately remembered the sad story of a short-timer dying when a water drum fell on him while taking a shower. Crushing his skull. With a week to go, I had about seven chances at a similar death. Either that, or not take a shower.

"Stand up, Walrus. Now stick one leg under the water."

He again followed my direction, ridding himself of puke one leg at a time.

"Thanks, Pinky. That really helped."

The instant we got back to my party, someone let out a "The cooler is empty. It's time!" Now it was my turn for the ceremonial dousing.

Grabowski, Eaton, Hoffman, and White each grabbed a limb and carried me to the bathtub-like container that kept the beer and soda ice cold. While they held me high in the air, I couldn't help but yell out: "Short is when you toss a wad of paper into a can and you DEROS before it hits the bottom."

"Toss him," Mr. Taguiped shouted.

"Wait a minute," McGuire cried out. Waving his arms for silence, he said, "I know I speak for everyone when I say good luck and good-bye, Pinky." The hint of a tear came to his left eye as he added, "We may be losing a friend, but a wife is gaining a husband."

"Do it!" Taguiped yelled.

Splash!

And, as was customary, I screeched: "Damn! That's cold!"

Chapter 21

GOODBYE,
VIETNAM!

As we often said in Vietnam, it was time to "get my shit together."
With DA Form 137 (Installation Clearance Record) in hand, I began
clearing Dong Tam. My first stop was to pick up my 201 File at
Team 1.

Although the last nine months had been spent with friends who
could provide the necessary diversion from the agony of being in
Nam, I wasn't in the mood to bullshit and start those long goodbyes.
Thankful I met no one in Team 1 whom I really knew, it took only two
minutes to get my records and the initials "MAC" next to Item 12 on
DA Form 137.

At finance, I signed DA Form 2139-1, collected a partial pay of $62
in MPC (for the last time), and got an "IT" initialed for Item 14.

When a medic handed me MACV (Military Assistance Command,
Vietnam) Form 270: Malaria Debriefing, I scrutinized the form before
signing it.

> *By virtue of having been in Vietnam, I recognize*
> *that I have been exposed to malaria. Malaria may*
> *develop long after departure from Vietnam. In order*
> *that I do not contract malaria, it will be necessary*
> *for me to continue my antimalaria tablets after leav-*

ing Vietnam. To not do so would be a violation of
Department of Defense orders as well as a violation
of a moral obligation not to endanger my country,
my friends and my family.

I put an *X* next to the block that stated:

I have been taking chloroquine-primaquine anti-
malarial tablets weekly (Salmon or orange colored
tablets) and I will take one tablet a week for 8 weeks
following departure from Vietnam.

Another *X* in the little box acknowledged I received the necessary tablets.

After getting an "excellent" rating from the Personal Affairs Officer for *Conduct* and *Efficiency*, the captain scribbled his indecipherable initials next to Item 18. Better than the ratings was the tingly feeling, which vibrated throughout my body, when I informed the Postal Officer (Item 20) that my change of address was *The World.*

My last two obstacles in Dong Tam were at the same location: the 9th Administration Company orderly room.

The company clerk put his "John Hancock" by Item 32, signifying I had cleared the Duty Roster. When our (new) first sergeant put his "WAS" by Item 31, I drifted back to the days of Sergeant First Class Smith's reign. Gone were his putrid black cigars and overweight frame. As the new Top stood up and extended a muscular arm to shake my hand goodbye, I had a vision of Smith doing the same. But in Smith's case, his fat arm resembled a broom handle with a loaf of pizza dough hanging from it. I didn't mention to the new Top that his initials (WAS) were prophetic.

Leg one of clearing Vietnam was now completed. My trusty M16 and TA-50 field gear would accompany me to Bearcat for final disposition.

A check of my wristwatch told me it was 4 p.m. (Even my watch talked *civilian* now.) I had skipped lunch and was hungry enough for anything our mess hall offered. Stopping by my hooch, I waited for the faithful troops to finish their workday, so they could buy the "condemned man" his last supper.

They must have been giving away free Alka-Seltzer, because the line at the mess hall extended a parade's length past the entrance.

"Hold it up, Pinky," Hoffman instructed.

I gallantly raised my short-timer's stick for all to see.

"Step aside," Hoffman bellowed, "short-timer comin' through."

With Hoffman, Eaton, Grabowski, White, McGuire, Wright, and Horvath in tow, I kept my symbol held high and said, "They're with me." Each of them had a mile-wide grin plastered on his kisser as we went to the head of the class.

Tears came to my eyes when I saw the evening menu. It was the same as the first meal I had shared with many of these guys almost nine months ago: hamburgers, fries, peas, and chocolate donuts.

"Oh, boy! Chocolate donuts," Horvath exclaimed. "My all-time favorite."

"Hey, Pinky," Hoffman said, "why don't you tell Walrus how the cook makes the holes in the donuts."

I did.

Horvath dropped his three donuts back onto the pile.

Halfway through the meal, Grabowski said, "I think it's time to do it, Pinky."

I smiled recognition.

Grabowski provided the necessary drum roll by beating his knife and spoon on his tray. The noise level in the mess hall dropped to whisper-quiet.

Grabbing the short-timer's stick in my left hand, I stood slowly up. I hoisted the emblem of my status high overhead. Waiting for Grabowski's crescendo to reach the appropriate level, I screamed: "*Fooour*. And a wake up!"

I drank in the thunderous applause from everyone in the mess hall. Sitting down, I observed the expressions of the guests at my table. Their faces beamed as brightly as mine: thankful for their coveted ringside seats. The next-best thing to *being* a short-timer was being *close* to one.

Foregoing a farewell drink at the NCO Cub before turning in for the night, it was time to say our goodbyes. With each handshake came the inevitable promise to keep in touch. When it came time to say goodbye to Eaton, it was a totally different scene.

Next to Dennis Bohnny, Eaton was my closest ally. The foundation for our friendship began my first day with the 9th Administration Company. I vividly pictured being in The Pit and his offering me a bandage for my wounded pinky. The allegiance intensified during our three wonderful days of R&R in Vung Tau. And it reached its peak in August when he was "all" I had left to keep me sane as Bohnny and Cohen deserted me and went back to *The World*.

Without saying a word, Eaton offered his hand. I accepted it warmly. We stood, frozen in a final handshake. When our smiles turned to blurry eyes, we released our grip, and walked away from each other for eternity.

By the time I rose the following morning, the hooch was empty: Everyone was at work. I packed my gear, hoisted the duffel bag on my left shoulder, and clutched my short-timer's stick in my left fist. My right hand found the handle of my M16. I looked around the hooch one last time. With a surprising sadness in my heart, I mouthed a "goodbye," and marched through the screen door.

At Dong Tam International, I joined hundreds of GIs waiting for a flight to Bearcat. The ones heading for R&R covetously eyed the short-timer's sticks of the lucky ones DEROSing. This time my stick did me little good, for I was lost in a forest of short-timers. With nothing to do but add my name to the bottom of the list and seek shelter from the punishing sun, I used my duffel bag as a pillow and hid in the relative shade of a deuce-and-a-half.

Morning turned to afternoon. I vaguely remembered eating something before darkness settled in. In droves, we found shelter for the night. With out-going rounds punctuating the stillness, most of us catnapped until daylight. After each explosion, I fell asleep while praying, and woke up clutching my short-timer's stick—and my manhood.

From 8:30 a.m. to 5:30 p.m., on Sunday, September 29, I waited again for a caribou to Bearcat. I was back to the same scenario as in January, when I played "hurry up and wait" for my final assignment.

Nothing in the Army had changed these nine months. Not a damned thing.

When the "That's the last flight out today" came over the loudspeaker, I joined a handful of short-timers who went to the flight desk with a plea.

"Isn't there some way we can get out of here tomorrow, Sir?" our spokesman asked the officer in charge. "We've been sitting around for two days—some of us even three days—waiting for a flight to Bearcat. All we want to do is finish clearing Nam and go back to *The World*."

"Well," the major began, "let me—"

"Not to interrupt you, Sir," our spokesman said, "but we've put in our tour. We just would like to get the hell out of Vietnam."

A few mumbled "yeahs" reinforced the plea.

"As I was going to say, Specialist," the major continued, "the best I can do is put your names on a manifest for a special flight to Bearcat at 1500 hours tomorrow."

"But—"

"*If* you don't get on an earlier flight, you'll be guaranteed a seat on the 1500-hours one. Okay?"

Mumble. Mumble.

"That would be great, Sir," Spokesman said. "And, thanks very much."

I spent another night of praying, catnapping, and clutching my dick—excuse me, my stick.

Morning. No flight. Noon. No flight. Afternoon. Same-same.

When 2:30 rolled around, I went to check on the special flight the major had promised some of us. Just like when I went to pick up my orders at R&R Headquarters for the trip to Tokyo, no one at the flight desk had been on duty the day before. And, of course, no one knew about the flight. Mumbling obscenities, I went back to my duffel-bag pillow.

At precisely 2:59 p.m., a miracle happened.

The loudspeaker barked a list of names to report to the flight desk. *Papp, John D.* was one of the chosen few.

The same clerk who didn't know anything about the special flight was telling our group to board the 1500-hours flight for Bearcat. *Should I have expected anything less from the Army?* One year and eleven-plus months and not a damned thing had changed in this man's Army.

I boarded the caribou, stowed my carry-on bags in the overhead compartment, fastened my seat belt, put my tray table in an upright position, extinguished the cigarette I wasn't smoking, and got ready for take off.

After what seemed like an eternity, the plane landed in Bearcat. We persuaded a couple of truck drivers to take us to The Academy so we could rid ourselves of TA-50 and weapons. However, by the time we stopped so the driver could get his kids from the babysitter, pick up his wife's dry cleaning, do his grocery shopping, pick up a pizza for supper, and buy a case of beer to go with Sunday's NFL game, we arrived at The Academy after official closing hours.

I said goodbye to September by drawing some linen and gleefully spending the night among the newbies who arrived for their mandatory training. *Welcome to Vietnam, troop!*

Item by item, I handed in my TA-50: sleeping bag, canteen, mess kit, flak vest, helmet . . . the four-page form went on seemingly forever.

"You were issued *two* canteens on 28 January. Where's the other one?" the supply sergeant demanded.

"I got only one."

"You *signed* for two." He shoved the DA Form 10-102 in my face and pointed to my signature on 28 Jan 68.

"I got only *one*."

"You signed for *two*."

Like a pendulum, we repeated our statements.

The supply sergeant made a notation in the far right-hand column.

"Where's your general purpose carrying strap?"

"My what?"

"Your 'Strap, Carrying, General Purpose.'"

"Guess I never got one."

"You signed for one on 28 January." Another faceful of DA Form 10-102.

"I never got it."

"You signed for it."

"I never got it."

"You signed for it."

"I never got it."

Mark number two in the far right-hand column.

After another scrutiny of my issued items, a third check mark was entered.

"Okay, Specialist Papp, you owe the—"

"What?"

"You have to pay for the missing items."

"You gotta be shitting me."

"I'm doing no such thing, Specialist."

"FTA," I mumbled.

"What did you say."

"I said how much do I have to pay?"

Money changed hands. A receipt went into my 201 File, along with another notation on the goddamned DA 10-102. And Item 29 of DA Form 137 was initialed, validating I had cleared yet another station.

Next came the arms room. The place where I was first issued my M16. I remembered being told by a PFC while at a weapons class at The Academy that, before the military got its hands on this fully automatic little baby known as the AR-15, it was lightweight and easy to handle. Then the Army changed the rifle's name, waved a magic wand, and the M16 jammed more often than not.

In typical Army screw-up fashion, I expected to be asked where the ammo was when I finally handed in the rifle. *You were issued four magazines of ammo on 28 January. Where are they? I never got them. You signed for them. I never got them. You signed for them.*

Instead, when I handed over my rifle, the clerk verified the serial number, checked that the slingshot was in working order, signed and dated the DA 10-102, and initialed Item 32 on the DA 137. Surprise! Surprise!

A rubber stamp came down on my forehead. It said: Congratulations, you have successfully cleared Vietnam. In much smaller type it added: We hope you don't get killed before you board your Freedom Bird.

With nothing but a change of clothes and the 201 File stuffed into my duffel bag, I jumped on a deuce-and-a-half for Long Binh: the last leg of my journey in Vietnam.

Relishing every minute of this ride, I finally saw the WELCOME TO THE 90TH REPLACEMENT BATTALION sign that first greeted me on New Year's Day. This time I walked through the cutout archway of a 12-foot-wide by 20-foot-high sign emblazoned with GOING HOME? REPORT HERE, BUILDING 1.

The anxiety of the final waiting game began. Along with 199 GIs scheduled for flight G2B4, I sat in a room expecting to be eliminated from the flight: the plane had room for only 160 of us.

My final bout of paranoia set in. My mind replayed the horror stories of guys getting bumped off their flights, returning to Long Binh, then eating a mortar round. Or a rocket. After finishing a tour in Vietnam, NOBODY wanted to cash in his chips for a coffin. Somehow, the Army should have had extra planes waiting around, just so a tragedy like that could be avoided. Somehow, the Army should have found a way to avoid the whole damned tragedy of Vietnam. It should have. But it didn't.

"Anyone who is *not* going to ETS when they reach the States," a staff sergeant instructed, "raise your hand. And sound off with your name, rank, and service number."

Since I *was* getting out of the Army when I got to Oakland, and not just being assigned to another duty station, I kept my hands glued to my lap.

One by one, hands slowly went up around the room. And voices reluctantly rang out. A total of *15* hands were raised. That left 25 destined for elimination.

"Okay," the sergeant called out, "now I want to see a show of hands for anyone with an official DEROS date *after* 18 October." Mine was 9 October. I was safe.

Two hands went up.

"Gentlemen. We have ways of checking for the truth. One quick glance at your 201 or 66 File will give you away."

Six more hands rose sheepishly. And voices squeaked.

Two and six were eight. That left 17 more.

"Okay, those with an official DEROS *after* 11 October."

Still safe.

Three went up. Four more. I looked behind me: another eight. That made fifteen; I needed another two.

"Okay, now anyone—"

"Excuse me. Did you say before 11 October?"

"No, Lieutenant, I said *after* 11 October."

The brown bar said, "Oh," and raised his hand. So did the officer sitting next to him.

Great! That made 25. Exactly what we needed. I breathed a sigh of relief.

"That's the official list," the sergeant said. "On your way out of the room, pick up a form," he pointed at the card table by the door, "and read it carefully. Especially Item #6. Dismissed."

The form didn't have an official Department of the Army number. This negligent omission *had* to be a court-martial offense.

In addition to my flight itinerary, the form listed my building assignment (#35) and my bunk number (33). It also stated that our final out-processing time was 0500 hours on 2 Oct 68. The rest of the form had the standard bullshit of what to do and not do while waiting for our flight. I skimmed through the B.S. until I found Item #6. In bold letters, it explained the importance of the bunk number: "Sleep in your assigned bunk. In the past, personnel have missed flights because they were in the wrong bunk."

Attached to the form was a hand-drawn map of the compound identifying the various buildings. Since it was time for supper, I ran my finger over the drawing until I found #12, Mess Hall. The description included these words: Best chow in the Army.

I found building #12. I ate supper. Maybe because it was my last (hopefully) meal in Vietnam, it *was* the best meal I'd had. In Nam.

Seeking out bunk #33, I tied myself to it and settled in for my remaining hours in this godforsaken place. I fell asleep to the symphony played by the artillery.

"Wake up," a voice said. "It's time to go home."

I woke up with a smile. My best in the last nine months.

During our final out-processing, we signed more forms, exchanged MPC for glorious greenbacks, and had a 100% inspection of our baggage. After changing from fatigues into Class-A khakis, we boarded buses to Bien Hoa.

Sitting in the bleachers at the terminal, awaiting our flight, we were assigned a number.

"Remember the number you have been given," a captain instructed us. "You will line up according to that number."

Then he dropped his bomb.

"If you hear your number called after you have lined up, it means you have been bumped off the flight for an emergency leave—"

Mumbles were heard throughout the bleachers.

"Report to the flight desk," he pointed to himself, "if your number is called."

A 30-day emergency leave was given for a tragedy at home—the death of a family member. A compassionate leave was granted so that a GI could return home for a "non-emergency" reason. One way to get a compassionate leave was to request permission to go home and marry the girl who was carrying your baby. However, someone on a compassionate leave did *not* have the authority to bump another GI off his freedom bird.

Then, the stupid, fucking Army changed the classification from compassionate to *emergency* if your intended purpose was to get married before the bun came out of the oven. So, all a GI had to do before he left home was knock up his girlfriend (or a complete stranger), and he could get out of Nam for at least a month. Plus, now the bastard-remover could bump someone who already had completed his entire tour. And risk getting the DEROSing GI killed.

"Can that really happen?" a naive PFC asked the Spec 5 sitting next to me.

"God did not give me enough fingers," the Spec 5 held up both hands, "to visually show you how many guys I personally knew who bought it that way."

It was a few minutes before 10 o'clock . . . a little more than an hour before our scheduled departure. I kept one eye glued on the second hand, watching it creep around the dial. The other eye was riveted on the runway, in search of our in-coming freedom bird. With less than an hour remaining in Vietnam, this should have been the happiest moment of my life. Instead of being filled with the anticipation of seeing family, friends, and home, I was distraught with the anxiety of hearing my number called.

10:30 drifted by.

I took my eyes off the runway and wristwatch and focused them on the bleachers. Not one word passed among the group. Those who weren't in a trance had adopted the same separate-eye technique of passing time.

10:45.

10:46.

10:47.

Two voices in the bottom row exclaimed, "I see it! I see it!"

Above the din, the unmistakable sounds of an approaching jet filled the terminal.

The captain behind the flight desk tapped the microphone. The loudspeaker came crackling to life.

"Line up for flight G2B4."

The bleachers emptied in organized chaos. I took position #38.

"Number 32 report to the flight desk."

A GI broke formation and walked toward the captain.

"Numbers 102 and 89. Flight desk."

Two more heads drooped, their bodies slumped as they crawled to the desk.

"Number 13."

A staff sergeant joined the captain behind the microphone. The two of them conferred for half a minute.

"Number 146," the captain said.

Checking the paperwork before him, the captain then called: "*38.*"

My heart stopped. My body went limp. One foot painfully went before the other as I inched my way forward. This was worse than that dreaded day in January when a lieutenant called my name for the 9th Infantry Division instead of for my originally listed unit.

The captain put his hand over the mike and got an earful from the staff sergeant.

"Negative. Negative," his voice rang out. "Number 38 return to your place in line," the captain ordered.

"Yes, Sir!" I shouted.

The plane disgorged its load. The newbies paraded by us. God! they looked so young.

Above the noise of the short-timers yelling their barbs at the cherries, the loudspeaker rang out: "Flight G2B4 will be boarding in one-zero minutes."

Barbs turned to shouts of joy. Minutes later, the shouts became an increasing chant: "We're going home. We're going home."

The line moved toward the plane. By the time I took my second step, I had to run to keep up with those before me. Leaving Vietnam behind, I boarded my freedom bird and got ready for the flight of my life.

"Please make sure your seatbelts are buckled," a voice from the cabin instructed. "We're cleared for takeoff."

In unified bedlam, 160 GIs erupted into a cacophony that didn't stop until Vietnam was the size of a pimple on my ass.

Chapter 22

When Vietnam disappeared from sight, I divorced myself from the window and noticed the GI seated next to me looked vaguely familiar.

"Hi, Sarge. Great to be going home. Isn't it?"

"Yes, Specialist, it is."

"You don't sound too sure."

He looked *very* familiar. His rugged features and military bearing bespoke a man who should be at ease in any country in the world.

"It's a long story," he said with mixed emotions.

"It's a long flight," I reminded him. "I've got plenty of time."

He smiled. "Okay."

When he turned toward me, so he wouldn't have to talk sideways, I was able to get a better look at his name tag.

"I'm going—"

"You're Sergeant First Class Johnson, aren't you?"

"Yes, I am, Specialist—Papp. Why?"

"You were you in Bearcat in January. Weren't you?"

"Why, yes, I was." He smiled faintly, giving my face a longer look.

"We spent several hours together—during in-processing." I recalled his telling me he was pissed at the Army. No surprise there! He had been in the service for nineteen years, including two previous tours in Nam. For thirteen of those nineteen years, he was separated from his family. He hoped for his last year before retirement he could spend it somewhere—*anywhere*—in the States, so that he could be with his wife and kids.

"Yes, Papp, I vaguely remember that now. But, if that was January, how come you're going home already?"

I explained the reason for my shortened tour and reminded him that he wasn't due to DEROS yet either.

"That's the long story," he said, the trace of a smile disappearing from his face.

"Refreshments, gentlemen?" the stewardess asked, offering a tray of sodas.

"Thank you," Johnson said, taking a Pepsi.

Helping myself to a 7UP, I held it before me and toasted Johnson. My mind unconsciously repeated the 7UP slogan: You like it, it likes you. *Well, what do you know? My brain is shifting gears from military to civilian. Aren't those little gray cells wonderful?*

"Maybe if you tell me your story," I took a sip of soda, "you'll feel better."

"As you may remember," he drank half his Pepsi, "I had one year to go before I retired."

"Yes."

"When we met in January, you had no way of knowing I had been kicking around Nam for well over a month."

That helped to explain why he looked so pissed the first time I met him.

"Three weeks ago, my mother died."

"I'm sorry."

"Thank you." He paused for a moment, his glance drifted away, evidently replaying the memory of his mother. "She was almost eighty and in poor health. So it was a blessing in one way." A tear worked its way down his left cheek. He wiped it away slowly. "By the time the Red Cross got word to my unit, it was too late for me to get home for her funeral."

I nodded.

"Anyway," he went on, "I was granted the emergency leave even though the funeral had passed. Since I had less than a month left in the Army after I'd eventually rejoin my unit," his smile slowly returned, "I was given an early out."

"So you'll be a civilian, too?"

He smiled and nodded.

"Well, you'll be home in a few days. And you can finally pay your respects to your mother."

"Actually, I won't be getting home for another three weeks. I'm making a few stops on the way."

"Oh?"

"My wife is meeting me in Oakland. We're going to stop by Oklahoma, Louisiana, Mississippi, Ohio, and Indiana on the way home."

That sounded like an odd itinerary. Unless they were the places he'd been stationed in the States, and he was taking a last look-see.

The sergeant must have read my puzzled expression, because he took a sip of soda, then answered my unspoken question: "We're going to visit the families of the men who were killed in my unit."

Unbelievable.

"I want to personally tell them what fine young men their sons and husbands were."

Tears came to my eyes. I never heard of a lifer doing anything like this before.

"You're a hell of a great man, *Mister* Johnson."

He smiled. "I'm not a civilian, yet." His smile grew at the sound of the soon-to-be title.

Along with the usual announcement to fasten our seatbelts came the long-awaited punch line: "We land at Travis Air Force Base in twenty minutes."

"That's *California*," someone behind me shouted.

As with takeoff, bedlam broke out. Shouts of jubilation lasted more than ten minutes. Then, as though everyone expected one final tragedy to take place, it became quiet as a eulogy.

I pushed my face against the window. Twilight was at hand. Gradually breaking through the clouds, I saw land far below. *The World.*

Moments after bouncing in our seats as the wheels made contact with the runway, the pilot's voice rang out: "Welcome home, gentlemen."

Take a handful of mayhem. Add a pinch of chaos. Throw in a good helping of bedlam. The cacophony of that mixture would have been dwarfed by the pandemonium that broke loose when the pilot uttered those three words.

Peace was miraculously restored when the plane stopped and the door opened. In an orderly fashion, happy GIs filled the aisle and began deplaning.

I stood at the doorway and looked at paradise. Guiding myself with the railing, I relished every step as I walked slowly down the ramp. After dispensing with the final one, I got on my knees, put the palms of my hands on the beloved ground, and, like the GIs before me, kissed the tarmac. It tasted so sweet, my face broke out with acne. I gave it another kiss.

"Come on, get on the bus," a voice instructed.

I hurried (I was too close to being a civilian to double-time-it) to one of the waiting buses.

"Look at the size of that thing."

My first thought was Hoffman had sprung another boomerang-sized erection. Instead, heads were turned to a humongous building. It looked like it could house a small city.

"It must be three blocks long," the same voice said.

When the buses stopped in front of the crude estate, a staff sergeant entered our bus and offered a cheerful greeting: "Good evening. Welcome to Oakland Army Base. And welcome back to *The World*."

Controlled pandemonium resounded throughout every cubic inch of the bus.

"All of your out-processing will be done in Building 640," he pointed to the obvious. "For those of you ETSing, you'll go to Bay 5 with your baggage. All others will report to Bay 2." His smile broadened. "We'll make this as short and sweet as possible."

Once inside the building, I made my way to Bay 5 with a group of happy campers. We were instructed to put our baggage on a numbered square and take a seat in the bleachers. After a Spec 4 gave a few opening remarks about the procedure we were about to go through, a second lieutenant took over.

"I'm Lieutenant Hoocairs, your reenlistment counselor."

Mixed responses filled the bleachers. Oblivious to our reactions, the brown bar continued.

"In a matter of hours, you will be separated from the Army."

The expected whistling and hollering erupted.

"So, this is your last chance to consider reenlisting before—"

An "FTA!" rang out in a far corner.

The lieutenant's face became red. Little puffs of smoke drifted out of each ear.

"I'll have none of that," he screamed. "The Army has been good to you."

"Bullshit!" a voice rang out.

Deeper red. Bigger puffs of smoke.

"Try saying that after spending a year in Nam," came another barb.

Clouds of smoke.

"Silence!" the lieutenant ordered. "I want silence."

"And I want out of the fuckin' Army," another voice said.

Above the din, the lieutenant shouted, "I have 19 years before I retire."

Catcalls erupted everywhere.

"So, I can wait as long as you want before I continue my talk. Do *you* have 19 years?" he threatened.

Silence.

"Good," he smirked, as though he had been given his little brother's favorite toy. "Now, as I was saying, this is your last chance to consider reenlisting." He waited for a response, but got none. "If you re-up now, you can have your choice of assignments." Another pause and scan of the bleachers. "That's more than you'll get if you choose separation instead."

He started pacing in front of us, from one end of the bleachers to the other. He either forgot the rest of his canned presentation, or was prolonging the agony for spite.

"One final word of caution," he continued. "If you change your mind after you walk out these doors, the Army will still take you back. But," he pointed a finger at a Spec 5 in the front row, "if you wait more than three-zero days, you'll lose one stripe." Evidently thinking he had a bunch of assholes before him, he restated his last words. "That means, if you're a Spec 5 now, you'll reenter as a Spec 4."

"What if you're a Private E1?" someone innocently asked. (A Private E1 was the lowest grade possible.)

Laughter broke out. From every corner of the bleachers.

"I'll ignore that wise-ass remark."

"But, sir, I *am* an E1," the private said.

More laughter.

"Then you become a *second lieutenant*," another GI shouted.

Total pandemonium.

With a "That's all I have to say," the lieutenant gave in to the masses and stormed out of the room. A standing ovation acknowledged his farewell.

The Spec 4 who made the earlier announcements returned. He attempted to conceal his laughter by covering his face with his right hand. After a few ahems! he began speaking.

"Gentlemen," he smiled, "the next step in your out-processing is a complete check of your personnel records to verify everything is in order." He surveyed the room to make sure he was the only one with us. "Unless, of course, someone wants to re-up?"

Laughter and foot-stomping filled the bleachers.

"I take that to mean no."

"Atsa Rog," a voice shouted.

"Okay," his smile broadened. "After that, you'll fill out a few forms—"

Groans punctuated every row of seats.

"It's inevitable, gentlemen. Then," he counted off the remaining steps on an upraised right hand, "you'll have your steak dinner, get new uniforms, take a physical . . . "

After my records were checked and double-checked, I was handed a form authorizing my free steak dinner.

"It's supposed to be a one-inch T-bone," a Spec 5 told me when I got in line behind him.

We exited Building 640, made a right down 10th Street, and hung a left on Midway Street. When the line began turning right onto 14th Street, I saw them: three rows of pay telephones. Having forgotten to reset my watch, I asked the time of the Spec 5 in front of me.

"It's a few minutes to 7."

That meant it was almost 10 p.m. at home.

I reached into my pockets and pulled out a few coins. I needed more than what I had.

"Anybody got change for a dollar?" I asked.

A few hands went into pockets. I exchanged one bill for the equivalent in coins. I needed more.

"Anybody else?"

Nothing.

Feeling like a hobo, I scrounged some loose change from two other guys.

I broke formation and ran to the closest phone. After pumping in coins and dialing numbers, I heard the voice of my mother-in-law.

"Hello?"

"Rose, it's Denny. I—"

"Denny! Let me get Annette."

Pause.

"Denny?"

"Yes, Annette. It's me," I cried.

"Where are you?"

"I made it, Annette. I'm in Oakland."

"Oh, thank God," she cried. I heard her whisper "He's in California" to her mother.

"I was on my way to my free steak dinner. I got out of the line to call you instead."

"Won't you get in trouble?"

"No."

"You sure?"

"Honest. I won't. Anyway, what can they do to me? Send me to Vietnam?"

"Don't even joke about that."

"Sorry." I hadn't been on the phone for a minute and already I was opening my mouth just to change feet.

"When are you coming home?"

"I don't know yet. We barely started out-processing. It'll be several hours at least."

"Oh, okay," she said a little dejectedly.

"If all goes well, I'll be home by tomorrow afternoon."

"Oh," her voice perked up, "that would be wonderful."

"Please let my folks—"

"I'll call them as soon as I hang up. I love you."

"I love you, too. As soon as I get an idea of what flight I can catch, I'll call you again. Okay?"

"Yes. Even if it's after midnight. Call me."

"Okay. Annette?"

"Yes, Denny?"

"Isn't it wonderful to talk on the phone and not have to say 'over'?"

She laughed a "Yes."

When we finally hung up, I was too psyched to eat. So I stuck the free steak dinner form in a back pocket and walked happily back to Building 640.

While the alterations were made on my new Class-A winter uniform, I underwent a thorough physical examination. After being probed and prodded, I got the medical stamp of approval. The next stop was finance, where I received my final pay, including unused leave time and my travel allowance.

"Here you go, Specialist Papp," the finance clerk said, counting out every penny due me.

"That's *Mister* Papp," I stated proudly, relinquishing my military ID card.

After exchanging my khakis for the winter uniform, I reported back to Bay 5. There I was handed my separation documents, wished a "Good Luck," and, with minimal baggage in hand, walked out of Building 640 a free man. *A civilian!*

Joining three other former GIs in a cab, we made our way to San Francisco airport.

Presenting my Military Standby Authorization to a gorgeous redhead behind the United Airlines counter, I purchased a one-way ticket to Philadelphia. After calling Annette and telling her I'd arrive shortly after 11:30 in the morning, I passed the remaining hours with two old friends: a beer and a hamburger. Both were made in the good old U. S. of A. And both were so damned good, I had two more friends join me.

Shortly after the pilot turned off the "Fasten Your Seatbelt" sign, a slender, attractive stewardess came up to me and asked, "Returning home from Vietnam?"

I managed to stop drinking in her beauty and gazed at her name tag. "Yes, Johanna, I am."

"We have a vacant seat in first class." With an obvious trace of emotion in her voice, she added, "We'd be proud to have you come forward and join us."

Johanna gave me an ice-cold beer and placed a delicious-looking steak before me. Digging into both, I felt as though I had waved my magic short-timer's stick and was being treated like royalty.

Totally stuffed and satisfied, I wiped the last nine months from my memory, and drifted off to sleep . . . to dream about home, Annette. My folks. The future lay before me. And it didn't include the Army.

A gentle tap woke me. Johanna towered over me, smiling. "We'll be landing in 15 minutes."

I wiped the slumber from my face, politely silenced a yawn, and sat up. I returned her smile and added "Thank you."

"Would you like to change seats?" asked the middle-aged gentleman seated next to me. "So you can look out the window?"

I stifled a "That would be right neighborly of you," and simply nodded. With face and window united, I consumed every inch of our remaining flight until the wheels touched the runway without a bounce.

Joining the mob as we deplaned, I walked on tiptoes, looking for a familiar face. Before seeing anyone, I heard my wife yell: "Denny, over here." Then I saw an arm thrust into the air, waving like a maniac.

I pushed impatiently through the crowd to the waving arm. There before me stood my wife. Arms open. Tears flowing.

Releasing the satchel, I passionately embraced her, making up for nine empty months. As I felt her warmth pressed up against me, I broke out in uncontrollable tears. We stood there like a soggy sandwich for untold minutes. Then another arm embraced me. And another. In addition to my wife, the welcoming entourage included my father-in-law and my buddy, Sam Tarcza.

Gaining control of her voice, my wife answered the unasked question.

"Your folks are at their house. They wanted to welcome you home there." With a twinkle in her eye and mischief in her voice, she added: "And leave you all to me at the airport."

Unwrapping my arms from Annette's body, I gave my father-in-law a bear hug.

"The last time I hugged you," I reminded him, "was nine months ago. In this very airport." As more tears mixed with my smile, I choked out, "This one feels a hell of a lot better, Ernie."

Another hug and handshake—this one with Sam—and the airport hellos were complete.

With arms entwined, the four of us walked to the baggage carousel to get my duffel bag.

During the hour's ride to Trenton, each passing sight brought back memories buried deep within. Memories that I thought I lost because of the inhumanity of being in Vietnam.

When we got to my in-law's, I said a tearful hello to my mother-in-law. This greeting freed me of yet another suffocating layer of the Vietnam shroud.

I looked around the kitchen and living room. I didn't see, or hear our dog.

My mother-in-law read my actions and said, "Honey is in the back-yard."

"I wonder if she remembers me." She was only a few months old when I left for Nam. "I'll go out the front door and wait for her at the side of the house." To Annette I said, "You go out the kitchen door and open the side gate for her. Okay?"

With the gate opened, Honey stood cautiously by it and sniffed the air. I bent down and let out one word, half-aloud: "Honey." When she heard her name, she came toward me slowly, cautiously. Halfway, the familiarity of my scent clicked, and she shifted into high gear. From five feet away, she jumped into the air and pounced on me, licking my face. I began crying at the near-instant recognition. When her joy showed itself in a little puddle of pee, I was grateful we said hello *out*side.

After saying goodbye to Sam and my in-laws, Annette and I jumped into our '65 Corvair with Honey in tow, and headed to my folk's home on Genesee Street.

Hanging beneath the second-floor windows of their red-brick row house was a "Welcome Home, Denny" sign painted on a full sheet of plywood.

My father must have heard the Corvair's doors slam, because he immediately stuck his head out their front door. Like a turtle, his head quickly disappeared into the house, and he shouted: "He's home, Helen. Our son's home."

Jumping off the porch steps, he greeted me with a tearful hug. Then he gave me the kiss he'd been saving for nine months.

"János," my mother yelled. She frequently called me by my first name (John) in Hungarian. "János," she repeated, while running down the porch steps, "you're home."

"Hi, Mom. I missed you."

"Oh, thank God, you're home."

After she planted a big one on my lips, she squeezed the living shit out of me with a hug that only a mother could give.

With these hellos, the memory of Vietnam was buried deeper in my subconscious. Not dead . . . just buried.

Twenty minutes later, we said goodbye, promising to pay a longer visit the next day.

With a look that told me she was anxious for me to see our new apartment, and get me all to herself, Annette gave me her car keys and said, "Take us home."

Heading down Genesee Street, I automatically made a right onto Beatty Street. At the light, I turned left onto South Broad Street. With an instinctive sense of radar, I took Broad all the way to our apartment.

When I parked in front of G-1, my hand shook as I shut off the ignition and handed Annette her keys. As soon as I opened the car door, Honey jumped out and raced to our porch. Looking at the front door and wagging her tail, she began barking.

"We'd better hurry or the neighbors will get upset," Annette warned.

I grabbed my luggage and followed the ladies inside our apartment.

Annette turned on the stereo. Old familiar songs filled my ears. Instead of the music putting me in the mood to read one of my wife's letters, as it had done those lonely months in Vietnam, I wanted to hold her and never let go.

"Let's sit on the couch," I said.

We sat at arm's length, my left hand entwined with her right. We looked at each other, without speaking, as tears of relief cascaded into our laps. The last nine months of uncertainty now were only a bad memory. Our six years of waiting to be "together forever" finally were over. We no longer had to live for the future . . . we could live in the present.

As tears choked me, I barely managed a "Come here."

She moved closer.

With a smile on my tear-stained face, and happiness in my pounding heart, I kissed her cheek and whispered into her ear: "I love you. *Over.*"

The Beginning

Made in the USA
Charleston, SC
15 April 2014